PERCEPTION

Perception is one of the most pervasive and puzzling problems in philosophy, generating a great deal of attention and controversy in philosophy of mind, psychology, and metaphysics. If perceptual illusion and hallucination are possible, how can perception be what it intuitively seems to be, a direct and immediate access to reality? How can perception be both internally dependent and externally directed?

Perception is an outstanding introduction to this fundamental topic, covering both the perennial and recent work on the problem. Adam Pautz examines four of the most important theories of perception: the sense datum view; the internal physical state view; the representational view; and naïve realism, assessing each in turn. He also discusses the relationship between perception and the physical world and the issue of whether reality is as it appears.

Useful examples are included throughout the book to illustrate the puzzles of perception, including hallucinations, illusions, the laws of appearance, blindsight, and neuroscientific explanations of our experience of pain, smell, and color. The book covers both traditional philosophical arguments and more recent empirical arguments deriving from research in psychophysics and neuroscience.

The addition of chapter summaries, suggestions for further reading and a glossary of terms make *Perception* essential reading for anyone studying the topic in detail, as well as for students of philosophy of mind, philosophy of psychology, and metaphysics.

Adam Pautz is a Professor of Philosophy at Brown University, USA. With Daniel Stoljar he is the editor of *Blockheads!: Essays on Ned Block's Philosophy of Mind and Consciousness* (2019).

NEW PROBLEMS OF PHILOSOPHY
Series Editor: José Luis Bermúdez

"*New Problems of Philosophy* is developing a most impressive line-up of topical volumes aimed at graduate and upper-level undergraduate students in philosophy and at others with interests in cutting edge philosophical work. Series authors are players in their respective fields and notably adept at synthesizing and explaining intricate topics fairly and comprehensively".

—*John Heil, Monash University, Australia, and Washington University in St. Louis, USA*

"This is an outstanding collection of volumes. The topics are well chosen and the authors are outstanding. They will be fine texts in a wide range of courses".

—*Stephen Stich, Rutgers University, USA*

The New *Problems of Philosophy* series provides accessible and engaging surveys of the most important problems in contemporary philosophy. Each book examines either a topic or theme that has emerged on the philosophical landscape in recent years, or a longstanding problem refreshed in light of recent work in philosophy and related disciplines. Clearly explaining the nature of the problem at hand and assessing attempts to answer it, books in the series are excellent starting points for undergraduate and graduate students wishing to study a single topic in depth. They will also be essential reading for professional philosophers. Additional features include chapter summaries, further reading, and a glossary of technical terms.

The Metaphysics of Identity
André Gallois

Consciousness
Rocco J. Gennaro

Abstract Entities
Sam Cowling

Embodied Cognition, Second Edition
Lawrence Shapiro

Self-Deception
Eric Funkhouser

Relativism
Maria Baghramian and Annalisa Coliva

Empathy
Heidi Maibom

Moral Disagreement
Richard Rowland

Perception
Adam Pautz

Thinking and Perceiving
Dustin Stokes

For more information about this series, please visit: https://www.routledge.com/New-Problems-of-Philosophy/book-series/NPOP

PERCEPTION

Adam Pautz

Routledge
Taylor & Francis Group

LONDON AND NEW YORK

First published 2021
by Routledge
2 Park Square, Milton Park, Abingdon, Oxon OX14 4RN

and by Routledge
52 Vanderbilt Avenue, New York, NY 10017

Routledge is an imprint of the Taylor & Francis Group, an informa business

British Library Cataloguing-in-Publication Data
A catalogue record for this book is available from the British Library

Library of Congress Cataloging-in-Publication Data
Names: Pautz, Adam, author.
Title: Perception / Adam Pautz.
Description: Abingdon, Oxon; New York, NY: Routledge, 2021. | Series:
   New problems of philosophy | Includes bibliographical references and index.
Identifiers: LCCN 2020051423 (print) | LCCN 2020051424 (ebook)
Subjects: LCSH: Perception (Philosophy)
Classification: LCC B828.45 .P38 2021 (print) | LCC B828.45 (ebook) |
   DDC 121/.34—dc23
LC record available at https://lccn.loc.gov/2020051423
LC ebook record available at https://lccn.loc.gov/2020051424

ISBN: 978-0-415-48604-0 (hbk)
ISBN: 978-0-415-48605-7 (pbk)
ISBN: 978-1-315-77193-9 (ebk)

Typeset in Joanna and Scala Sans
by KnowledgeWorks Global Ltd.

In memory of Cecile Pautz

CONTENTS

Preface and acknowledgments   x

Introduction: What is the puzzle of perception?   1
1   The character question   2
2   Why the character question is hard: the external-internal puzzle   6
3   Why the character question is important: the significance of
     experience   12
4   The organization of this book   14

1   **The sense datum view: Experiencing virtual reality**   17
1.1   Naïve realism: the window shade model   18
1.2   The sense datum view: the brain as a virtual reality device   21
1.3   The act-object assumption   27
1.4   The argument from hallucination for the sense datum view over naïve
      realism   30
1.5   The argument from illusionism about sensible properties for the sense
      datum view over naïve realism   36
1.6   The sense datum view neatly solves the external-internal puzzle   42
1.7   The *percipi* problem about pain   44
1.8   Can the sense datum view explain our access to the external world?   45
1.9   Do simplicity considerations undermine the sense datum view?   48
1.10 Where are sense data?   50
1.11 Hard cases: perceptual imprecision and incompleteness   52
Summary   56
Further Reading   56

2   **The internal physical state view: Experiences as inner modifications**   **59**
2.1   What is the internal physical state view?   60
2.2   From experiential internalism to the internal physical state view   65
2.3   Can the internal physical state view accommodate the transparency observation?   68
2.4   The externally directed nature of some experiences   72
2.5   The argument from essential external directedness against the internal physical state view   77
2.6   Could a brain-in-the-void have a favorite shape?   81
2.7   Papineau's reply: rejecting essential external directedness   84
Summary   90
Further Reading   91

3   **The representational view: Experiencing as representing**   **93**
3.1   What is the representational view?   94
3.2   The argument for the representational view: an inference to the best explanation   102
3.3   Can the representational view explain all sensory-perceptual experiences?   110
3.4   How rich is the content of experience?   116
3.5   The question of skepticism and the dogmatist answer   120
3.6   Does the representational view explain perceptual presence?   126
3.7   Is the representational view intrinsically implausible?   128
3.8   Can the representational view explain the laws of appearance?   130
Summary   135
Further Reading   136

4   **How does experience represent the world?**   **139**
4.1   Two questions for representationalists   140
4.2   Response-independent representationalism   142
4.3   Armchair arguments against response-independent representationalism?   148
4.4   The problem of internal dependence about sensible properties   151
4.5   Other problems about sensible properties   161
4.6   Response-dependent representationalism   164
4.7   Two problems with response-dependent representationalism   167
4.8   Internalist-nonreductive representationalism: the basic idea   170
4.9   Must internalist representationalists treat color as illusory?   175
4.10   Is internalist representationalism plausible for spatial experience?   178
4.11   Is internalist representationalism mysterious?   182
Summary   185
Further Reading   185

5   **The return to naïve realism: Experience as openness to the world**   **188**
5.1   A basic form of contemporary naïve realism   190
5.2   How naïve realism differs from representationalism   195
5.3   Naïve realism v representationalism: intrinsic plausibility   198
5.4   Naïve realism v representationalism: explanatory role   202

5.5 Representationalism *v* naïve realism: hallucination and illusion   207
5.6 Representationalism *v* naïve realism: two arguments from science   215
5.7 Can internalist-selectionist naïve realism answer the arguments
     from science?   222
5.8 Can ways-based naïve realism answer the arguments from
     science?   226
Summary   232
Further Reading   232

6   **Conclusion**   **235**
6.1 Explaining essential external directedness at the cost of denying
     internal dependence   236
6.2 Explaining internal dependence at the cost of denying essential
     external directedness   237
6.3 Accepting both essential external directedness and internal
     dependence   238
Further Reading   240

Glossary   241
References   244
Index   260

PREFACE AND ACKNOWLEDGMENTS

The *New Problems of Philosophy* series provides accessible and engaging surveys of the most important problems in contemporary philosophy. This book is an introduction to the main positions in the philosophy of perception intended for graduate students and advanced undergraduates.

I tried to write the chapters so that they form a narrative, with each chapter leading to the next in a natural progression. But I have also tried to make each of them self-standing, so that teachers can use them separately.

In keeping with the aim of the series, this book mostly has a contemporary focus. I do begin with a chapter on the traditional sense datum view, because it appeals to students' imaginations and it is a good vehicle for introducing the problem of perception to them. The rest of the book focuses on contemporary alternatives to the sense datum view.

Like some other books in the series, this is an opinionated introduction. I do not stake out my own position. But my opinions naturally affected what issues and arguments I decided to cover and how I presented them.

I am grateful to many people for helpful discussion of various parts of this book.

Parts of the book were tried out on audiences at Oxford's Jowett Society, the University of Southern California, the University of California at Berkeley, and New York University. I am grateful to audience members on those occasions for helpful comments.

I have used drafts of this book in undergraduate seminars at Brown University and in a graduate seminar at MIT (co-taught with Alex Byrne and Jack Spencer). I am grateful for the invaluable feedback I received in those classes.

I am grateful to many people for reading parts of the manuscript and helping me to revise it. Farid Masrour, John Morrison, Jacob Beck, and James van Cleve used parts of the book in their undergraduate classes and gave me useful feedback. Brian Cutter, Matt Duncan, Boyd Millar, Alex Moran, Brad Saad, and Jeff Speaks read drafts of the book in whole or in part and kindly provided me with invaluable comments. I am also grateful to Neil Mehta and the members of his summer 2020 perception group (especially Chris Hill, Farid Masrour, Boyd Millar, David Papineau, and Susanna Schellenberg) for reading parts of the book and giving me a lot of helpful advice.

Finally, I would like to thank two anonymous referees for Routledge for their encouraging and very helpful reports. And a big thanks to Tony Bruce and Adam Johnson at Routledge. They have been consistently patient and kind during what turned out to be a very long process.

INTRODUCTION
WHAT IS THE PUZZLE OF PERCEPTION?

In cases of illusion or hallucination of a pink vase ... one's state of mind can hardly be vase-shaped or pink, so what is one describing when one asserts that it looks to one as if there is a [vase-shaped, pink] vase before one?

—M. G. F. Martin (1995)

The qualitative difference between red and green, the tastiness of fruit and foulness of carrion, the scariness of heights and prettiness of flowers are products of our common nervous system.

—Stephen Pinker (2008)

The subject of this book is perception – the mind's first point of contact with the world. We will mainly focus on visual perception but we will also consider our experience of sound, smell, and pain.

There are many questions about perception. What constitutes how things appear to us – the character of our experiences of the world? What is it to perceive an object? How does perception enable us to think about objects and form a conception of the world? How does perception give us knowledge of that world?

In this book, we will focus on the question of what constitutes the character of experience, although here and there we will address the other questions too. The main views in the philosophy of perception are defined by how they answer this question. This book covers four of them: the sense datum view, the internal physical state view, the representational view, and naïve realism.

In this introduction, I will first explain the "character question". Then I will explain why it is puzzling. Finally, I will explain why it is important.

1 The character question

Suppose you first view a tomato and then a lemon. The object you now perceive is different from the one you first perceived. The *character* of your experience is also different. In ordinary language, we would simply say that "you have a different experience". And we would convey the difference by talking about the difference in how things "appear" or "seem" to you.

In this example, the character of your experience changes, and so does the object you experience. However, the character of your experience can change even if the object you perceive doesn't change in its intrinsic features. For instance, if you move closer to a table, the table doesn't change, but your experience of it does, because your perspective on the table changes. Again, if you take off your glasses, the character of your experience changes because things look blurry, but the objects you see don't change.

There are also illusions. In an illusion, you experience a real thing, but it seems other than it is. A recently famous example is "the dress", which became a viral internet sensation in 2015. This is an image of a dress which to some people looks white and gold and to other people looks black and blue. The explanation is that the color signal is ambiguous and different individuals' visual systems resolve the ambiguity in different ways. If the dress cannot have multiple colors, at least one of the groups must be subject to an illusion, but it is not clear which one. This caused heated debate on twitter, with many celebrities chiming in. The dress nicely illustrates important philosophical worries about how we could know whether perception is a reliable guide to reality. Taylor Swift tweeted that thinking about it left her "confused and scared".

After-effect illusions can also be very powerful. My favorite examples can be found on YouTube (just search "color after image"). For example, in one video, you start off by seeing an image of a castle on top of a grassy hill with the sky in the background. At first the castle, the sky, and the grass are shown with very odd colors. Then in fact the odd colors are replaced with black and white. But, because of the after-effect, even though image is now in black and white, you experience the grass as being vividly green, the sky as vividly blue, and so on. Your brain "projects" onto the black and white image a variety of colors that aren't really there. The illusion is perfect. The illusory colors really appear "out there", and there is nothing that could tip you off that they are not. After a while, the illusion goes away: the illusory colors go away and the image begins to look black and white, just as it really is.

Hallucination is a more extreme perceptual failure. In a visual hallucination, you have a visual experience but you don't experience any real thing at all. For example, there is a fascinating condition called "Charles Bonnet syndrome" (CBS) that is common among those who have lost their sight, often through an age-related condition (e.g., macular degeneration). While they lose the ability to see, they acquire a tendency to have extremely vivid hallucinations. For instance, on a webpage about CBS, you can find the following description:

> I have macular degeneration and about six months ago, I started to see these super colorful shapes and figures. Fortunately, I was told about CBS by my eye doctor so I then began to enjoy them. Sometimes I see these climbing vines or plants which are such a rich green. I love seeing the strong colors but sometimes they are really, really colorful like when you put up the colour control on the TV to the maximum.

So far, I have given examples of radical changes in the character of your experience. Other changes are more subtle. For instance, you can see the drawing below as a rabbit or as a duck. This is called a "gestalt" (German: "shape, form") shift.

In other cases, it is hard to tell whether there is a difference in your experience or in your cognitive reaction to the experience. For instance, if you see a long-lost friend from childhood, and don't recognize her at first, and then all of a sudden recognize her, there is a change in your overall mental state. But is it a change in your visual experience?

In spite of such tough cases, we have a pretty good grip on the idea of having two sensory-perceptual experiences with "the same character". In ordinary language, we would simply say that you "have the same experience" (so that perhaps the term "character" can be eliminated).

We can use our grip on this idea to introduce another idea that will be very important in this book: the idea of having an experience of a certain

Figure 0.1 Duck-rabbit.

maximally-specific type. Suppose you see a tomato on one occasion and then an identical tomato on another occasion. Or – to take a more extreme case – suppose you have an identical hallucination of a tomato. Even though the cases are very different in certain respects, we all recognize a sense in which you "have the same type of experience" in each case. You have an experience of a different type when you view a lemon. Likewise, when you view the table from different places, or interpret the image in Figure 0.1 differently, then you have different experience-types. When you hear a sound or feel a tickle, you again have different experience-types.

This brings us to:

> **The character question.** What is it to have a certain specific experience-type? For instance, what is it to have the tomato-like experience, or the quite different lemon-like experience? Or a specific experience of the table from a particular vantage point, or a specific experience of the figure shown above? What is it to have a specific type of auditory experience? And so on.

An answer to this question will tell us what differences in the character of experience consist in. It will take the form of a definition:

> To have an experience with a certain character (that is, to have an experience of a certain type) *just is* to ＿＿＿＿＿＿＿.

This whole book will be devoted to filling in the blank here. Different views fill in the blank in different ways.[1]

I have mentioned many examples where there is variation in experience without variation in the world: change of perspective, blur, color illusion, gestalt shifts. So any adequate answer to the character question must answer the following question: in such cases, what does the variation in experience consist in, if not variation in the world you perceive? This is part of what makes the question difficult.

You might wonder how we can give an interesting "definition" of something as basic as having an experience with a certain character. What would such a definition look like? So let me briefly describe some examples of the main answers to the character question that philosophers and scientists have proposed through the years in order to give you a rough sense of them. Each of these views will be the subject of a subsequent chapter.

> **Naïve realism.** This view holds that, at least in normal cases, to have an experience with a certain character is just to experience the actual character of external things. Normally, differences in the character of your experience just consist in differences in the world you experience. Naïve realists face a big problem: how can they explain cases, such as the above-mentioned cases of illusion and hallucination, where the character of your experience changes but the world doesn't change? (Chapters 1 and 5)
>
> **The sense datum view.** Sense datum theorists think that illusion and hallucination show that your brain is always creating non-physical images ("sense data") in a kind of virtual world; it is this virtual world that you perceive, not the real world. To have certain experience-type is just to be aware of a certain array of images (and also perhaps to "interpret" them in a certain way) created by neural activity in the brain. Differences in experiences are constituted by differences in the images in the virtual world (or, perhaps in some cases, your "interpretation of them"). (Chapter 1)
>
> **The internal physical state view.** This view gets rid of non-physical images created by brain states and instead maintains that to have a certain experience-type is just to be in a certain brain state. Modulations in experiential character *just are* modulations in brain states. (Chapter 2)
>
> **The representational view.** This view holds that to have a certain experience-type is just to "experientially" represent the external world to be a certain way, where this is somewhat akin to believing the world to be a certain way, but more automatic and vivid. Our experiences are, so to speak, hypotheses about the world that the brain arrives at. These representational states are enabled by brain states but they are more than brain states (just as a story is more than a series of marks and lines in a book). Differences in the character of experience are constituted by differences in how your experience represents the world to be. In cases of illusion and hallucination, the world is not that way. (Chapters 3 and 4)

We are not assuming from the start that one of these theories applies to all types or aspects of experience. That is one possibility. But another possibility is that one theory is correct for some types of or aspects of experiences, and another theory is correct for other types of or aspects of experiences.

It is important to understand that the character question is not just about what causes or explains or enables your experiences. It is about the *definition* of experience. It is about what your experience, and what changes in your experience, consist in. For example, we know that a neural activation state in your brain is a cause or enabling condition of your experience of a tomato. But that doesn't automatically mean that having a tomato-like experience consists in nothing but undergoing a certain brain state. Maybe this "internal physical state" view is correct, but it cannot be established so easily. Maybe instead having a tomato-like experience is dependent on a brain state but something more than a brain state. For instance, maybe it consists in perceiving a tomato in the world (naïve realism), or in perceiving a non-physical, tomato-like sense datum created by your brain (sense datum view), or representing the presence of a tomato-like object (representational view).

2 Why the character question is hard: the external-internal puzzle

There are many philosophical puzzles about perception. But I think it is helpful to understand the main puzzle in the following way. Experience has a Janus-faced character. Many experiences are essentially "externally directed". But experiences are also "internally dependent". Experiences spring from the inside but they also point outward. And this is puzzling.

The external-internal puzzle will be a unifying theme of this book. For each view we will look at, we will consider whether it can adequately solve the puzzle. For now, it will be enough to explain roughly what it means to say that some experiences are both "externally directed" and "internally dependent", and to give you some sense of the resulting puzzle. As we go along in the book, these ideas will become clearer.

The puzzle comes in two forms. One concerns abnormal perception: illusion and hallucination. The other concerns the experience of "sensible properties" in normal perception.

To illustrate the first puzzle, imagine that you have an experience as of a tomato on a white table. You know simply by reflecting on what the experience is like that it is essentially externally directed. To a first approximation, by this I mean that, necessarily, if you have this type of experience, then you in some sense have an experience of a red and round thing in space. It seems to you that there is a red and round item present. Having an experience like this is *inseparable* from the seeming presence of a round thing. It is strictly impossible to have the one without the other. Thus, this type of experience is always essentially "directed" at a certain type of item in space, a kind of item that doesn't exist inside your brain when you have the experience. It is not like a headache, which doesn't seem to present any item in space. That some experiences are externally directed should be one of our starting points in theorizing about perceptual experience.

While simple reflection on what the experience is like supports external directedness, the empirical fact that there are illusions and hallucinations supports a form of internal dependence. For instance, imagine that you have CBS (described above). Then you might have a vivid hallucination of a tomato that is just like your normal perception of a tomato because of aberrant neural activity.

These two ideas generate a puzzle. The puzzle can be put like this:

> **External-internal puzzle about hallucination.** Even in such an hallucinatory case, your tomato-like experience is externally directed: it seems you as if a red and round thing is *right there*. Yet, in this case, no physical red and round thing is there. *So how can we account for your vivid impression that a red and round thing is there?* How is it that in this case the experience is both externally directed and internally generated? Does your brain perhaps create a ghostly red and round "mental image" and project it into space? Or what?

As M. G. F. Martin puts the puzzle in the quote I started with, in such a case, "what is one describing when one asserts that it looks to one as if there is a [red and round thing] before one?" Any good answer to the character question must address this question.

The experience of pain provides another example of the same puzzle. Experiences of pains are externally directed. We experience pains in space in various bodily regions and as standing in spatial relations. The apparent location of one pain in your forearm can really be close to the apparent location of a second pain in the same forearm. But, in abnormal cases, experiences of pain are internally dependent. An example is phantom pain. People who have lost a limb continue to feel "phantom pain" there because of aberrant neural activity. Again, the external-internal puzzle is this: in such a case, how come it feels as if there is a pain in the relevant region, even though there is no physical disturbance there at all?

This instance of the external-internal puzzle concerns abnormal experience. The other instance of the puzzle concerns our experience of "sensible properties" in normal experience.

Let me first define the idea of a "sensible property", which has been a central focus of the philosophy of perception. (In this book, I will also sometimes use the synonymous term "sensible quality". Others use the term "qualia".) In experience, we are presented with spatial properties, such as shape, location, and depth. But that is not all we are presented with. We presented with properties together with spatial properties. *Sensible properties* are among the distinctive properties presented to us in experience together with spatial properties. They belong to various "families". It is difficult to locate them in the quantitative world of physics. Here are some examples:

sensible colors

audible qualities

smell qualities

taste qualities

pain qualities

For instance, when you view a bowl of fruit, you experience a number sensible colors in a spatial arrangement. At the same time, you might hear a high-pitched bird call outside the window. You might feel a dull ache in your foot. The sensible properties presented in your experiences are bound up with the character of those experiences.

The sciences of psychophysics and neuroscience suggest that, even in normal perception, our experience of sensible properties is especially dependent on our internal neural processing – even more so than our experience of spatial properties. In Chapter 4, we will formulate this claim more exactly and describe the empirical evidence. But here we can work with the rough idea.

For example, consider again the case of pain. We saw that the experience of phantom pain is internally generated. But there is plenty of evidence that even in normal cases what pain we experience depends more on our internal neural response than on the external bodily disturbance. For instance, when put your hand in scolding hot water, the explanation of why you experience pain of a certain specific intensity (and not a higher or lower intensity) resides most directly in what happens in your brain (namely, firing rates of neurons in the pain-matrix), not anything that happens in your hand itself.

Or consider the experience of smell. There is a lot of empirical evidence that how something smells to us is more closely dependent on our neural response than on the external odorant. For example, the explanation of why you experience a citrus smell and not a minty smell resides most directly in your neural processing – not the objective character of the odorant.

The same applies to the experience of color. You might have thought that things just have certain colors "out there" and that is why we experience the colors we do. But the empirical evidence suggests that the experience of color is just as dependent on neural processing as the experience of pain or smell. For example, light varies continuously but we experience discrete color categories (red, green, yellow, and blue). When you look at a tomato, the reason why you experience red and not green is more directly explained by your neural response to the tomato than it is by the objective reflectance of the tomato (i.e., the way it reflects light). A different species could respond to the same reflectance of the tomato but experience green rather than red because of different neural processing.

So science suggests that the experience of sensible properties is internally dependent. At the same time, first-person reflection shows that the experience of sensible properties is externally directed. You experience sensible properties as "out there", as filling shapes and spatially arranged in various locations, often at a distance from you. As a result, a form of the external-internal puzzle extends to normal perception:

> **External-internal puzzle about sensible properties.** Even in totally normal perception, and not just in illusion and hallucination, your experience of sensible properties (pain qualities, smell qualities, color qualities) is shaped by internal processing. Yet you experience sensible properties as "out there", together with shapes and in various locations, often at a distance from you. How is it that what you seem to experience as "out there" is shaped by internal processing "in here"?

One traditional response is that sensible properties are "unreal" or "projections of the brain". But what does this mean? And even if nothing has ever been objectively minty or objectively red, the *appearance* of these qualities still needs to be accounted for. How did our brains enable us to have illusory experiences of unreal properties of a wholly novel sort (colors, smell qualities, pain qualities, audible qualities), properties that are totally unlike any of the properties (charges, masses, spin) that have occurred in the real world?

Traditionally, the first puzzle is called the "problem of illusion" or "the problem of hallucination" while the second is called "the problem of sensible properties". But there is a rough similarity between the two problems. So we can see them as instances of the same kind of puzzle: the external-internal puzzle. The external-internal puzzle is what makes the character question so hard to answer.

For example, pretend we didn't know anything about how our visual and other experiences are internally dependent. We didn't know about illusions and hallucinations and we didn't know about the empirical evidence for the role of the brain in shaping our experience of colors and other sensible properties. In that case, we would not think that there is any big problem concerning how to answer the character question. We would probably just accept the simple position of "naïve realism". It is only when we discover that our visual and other experiences are internally dependent that naïve realism becomes problematic. Naïve realists are hard-pressed to explain why an external object might seem to be present in a hallucination case where no physical object is present. And they cannot easily accommodate the big role of internal processes in shaping what sensible properties we experience in normal perception. In short, while naïve realism nicely explains the externally directed character of experience, it has trouble accommodating internal dependence.

Conversely, if all of our experiences were internally dependent but none were externally directed, like diffuse head pains or bouts of nausea, then again experience would not pose such a formidable philosophical puzzle. For instance, if you have a diffuse headache that is not caused by an external object, there is no problem of the form "why does it seem to you that an external object is out there even though there isn't one?", for the simple reason that in having a headache it *doesn't* seem that an object is out there. Headaches are just internal sensations that aren't externally directed in the same way as ordinary visual experiences. Unlike visual experiences, they don't involve the vivid impression that an external thing with certain sensible properties is *out there* in space. Because many of our experiences are both externally directed and internally dependent, experience poses a difficult philosophical problem. How can we have vivid experiences as of objects and sensible properties "out there", because of internal neural processing "in here" – even in hallucination cases where no physical object is really present at all?

What kind of answer to the character question *would* solve the external-internal puzzle? That is what this book is going to be about. But, in order to get across the difficulty of the external-internal puzzle, let me briefly explain to you one quite complex and strange solution: the traditional sense datum view, which will be the focus on our first chapter. This view had its heyday in the early 20th century and it traces back to John Locke (1632–1704). It could not be more different from the simple, cozy position of naïve realism.

To illustrate, suppose you view a tomato on a table. According to the sense datum view, the physical objects reflecting light into your eyes are in fact intrinsically colorless, made up of colorless subatomic particles. The red and round item in your visual field and the other colored items in your visual field are in fact very detailed images created by your brain. All this – this whole realm of colored items – is a figment of your brain. You think all these colored items are physical things in a public space, but in fact they are mental images in a private mental realm created by your brain. Likewise, when you feel pain (real or phantom), the brain creates non-physical pain sense data in a kind of private bodily space. In general, each of us lives in her own virtual reality created by her brain. So the perceptual process works like this: first the world, then a brain process, and finally a highly embellished virtual model of the world. Why does your brain go to the trouble of creating for you a virtual reality filled with colors, pain qualities, audible qualities, and so on, even though these qualities are absent from your physical environment and body? Because it helps you to tell objects apart and react appropriately to them.

This "sense datum view" view may seem extreme, but it would at least have the merit of solving the external-internal puzzle. Even though sense data are internally generated, the sense datum view explains the externally directed character of the tomato-like experience: on this view, whenever you have this experience, it vividly seems to you that you experience a red and round item in space, for the simple reason that you really do experience a red and round item in space – even in a hallucination case. At the same time, it also explains internal dependence, by holding that this red and round item is a "sense datum" created by your brain in a private mental space.

I hope the foregoing gives you a sense of the external-internal puzzle and why it may challenge our pretheoretical ideas about perception. Many have thought that its proper solution requires recognizing that there is a big difference between the way things appear and the way they really are.

How might we figure out the correct solution to the puzzle of perception? We can rely on simple reflection on what our experiences are like. For instance, that is where we get our reason to accept external directedness. We can also rely on empirical findings. That is where we get our reason to accept internal dependence. Our aim is to come up with a simple theory that fits as best as possible with the things we have reason to believe about experience. To do this, we must try to weigh up the costs and benefits of the different theories.

3 Why the character question is important: the significance of experience

I have explained why the character question is hard: the reason is the external-internal puzzle. But what is it important?

The answer is simple: we hold dear certain beliefs about the nature of experience that may be thrown into doubt by the correct answer. Some of these beliefs come from commonsense and reflection; others derive from more general theoretical commitments about the world. Here are some of the beliefs I have in mind.

We perceive elements of the external world in a strong sense. We don't think we perceive things indirectly by perceiving "images" made by the brain (as on the "sense datum view"), in the way we perceive a football game by watching images on a TV screen. Rather, we perceive ordinary physical things themselves in the strong sense upheld by naïve realists: the very character of our experience is *constituted by* our perceiving the character of real things, events, and other items in the external world. In this sense, on occasion, the real, concrete states of things themselves shape the contours of our experience.

We take it that this is part of what gives experience its distinctive value. For instance, we take it to be a good thing that we can in this sense perceive a sunset, or the smile of a friend. So if we do not in this strong sense perceive elements of the external world, then experience doesn't have the value we take to have.

Many theories imply that we do not in this sense strong perceive elements the real world. Clearly, the sense datum view has this implication. But the internal physical state view and representationalism have this implication as well, because they reject naïve realism.

The external world is generally the way it appears. Relatedly, we believe that, at least normally, the world is pretty much as it appears. The world is *not* devoid of colors, sounds, smells, and so on. Things really do have the colors, sound qualities, tastes, smells, and so on, that they seem to have. They also have the spatial features they seem to have.

As we shall see, many theories of experience go against this common-sense belief as well. As just explained, the "sense datum view", to be discussed in Chapter 1, goes against this belief. The position of "illusionist representationalism", to be discussed in Chapter 4, does as well.

Perceptual experience is a natural, physical phenomenon, not radically different from other physical phenomena in the natural world. This belief flows from a general kind "physicalism" about the world that many people embrace. Roughly, physicalism is the idea that all facts about the spatio-temporal realm amount to physical facts. So perception is an entirely physical phenomenon, like digestion or photosynthesis. In response to the "mind-body problem", physicalists insist that states of the mind are just purely physical states of the body. This view is recommended by its simplicity.

Some prominent theories of perception cast doubt on this simple physicalist picture of the mind. Consider for instance the sense datum view. If the physical world is colorless, and the detailed colored images you experience are creations of your brain occupying a kind of private "virtual reality", then those colored images must be non-physical. For instance, a neuroscientist looking into your brain would not find them there. So if the sense datum view is true, physicalism fails. Or again, "internalist representationalism", which we will consider in Chapter 4, creates another puzzle for physicalism. On this view, the brain has an intrinsic capacity to enable us to experientially represent (be "acquainted with") properties that are not instantiated in the brain – including properties like color properties that have never occurred in the world at all. This is mysterious, and it is unclear whether it can be explained in purely physical terms.

It follows that you cannot tackle the mind-body problem without taking a look at the philosophy of perception. Many discussions of mind-body problem are conducted at a very abstract level; they are focused on general arguments ("the zombie argument", "the knowledge argument", and so on) and grand views (physicalism, pansychism, and so on). But the details matter too. The grand views need to account for the facts of perception. No discussion of the mind-body problem would be complete without a look at the puzzles of perception.

Experience has a unique explanatory and reason-giving significance. It's natural to think being experientially acquainted with certain things or qualities is necessarily *sufficient for having certain kinds of reasons.* For instance, necessarily, if you have a vivid experience of a lemon, you have at least some reason to think a yellowish, round thing is there (although the reason could be defeated if, for instance, you are told you are hallucinating). This is related to the essentially "externally directed" character of experience.

Experiences are not just sufficient to give us certain reasons for having certain beliefs about things; it is also sufficient to give us the very capacity to have those beliefs in the first place. For instance, your experiences are enough to enable you to have beliefs about the colors and shapes of things.

In fact, some philosophers find it intuitive that experience is *necessary* for having the relevant beliefs, and for having reasons for those beliefs. For example, a robot lacking experiences couldn't have the same reasons to believe things about the external world, and indeed maybe could not really understand and believe things at all, even if its internal physical states are reliably connected to the environment and it is indistinguishable from a normal human in its behavior and appearance.

We might put these ideas in slogan form: *experience first*. Experience lies at the foundation of our most basic mental capacities and knowledge. In fact, it may be that, before you can have these capacities at all, you need experience first.

4 The organization of this book

The organization of this book is simple. We will start with the traditional sense datum view already touched on and then by a natural train of thought move through the more contemporary views. Here is a brief guide to the book.

Chapter 1 is about the traditional sense datum view. On this view, experiences involve arrays of non-physical "sense data" created by brain processes. As already noted, this provides an interesting solution to the external-internal puzzle. It explains how experience is both "externally directed" at items arranged in space, but also dependent on neural processing. But it requires belief in sense data. Sense data would be very strange items. If you were to hallucinate a tomato, would there really exist a reddish and round mental image? If so, where is it? It is not in your physical brain (there is no physical reddish and round thing in your brain). Maybe the right thing to say is that, even though there vividly seems to be a reddish and round item, there doesn't really exist such a thing – not even a reddish and round image or sense datum.

Chapter 2 is about the internal physical state view. This view is a natural option after setting aside the sense datum view. Instead of holding that experiences are relations to non-physical sense data created by states of the brain, this view holds that experiences are identical with those brain states themselves. It simply removes the additional step. Changes in the character of experience *just are* changes in brain states. All experiences are therefore entirely "internal" phenomena like headaches. The trouble: this view may not fully solve the external-internal puzzle. It explains the fact that experiences are internally dependent but may not be consistent with the fact that some of them (e.g., visual experiences) are also essentially externally directed. Some recent internal physical state theorists (for instance, David Papineau) are willing to reject or weaken the idea the strong thesis that experiences are essentially externally directed. Thus, they solve the external-internal puzzle by rejecting or weakening one of the ideas that generate the puzzle. However, opponents will say that rejecting essential external directedness flies in the face of phenomenological observation.

Chapter 3 is about the representational view. The lessons of the previous chapters will lead straight to it. Many experiences are essentially externally directed (contrary to the internal physical state view), but they also existence-neutral (contrary to sense datum theorists). These are features that experiences share with "representational" states like beliefs. For instance, your belief that there is a round tomato in the next room is externally directed but existence-neutral: there might be no such thing there. Representationalists propose that experiences are a species of representational states like beliefs, only they are much more vivid and detailed. In this chapter, we will mostly focus on the *basic idea* and how it explains the *externally directed character* of experience.

Chapter 4 continues the discussion of the representational view. Whereas Chapter 3 is about the basic idea of representationalism and focuses on how it explains the externally directed character of experience, Chapter 4 focuses on how the basic idea can be developed in detail, with a view to determining how it might fully accommodate the dependence of experience on internal factors. We will find that some "externalist" forms of representationalism may not fully accommodate the empirically-supported fact (mentioned above) that our experience of sensible properties is especially dependent on internal neural processes. By contrast, "internalist" forms of representationalism may accommodate the way in which many of our experiences are both externally directed and shaped by internal processes. The idea is this: experiencing consists in representing things and qualities in space, but in some cases how we experientially represent the external world is due to our own internal processing, rather than to the character of the world itself. For many, such an internalist form of representationalism offers the best solution to the external-internal puzzle. However, it also faces many problems.

Chapter 5, the final chapter, is on contemporary forms of naïve realism. In particular, it is about the debate between contemporary naïve realism and representationalism. Traditionally, naïve realism had been cast aside because of internally-generated illusions and hallucinations. But contemporary forms of naïve realism show promise in accommodating illusions and hallucinations. Moreover, there is something to be said for naïve realism: it just seems right. But there is a problem: while it nicely explains the externally directed character of experience, it doesn't fit well with empirical evidence for the robust role of internal factors in shaping our experience of sensible properties. The problem for naïve realism is therefore the opposite of the problem with the internal physical state view, which accommodates internal dependence but has trouble with essential external directedness. Some naïve realists are prepared to reject internal dependence. For instance, John Campbell writes, "what I disagree with is the idea that our brain makes a big contribution to experience] ... the function [of brain processing] is just to reveal the world to us" and "looking for the qualitative character of experience in the nature of a brain state is looking for it in the wrong place". Thus the viability of naïve realism depends to a large extent on empirical issues in neuroscience and psychophysics.

Finally, the *Conclusion* summarizes the advantages and disadvantages of the main views and points out some important unresolved issues.

Notes

1   In this book, then, I will typically assume that answers to the character question take the form of "real definitions" that apply in all possible cases (Dorr 2016). However, as we will see, answers to the character question might also be understood as specifying what "constitutes" or "grounds" the character of experience (for this notion see Fine 2012). And it may be that different things can constitute or ground the character of experience in different cases. For instance, as we will see in Chapter 5, some say that "naïve realism" is right for normal experiences but some other theory is right for hallucinatory experiences. And sometimes "representationalists" (Chapters 3 and 4) say that naïve realism is wrong for actual humans but allow it might be right for individuals in other "possible worlds" (e.g., Chalmers 2010: chap.12).

1

THE SENSE DATUM VIEW:
EXPERIENCING VIRTUAL REALITY

When I see [or hallucinate] a tomato ... I cannot doubt that there exists a red patch of a round and somewhat bulgy shape, standing out from a background of other colour-patches, and that this whole field of colour is directly present to my consciousness.

—H. H. Price (1932)

It becomes evident that the real table is not the same as what we immediately experience by sight or touch or hearing.

—Bertrand Russell (1912a)

When you see a sunset, you take it that the vivid colors you experience are really out there. In general, the character of your experience is inherited from the character of the world. This is called *naïve realism*. We value experience because we take it to reveal the world in this way.

The sense datum view of experience tells us that this is all wrong. Experience is not what it seems. It does not reveal the world at all. Experience is a rip-off, an elaborate hoax. The vivid colors of the sunset are not really out there. Sounds, smells, tastes, and so on, are also not out there in the world of physics. All that is out there are colorless particles and fields, or an evolving multidimensional wavefunction, or something equally alien.

The life-like colored "objects" you experience are in fact mental images ("sense data") constructed by the brain, and the space in which they reside is in fact a private mental arena. They are so life-like that you take them to be physical things (so you are duped into accepting naïve realism), but in fact they are quite different from physical things. Likewise sounds, smells, tastes, and so on, are only "in the mind".

The 18th-century Scottish philosopher Thomas Reid remarked that "all philosophers, from Plato to Mr. Hume, agree in this, that we do not perceive external objects immediately, and that the immediate object of perception must be some image present to the mind" (1875: Essay 7). In the early 20th century, it was defended by two luminaries of "analytic" philosophy, G. E. Moore and Bertrand Russell. It was very popular until the 1950s. However, it has largely fallen out of favor and now has very few defenders.[1]

Nevertheless, the sense datum view is important. First, there is a formidable case for the view. As we shall see, it provides a neat solution to a central puzzle about perceptual experience, the puzzle of how experiences present items in space but also depend on our internal sensory processing. Second, the problems with the sense datum view lead to the contemporary views we will discuss in the rest of the book.

Traditionally, the sense datum view is pitted against naïve realism. So in Section 1.1 we will begin with naïve realism. Then in Section 1.2 we will formulate the sense datum view. Finally, in Sections 1.3–1.10 we will look at arguments for and against the sense datum view.

1.1 Naïve realism: the window shade model

Suppose you view a ripe tomato on a table. Your experience has a distinctive phenomenological character. An experience of a lemon on the table would have a very different character. The central question in the philosophy of perception is the *character question*. What is it to have an experience with a certain character? What do differences in the character of experience consist in?

Naïve realists answer that for you to have the tomato-experience on this occasion is simply for you to experience the objective color and shape of the physical tomato itself. Experience involves a special mental relationship that "leaps the spatial gap" between you and the tomato. The character of your experience is simply constituted by your experiencing the bright redness of the tomato, its bulgy shape, and so on (see Figure 1.1).

Figure 1.1 Naïve realism. Thanks to Stuart McMillen (http://www.stuartmcmillen.com/) for the drawing.

More generally:

Naïve realism. At least in normal cases, differences in the character of your experiences are constituted by your experiencing different states (colors, shapes, spatial layouts, sounds, smells, etc.) of mind-independent objects.

Here I am using "objects" very broadly to include ordinary things like tomatoes, pure *visibilia* like the sky and rainbows, events like the movement of a bird in your peripheral vision, and whatever else you might experience.

Naïve realism is in the first instance an account of the character experience. But it also makes a big assumption about the character of the world. In particular, it presupposes *realism about sensible properties*, such as colors, audible properties, taste qualities, and smell qualities. It requires that, even before we evolved, the physical world was replete with all these sensible properties. Tomatoes were red, the sky was blue, the whistling wind made a high-pitched sound, sulfur had a bad smell, and so on. The so-called "qualia" were already in the world. In some versions, these sensible properties *just are* objective physical properties, even if they seem very different from physical properties: redness-as-we-see-it *just is* a way reflecting light, smells are just chemical properties, audible qualities are complex physical properties involving frequency and intensity, and so on.

You might wonder how naïve realism coheres with scientific thinking about experience. Many ancient thinkers, including Plato, Euclid, and Ptolemy, accepted the *extromission theory* of the physical process underlying seeing. They speculated that we experience the world by way of rays emanating from the eye (perhaps with infinite velocity). As Euclid said, "Rays [proceed] from the eye [and] those things are seen upon which the visual rays fall and those things are not seen upon which the visual rays do not fall" (Gross 1999). If the character of experience is constituted by what objects and states of affairs we see, *via* the rays emanating from the eye, then this is a form of naïve realism.

In the early part of the 17th-century scientific revolution, the work of Da Vinci and Kepler established the opposing "intromission model" that we now all accept. In fact, well before them, Alhazen (c. 965–c. 1040) had already mounted an empirical case for the intromission theory. It is now part of educated commonsense that objects reflect light into the eyes. (However, it is interesting to note in passing that, according to a recent study (Winer *et al.* 2002), 60% of college students still accept the extromission theory!)

Now you might think that the intromission model of the causal process underlying experience immediately refutes the naïve realists' account of the character of experience. As Bertrand Russell said, "The observer, when he seems to himself to be observing a stone, is really, if science is to be believed, observing the effects of the stone upon himself [and so] naïve realism is false" (1940: 15).

But naïve realists can resist this argument by accepting the *window shade model* of the role of the brain. For instance, go back to the example of viewing a tomato. Naïve realists can say that the long causal process from the object to the brain (the "inward-pointing arrow" in Figure 1.1) is what "opens the window shade" and enables you to experience the character of the object (the "outward-pointing arrow"). On this view, you do not experience *the end result* of the causal process that starts when light is reflected from the tomato and stimulates the receptors in your eyes, as Russell assumed. Rather, it is just a fact about the way perception works that you only experience the tomato that starts off the causal process. The brain processes play an *enabling role*: they enable you to experience the pre-existing color and shape of the tomato. They select what elements of the mind-independent world you get to experience.

You might wonder what naïve realists say about illusions and hallu-cinations. We will discuss that later. First we must understand the sense datum view.

1.2 The sense datum view: the brain as a virtual reality device

Since the sense datum view is strange, understanding it will take some time. That is the goal of this section; potential reasons to believe it will come later.

Briefly, sense datum theorists accept a "virtual reality model" of the role of the brain instead of the "window shade model". The brain doesn't ena-ble us to experience what it is already there; rather, it constructs a virtual model and it is this model that we experience.

The first thing to understand is that sense datum theorists differ from the naïve realists concerning what the world is like. We just saw that naïve realists accept realism about the sensible properties. The physical tomato on the table before you really is red. By contrast, sense datum theorists accept *illusionism* about sensible properties. In this, they follow a long tra-dition that started with the scientific revolution. Science shows that the tomato is nothing but a collection of extremely small, colorless particles, which reflect some other colorless particles into our eyes (Newton called them "corpuscles"). So the tomato may have the spatial property *round*. But it lacks the sensible property *red*. Similarly, a tree falling in a forest with no one around to hear it doesn't make a sound with pitch, loudness, or timbre. High mean molecular kinetic energy in a body of water can cause you to feel pain, but the pain is not in the water. As Galileo famously wrote:

> I think that tastes, odors, colors, etc., only exist in consciousness; so that if the animal were removed, every such quality would be abolished and annihilated.
>
> (Galileo 1623/1957)

But if, contrary to naïve realists, the tomato is not red, why does it so viv-idly seem to you as if a round and red object is there? The appearance of color needs to be accounted for.

We can approach the answer offered by sense datum theorists using a modern analogy. Consider a "virtual reality" (or "augmented reality") headset that displays highly detailed images on a screen right before your eyes. Suppose it is wintertime and everything outside is white and grey. So you decide to program your headset so that it creates vibrantly colorful and detailed images in real time of the things in front of you. If you pick up a white and round snowball, a *reddish* and round image appears on the display that you see within the headset. If you wore the headset long enough and walked around, then you would be "fooled": the colored images would appear to be in three dimensions and you would mistake them for real objects. It would be an immersive experience.

On the sense datum view, you already occupy a similar virtual reality scenario. Your own brain is an elaborate virtual reality device. For instance, return to your experience of "a tomato on a table". On the sense datum view, even though you take all the colored items in your field of vision to be physical and public (a tomato, a table, your arms, etc.), they are in fact all parts of a super-realistic, ostensibly three-dimensional, non-physical "image" constructed by your brain. This image is akin to a super-realistic, elaborate hologram. On the traditional sense datum view, it is not to be found anywhere in physical space; it is neither located in the physical space before you nor in the physical space occupied by your brain. Instead, the entire spatial arena in your field of vision is in fact a non-physical, private space that is newly created by your brain whenever you open your eyes. The non-physical parts of this image – the red and round part, the table-shaped part – are called "visual sense data". Sense data exist no less than physical objects – they are just very different from physical objects. You instinctively take these visual sense data to be the facing surfaces of physical objects (Russell 1912a: 24), but that is not what they are. It is all a big fake.

If you find the sense datum view impossible to believe, suppose you cross your eyes. Then everything in your visual field will "move" and "become double". Then you can get the sense that it is all an image constructed by your brain, an image that you can move around by screwing up your eyes.

Likewise, if a friend comes in the room at looks at the tomato, she is really experiencing a distinct, ostensibly three-dimensional image in the different mental arena created by her brain.

Now we can see how sense datum theorists answer the question: if the physical tomato is not red – and indeed the entire physical world is color-less and alien – why does it so vividly seem to you (and your friend as well) as if a round and red object is there? The answer is that the physical tomato reflects light into your eyes, setting up a cascade of neural processing. This neural processing somehow conjures up a new little world: an ostensibly three-dimensional mental realm containing a red and round sense datum and other colored sense data.[2] It is this temporary and private world of sense data that you experience. So appearance corresponds to reality; but it is a mental reality constructed by your brain.

While the sense datum differs from the physical tomato in that it is colored while the physical tomato is not, it resembles the physical tomato in its spatial features. So it is a kind of simulacrum of the physical tomato, but with colored added.

Sense datum theorists, then, deny the naïve realist claim that our experiencing physical objects themselves constitutes the character of experience. On the sense datum view, then, we don't really experience objects in the way we thought we did. We can only be said to "perceive" physical objects in a less-than-full-blooded sense: we do so by experiencing sense data that are "pictures" of those physical objects – somewhat as, in the above virtual reality example, you "perceive" physical objects by experiencing images within your headset.[3]

Sense datum theorists focused on visual experience. However, Russell (1912a: 10), Moore (1953/1910: 46–47), and Price (1959) applied the theory to all sensory-perceptual experiences. So, when you smell a rose, there exists an item created by your brain that occupies a diffuse region in some kind of mental space (even though you naively locate it in or around your nose in physical space). This item is *rosy* – nothing more can be said about its nature. Moreover, you stand in the relation of *experiencing* to the rosy character of this item (unlike someone else who has only been told about the rosy character but does not experience it). Likewise, when a soldier who has lost a leg feels phantom pains where their leg used to be, they experience painful sense data in a private "body space".

I haven't yet fully explained how the sense datum view answers the "character question". Before I do that, let me pause to address some questions you might have.

Question 1: *Isn't it just obvious that the colored things we experience are physical things with mass, not ghostly non-physical images (sense data) created by the brain?*

To answer this question, sense datum theorists might return to the virtual reality headset. Suppose that, in addition to such a headset, you also wear gloves that supply tactile information. And now imagine that you are wearing the headset and gloves in an empty room, although you don't yourself know you are in an empty room. Then, on the screen, there appears a very vivid image of a table. When you move around, the table-like image changes according to the laws of perspective. You move your real hand toward where you think the table is. The virtual reality program is very well-designed, so that, as soon as you see the image of your hand meet the image of the table, the glove you are wearing creates a sensation of resistance and a sensation of touch. In this scenario, you would think that the table-like image you experience is solid and has a mass. In fact, you would be wrong: it is just an image on a screen.

In the same way, the sense datum theorist can explain why you might be "tricked" into thinking that the colored objects you experience have mass, when in fact they are non-physical images on a "screen" created by your brain. For instance, when you view a real table, and you move your image of your hand toward the image of a tomato, then your physical hand also touches the physical table, and you have a sensation of resistance. So you mistakenly think that the image of the table has mass.

Question 2: Where are sense data supposed to be located? Are they on the retina, or inside your brain, or what?

Sense data cannot be physical things in the brain or images on the back of your retinas or indeed anything physical at all. The reason is that, when you view a tomato, the sense datum you experience is literally round and red, but there is no physical object like that in your brain. As I said, sense datum theorists typically thought sense data reside in a kind of private mental arena ("phenomenal space"). This mental arena is created by your brain but itself has no physical location.

Question 3: Are sense data "flat", that is, two-dimensional, just like on a TV screen? But the colored objects we experience are clearly three-dimensional.

Many sense datum theorists said that visual sense data are indeed flat or two-dimensional. For instance, the image of the plate viewed from the side is elliptical. But, because of unconscious inferences, it *strikes* you as round and tilted, where its striking you this way is an automatic, pre-cognitive result of visual processing. Again, if you view a tomato, you experience a flat sense datum, but it appears to be three-dimensional and to have a backside.

However, other sense datum theorists, for instance H. H. Price (1932) and Frank Jackson (1977), said that sense data are three-dimensional just as they seem to be. They are like holograms in that they are three-dimensional pure *visibilia* (except that, unlike holograms, they are created by the brain, not a split laser beam). This view agrees better with phenomenology: after all, there is an experiential difference between seeing with one eye and seeing with two eyes (stereopsis) and this can only be explained if depth is given in experience.

Question 4: What are "you", the subject who experiences sense data? And, whatever you are, how do you experience and peruse these non-physical sense data? Sense data don't reflect light!

Sense datum theorists have various options. They might say that you are a physical thing (an animal) but the things you experience are non-physical – they are sense data created by your brain. Or they might say that you are a non-physical thing ("soul") dependent on your brain, just as they say that sense data are non-physical things dependent on the brain. In any version, your experiencing a sense datum is not mediated by any physical process between you and the sense datum. It is a purely mental, non-physical relationship. When your brain generates sense data, it simultaneously causes you to stand in this purely mental relationship to the sense data.

Having answered some basic questions about the idea of "sense data", let me explain how sense datum theorists might answer the character question.

First, we must understand individuals and properties. Roughly, *individuals* are specific existing items that have properties. Visual sense data are examples of individuals. (Other examples would be electrons, tables, and me and you.) *Properties* "characterize" individuals. They are the ways individuals are. So, for instance, the properties of a sense datum include its color and shape. They are repeatable entities that are more "abstract" than individuals. The ways individuals are include how they are related to other individuals. These are "polyadic properties", more commonly called "relations". In ordinary English, we talk about properties and relations all the time. For instance, we talk about the "characteristics" of things and their "relationships". We are focusing here on the perceptible properties of sense data. But all things have properties. For instance, electrons share a certain charge.

Next we can introduce the idea of a "state". A state (or a "trope") is a specific condition of an individual having a certain property, or some things standing in a certain relationship. For instance, Bertrand Russell gave as examples *the-yellowness-of-this, this-above-that, this-before-that, this-moving-from-place-1-to-place-2* (1912a). H. H. Price (1932: 63–64, 103) called them *instances*. He said that, when you look at a tomato, it is clear that what you experience is an *instance* of redness. That is why it looks *red* to you.

Finally, we can give the sense datum answer to the character question.

Sense datum view. To have a sensory-perceptual experience with a certain character is to stand in the *experiencing* relation to certain states, like the redness and roundness of something or the movement of something from one place to another. People have different sensory-perceptual experiences if, and only if, they experience different such states. In the actual world, these states always wholly concern sense data. *Sense data* are non-physical objects (images) created by the brain and occupying a kind of private space. In normal perception, they have spatio-temporal properties that more-or-less match the spatial properties of the corresponding physical objects and events in the world. But in another respect sense data are totally different from physical objects and events: they have sensible properties (sensible colors, audible properties, taste qualities, smell qualities) which are entirely absent from the physical world.[4]

Let us look at how the sense datum theory might handle some cases. First, consider illusions and hallucinations. To take an old example, suppose you view a straight stick that looks bent because it is half-submerged in water. On the sense datum view, it looks bent because it causes an image of a stick to appear on your inner cinema screen that really is bent. In general, the character of your experience coincides with the character of the sense data you experience. As for hallucinations, sense datum theorists explain them neatly. There is on this view no real difference between normal experience and hallucination. In both cases, life-like images (sense data) occupy your internal spatial arena as a result of brain activity. It's just that in normal experience the brain activity is controlled by your environment, whereas in hallucination it occurs off-line.

The sense datum theory can also explain how there can be shifts in the appearance of the same scene. For example, suppose you look at some dots arranged in a six-by-six pattern. You can see them as organized into vertical rows and then as organized into horizontal rows (Green 2016). This is called a "Gestalt shift". In this example, sense datum theorists might say that, even though the sense data don't change, there is a change in what *states* involving these sense data you experience: maybe you first experience the state of the horizontal dots *being co-linear* and then you experience the state of the vertical dots *being co-linear*. Your experience divides the visual array into larger visual objects having certain properties.

Other cases might require that the sense datum theory be supplemented. For instance, if you see an irregular stick-figure on a drawing, it might "strike you" differently depending on how you interpret it: for instance, it might first appear as a kite on its side and then as a crushed square (we will discuss this example later on in this book in Section 3.3). There are also switches regarding what is the "foreground" and what is the "background". (A famous example is Rubin's "vase/face figure".) In addition, your distribution of attention can change, even if the sense data you experience do not change. To handle these cases, sense datum theorists might complicate their view by offering a "dual-component" account (Price 1932; Farkas 2013). When you experience states involving sense data, you automatically form a higher level "response" to these states. This involves the distribution of your attention, together with how the sense data "strike you". So you can experience the states in different ways. In what follows, however, we will ignore this complication.

1.3 The act-object assumption

So far, I have only said what the sense datum view is. But why believe it?

In Sections 1.4 and 1.5, we will consider two arguments for the sense datum view: the argument from hallucination and the argument from illusionism about sensible properties. They both start from the general *act-object assumption* about how to explain experience, which leads to the choice between the sense datum view and a form of naïve realism I will call "normal-abnormal" naïve realism. Then they use additional considerations to support across-the-board sense datum view over normal-abnormal naïve realism.

Therefore, before we examine the arguments for the sense datum view, we must take a moment to understand the general act-object assumption, and how it leads to the choice between the sense datum view and normal-abnormal naïve realism.

> **Act-object assumption.** To have any experience with a certain character *just is* to experience the actual state of some *existing "object" or "objects"*, where it is left open what those objects are (physical objects, mental images, whatever). Experiencing an object is an "act of the mind". In the case of visual experience, the relevant objects always possess the apparent shapes and colors. In the case of auditory experience, the "objects" are events with audible qualities; and so on. The relationship of experiencing is the same in each case; so all differences in the character of experience consist in differences in states of the objects we bear this relation to (together with the distribution of attention).

Roughly, then, the act-object assumption is the initially plausible idea that an experience is always an experience of something, and that we always must explain the character of your experience in terms of *what* you experience. So all experience has the following structure: *subject–experiencing–object*.

The act-object assumption is a general framework because it leaves open what the relevant "objects" are – mental images (sense data), physical objects, or a mix of the two. So the framework assumption leads to different theories, depending on what we plug in for the "objects".

In effect, the sense datum theory is the act-object assumption together with the claim that the relevant "objects" are always non-physical sense

Figure 1.2 The sense datum view. The sense datum is red but the physical tomato lacks color.

data created by the brain. These objects exist, even though they are non-physical. Thus, in both normal experience and hallucination, to have a tomato-like experience is to experience a tomato-like sense datum on your private screen (Figure 1.2).

But there is another theory that fits with the act-object assumption. For we also might combine the act-object assumption with the claim that the relevant "objects" are heterogeneous: almost always they are simply physical objects in public space but rarely they are brain-created "sense data". I call the resulting view *normal-abnormal naïve realism* because it supplements naïve realism with a sense datum theory of abnormal experience (see Figure 1.3).

On normal-abnormal naïve realism, when you look at a tomato, the red quality you experience belongs to the physical tomato, rather than a brain-generated "sense datum". Your neural processing merely opens the "window shade" to reveal this pre-existing quality of the physical tomato. If later on you should hallucinate an identical tomato, what is going on is that your brain is creating a sense datum "copy" of the tomato. In this special case, your brain is working as a "virtual reality device". The physical

Figure 1.3 Normal-abnormal naïve realism.

tomato and the image have the same visible properties, somewhat like a real tomato and plastic look-alike. That is why hallucination can resemble normal experience.

In general, according to normal-abnormal naïve realism, naïve realism is *almost always* true. But in some rare abnormal cases – cases of hallucination or internally-generated illusions – the "object" is a look-alike image of a thing made by the brain (the "brain is a virtual reality device"). John Austin flirted with this view in his influential book *Sense and Sensibilia* (1962: 32, 50, 52).

In sum, the act-object assumption is roughly the assumption that "appearance is always explained by reality". If we accept this assumption, the only choice we face in the philosophy of perception is between the sense datum view that that appearance is always explained by *mental* reality or the naïve realist view that it is typically explained by *physical* reality and only rarely by mental reality (Figure 1.4).

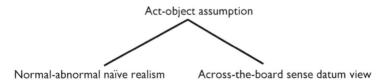

Figure 1.4 If we accept act-object assumption, we have two options.

1.4 The argument from hallucination for the sense datum view over naïve realism

To illustrate the famous *argument from hallucination* for the sense datum view, let's work with a very simple experience. In particular, imagine that you are viewing a blue-looking sphere on a white background. (We will discuss more exciting experiences when we turn to arguments against the sense datum view.)

The first step of the argument is the general act-object framework introduced in the previous section, applied to this experience:

> (1) The blue-sphere experience has an act-object structure. For you to have the blue-sphere experience (in the present ordinary case, and indeed in any possible case) *just is* for you to experience the blueness and roundness of an existing object *of some kind or other*.

Why accept this starting point? In a famous passage at the start of his book *Perception*, H. H. Price said that the act-object assumption is "certain" and something "we cannot doubt" (1932: 3, 63); the quotation from him that starts this chapter is drawn from that passage. This is sometimes called *Price's intuition*. Likewise, Bertrand Russell said, "from mere inspection of experience, I for my part should hold it obvious that perception is in its intrinsic nature a relation involving an act [of experiencing] as well as an object" (1912b: 574). G. E. Moore (1957: 208) said that the act-object assumption is "quite plain", and C. D. Broad (1923: 240) said it is "highly plausible".

In fact, the basic act-object model is quite plausible in the case of the experience of a blue-looking sphere. In this case, it just seems obvious that there really and truly exists a blue and round object of *some* kind. Such an object is *right there* and it is clearly *blue and round*. True, it is not obvious what kind of object this is: whether it is a physical object (as naïve realists hold) or a life-like blue and round image created by the brain (as sense datum theorists hold). That requires further argument. But the basic claim that there is *some* kind of blue and round object then and there is hard to doubt.

Similar remarks apply to a hypothetical case where you knowingly have an identical hallucination of a blue sphere. Even though there is no blue and round *physical* thing there, it would seem obvious to you that there is a blue and round *something* – a blue and round *image*. It is just *right there* for you to attend to. It is not like believing that there is a Tooth Fairy and then finding out there isn't one. Belief is not directly presentational in the same way as experience.

When you view a blue-looking sphere, not only does there exist a blue and round object; you also stand in a special relation to this object: you experience it. For the object is insufficient to account for the experience, since it is conceivable that the object should exist without being experienced at all; so your experience is constituted by the object *and* by your experiencing it. Thus, it "takes two" to have the experience, just like it "takes two to tango". There is, moreover, no aspect of the character of this experience that cannot be accounted for in terms of your standing in the relevant experience relation to the shape, color, and other features of the object. Just try to find such an aspect – you cannot do it.

Rene Descartes (1596–1650) doubted everything but had the revelation that he could at least be certain that he exists: "I think, therefore I am", he famously said. If Price was right, then Descartes was being unduly modest. Descartes should have added, "I experience, therefore something I experience is". When you have experiences, you can not only be certain that you exist; you can also be certain that the objects you experience exist – color patches, sounds, and so on.

However, when you view the blue-looking sphere, while it may be certain (or at least "highly plausible") that there exists a blue and round object of some kind, you cannot be certain *what it is*. That is the big issue. As Figure 1.4 illustrated, there are two main options here, and this brings us to the next step:

(2) Either the blue and round object you experience is the physical sphere itself (naïve realism) or a non-physical object – a *sense datum* – standing "between" you and the physical sphere (sense datum view).

The next steps of the argument are meant to support the surprising claim that in fact the blue and round object before your mind is a non-physical object, that is, a sense datum, as sense datum theorists maintain.

To show this, the argument from hallucination leaves behind your actual experience as of a blue sphere. It goes on a detour concerning a hypothetical hallucination of a blue sphere and then returns back to your actual experience. In particular, it argues that you would experience a blue and round non-physical object in the hypothetical case; and that, if this is so, then, in the actual case, too, you must be experiencing a non-physical blue and round object, rather than the physical sphere itself.

To argue that your blue-sphere experience could be duplicated in the absence of a sphere, we note that your underlying neural state (the total pattern of neuronal activity in your brain) could be duplicated in the absence of a sphere. In particular, let N name the neural state that underlies your present blue-sphere experience on an all-white background. In the actual situation, your undergoing neural state N is caused by light being reflected by a sphere and hitting your eyes. Now consider a hypothetical case where no sphere is present and you undergo N because of spontaneous activity in your brain. Then our next step is:

> (3) You could have a total hallucination as of a blue sphere on a white back-
> ground as a result of being in the same neural state, N – the same neural
> state that underlies your actual blue-sphere experience.

The case for step [3] comes from actual hallucinations. For example, H. H. Price, who was Wykeham Professor of Logic at Oxford University, regularly took the potent drug mescaline (he was an "experimental philosopher"). In his paper, "A Mescaline Experience" (Price 1964), he reported having a drug-induced hallucination of "a pile of leaves" whose "shapes were very clear and vivid" and "three-dimensional". It "looked as real as could be" and lasted two or three minutes, so that he "had ample leisure to study it and enjoy it" (Price 1964: 15). People with Charles Bonnet syndrome (CBS) also have super-vivid hallucinations. These people have impaired eyesight. However, due to spontaneous internal neural activity, they have hallucina-tions that are so vivid and detailed that they often cannot tell them apart from real life. Moreover, there is evidence that the neural activity under-lying these hallucinations is broadly similar to the activity that underlies normal visual experience (Penfield and Perot 1963; ffytche 2013).

The act-object assumption [1] is meant to apply to *any* blue-sphere expe-rience – even a hallucinatory one. So the act-object assumption [1], plus the further claim [3] that you could have the blue-sphere experience in a hallucination, implies our next step:

> (4) Even in this hypothetical hallucination, there exists a blue and round object
> that you experience.

The next step:

> (5) In the hypothetical hallucination, the relevant blue and round object you expe-
> rience must be *non-physical* (a "sense datum") generated by neural state N.

The case for this step is simple. In the hypothetical hallucination case, there is no blue and round physical object in your environment. And there is no blue and round physical object in your brain (*contra* Russell 1927). So, in this case, the blue and round object you experience cannot be a physical thing. It must be a *non-physical object* — a very life-like "image". And, since it can be altered by altering your neural state, your neural state brought it into existence.

With our detour through hallucination complete, we can turn back to the actual case where you are viewing a blue-looking sphere, and argue for the sense datum theory over naïve realism. The "normal-abnormal" naïve realists will agree that, in the hypothetical hallucination case, you experience a non-physical blue and round image. But they will want to say that the present case is very different. In this case, the blue and round object you experience is just the physical sphere itself; your neural processing "opens up the window shade" to reveal this pre-existing, blue physical object.

In order to rule out normal-abnormal naïve realism, and support across-the-board sense datum theory, the following final premise of the argument from hallucination is crucial:

> (6) If you would experience a non-physical, blue and round object in an internal mental arena in having a blue-sphere hallucination, then even now, in the "normal case", you are likewise experiencing a blue and round non-physical object in an internal mental arena, in favor of the sense datum view and against naïve realism.

Let us call this the *generalization premise*, because it generalizes the sense datum theory from hallucination to normal experience. After the act-object assumption [1], this is the most important step of the argument. Why believe it?

The best case for step [6] is the *law-based* argument. Suppose we accept step [5]: at least in the hallucination case, you would experience a non-physical, blue and round image as a result of being in neural state N. This is not an accident; there must be some *law of nature* that explains this. This law governing the generation of sense data is distinct from the physical laws, since it connects your physical neural state with the creation of a non-physical sense datum and the obtaining of the psychological relation of *experiencing* between you and this sense datum. Call it a *psychophysical law*. Here is the simplest hypothesis about the form of this law:

> [L] It is a general law of nature that, if someone undergoes neural state N, then as a result there exists a blue and round non-physical image, and they experience this image.

Now turn to the actual, "normal" case. In the actual case, you undergo neural state N because of the light reflected from a sphere into your eyes – the same neural state you undergo in the hypothetical hallucination case. [L] implies that even in this case your neural state N causes a non-physical blue and round image to come into existence, and moreover causes you to experience this image. So the blue and round object you experience *now* must be the same kind of life-like image ("sense datum") your brain would create in a hallucination case.

The only response available to normal-abnormal naïve realists is to say that whether the neural state N causes a blue and round image to come into existence is *sensitive to how N itself was caused* (Moran 2019a). This would require the following pair of more complex laws:

> [L*] It is a law of nature that, if someone undergoes neural state *N, and* their being in neural state *N* is *not* caused in the normal way by the presence of a blue and round physical object, then as a result there exists a blue and round non-physical image, and they experience *this image*. It is also a law of nature that, if someone undergoes neural state *N*, and their being in *N* is caused in the normal way by the presence of a blue and round physical object before them, then this merely "opens the window shade" and enables them to stand in the very same kind of experiential relation to this blue and round physical object (and here no non-physical blue and round image is created).

Now [L*] rather than [L] *could* be true. But [L*] is more complex than [L]. [L*] is also arbitrary-looking. Why should the psychophysical law governing the generation of sense data be exactly what is required to save naïve realism? Finally, since the distinction between "normal" and "abnormal" cases is unclear and vague, it is hard to see how [L*] could even be adequately formulated. These points favor [L] over [L*].

So now we have our conclusion:

> (7) *Summary and Conclusion.* Step 1 says that the act-object assumption holds for having a blue-sphere experience. The remaining steps show that, in the actual world, the relevant object is in every case a non-physical blue and round image created by the brain.

To show that the argument for sense data generalizes to other cases (all other visual experiences, auditory experiences, bodily sensations, etc.), we would have to proceed case by case (Broad 1923: 254–257; Price 1959). This would establish the sense datum theorists' answer to the character question. We will briefly address this issue in Section 1.6; for now, we will continue with the blue-sphere example.

Is the argument from hallucination persuasive? In fact, the most crucial step is the initial act-object assumption [1]: to have the blue-sphere experience – in a normal case or a hallucination case – is always to experience the blueness and roundness of an object of some kind or other. After this step, the argument is persuasive. This assumption is crucial because the basic strategy of the argument is to establish the radical conclusion that the blue and round object you now experience is a non-physical object (image) and not the physical sphere by first showing that in the hallucination case there really exists a non-physical object that you experience and then generalizing this account to the normal case.

But is the act-object assumption [1] really correct? There is an alternative that I haven't yet told you about. The alternative denies the act-object assumption that there exists a blue and round object of *any* kind in the hypothetical hallucination case. Rather, it merely vividly *seems* to you that there is such an object. Of course, if you have a hallucination, you might speak *as* if there is such an object – you might say "I'm seeing a blue and round object". But that is just a manner of speaking, according to this alternative. In fact, *there is nothing that you see* – it only seems as if there is such an object. Not only is there no physical blue and round object; there is not even a blue and round "image" or "sense datum". In general:

> **Seems-gambit.** In typical cases where it seems that there exists an object with a certain perceptible property F (round, blue, etc.), there may exist an object before you that is really F. But, in *some* such cases, there doesn't really exist such an object. It merely seems to you that there is one.
>
> (Moore 1918; Barnes 1944–1945; Chisholm 1950)

To be clear, to employ the seems-gambit and deny the reality of the *ostensible object* of your experience in the hallucination case is not to deny the reality of *your experience*. The idea is that your experience is real. In having this real experience, it seems that there is a blue and round object. But that object is not real.

This is not yet a positive theory of the character of the experience. It is just a denial of the act-object theory that the character of experience is always inherited from the character of an existing object that you experience. In the rest of this book, we will be looking at positive theories of what your experience consists in, if not a relation to an object. For now, we only need to be concerned with the basic idea.

If we deny the act-object assumption for the blue-sphere hallucination, and instead apply the seems-gambit, then the argument from hallucination for the sense datum view collapses. For, in that case, we cannot prove that in the hallucination case there exists a non-physical blue and round sense datum. So we can no longer use the generalization step to prove that such a peculiar object is present in the normal case too. Instead, here is what is going on. In the hallucination case, it merely seems to you that a blue and round object is present. In fact, no such object is present (not even a sense datum).[5] In the present normal case, likewise, it seems to you that a blue and round object is present. In this case, there really is a round object present: the physical sphere itself. The way things seem coincides with the way they are. In neither case is there a blue and round non-physical sense datum that interposes between you and the world.

As a matter of fact, the eminent sense datum theorists of the past – for instance Broad (1923: 237–240) and Moore (1957: 208) – were aware of the seems-gambit for avoiding sense data but they found the rival act-object assumption "highly plausible" and "quite plain". So they thought that the argument from hallucination was sound after all. However, in Sections 1.10 and 1.11, we will see that there may in fact be good reasons to prefer the seems-gambit to the act-object assumption. If those reasons are cogent, then the argument from hallucination fails at the first step.

Therefore, our final appraisal of the argument from hallucination will have to wait until we look at those reasons.

1.5 The argument from illusionism about sensible properties for the sense datum view over naïve realism

The *argument from illusionism about the sensible properties* starts out with the act-object assumption, just like the argument from hallucination:

> (1) The blue-sphere experience has an act-object structure. For you to have the blue-sphere experience (in the present ordinary case, and indeed in any possible case) *just is* for you to experience the blueness and roundness of an existing object of some kind or other.

As we saw, this framework assumption is intrinsically plausible, even though it can be avoided with the "seems-gambit". And it leads to:

> (2) Either the blue and round object you experience is the physical sphere itself (naïve realism) or a non-physical "image" created by your brain (sense datum view).

At this point, in order to support the sense datum option, the argument from hallucination took a detour through a hypothetical hallucination. The argument from illusionism about the sensible properties provides a second, independent line of argument for the sense datum option that doesn't involve such a detour. This additional argument depends on illusionism about the sensible properties:

> (3) Science shows that the physical sphere in front of you is not blue – in general, there is no blue and round physical object in your environment or brain, just a bunch of colorless atoms arranged in space.

This, together with step [2], implies:

> (4) Contrary to naïve realism, since the physical sphere is *not* blue, the blue and round object you experience must be an "image" *distinct from* the physical sphere itself, in accordance with the sense datum view.

The reasoning here is similar to that used by the argument from hallucination, but now it is being directly applied to your present "normal" experience. The idea is that, in this normal case no less than in hallucination, the blue object you experience has no matching counterpart in the physical world. So it cannot be a physical object. And since it can be altered by altering your neural state, it must have been generated by your brain.

The argument generalizes. Suppose you hear the sound of a tree falling the forest. By the act-object assumption, you experience a sound (the "object" of your experience) with loudness and pitch. By illusionism about the sensible properties, the physical perturbation in the air does not *itself* have these properties – it is merely the initial cause of your experience of them. So the sound you experience is distinct from that physical event. It is a subjective item dependent on the right kind of neural processing.

Is the argument from illusionism about sensible properties persuasive? Let's start by looking at step [3]. The leaders of the scientific revolution from Galileo to Newton thought that science shows that colors and other sensible properties do not belong to the physical world. Is this right?

One argument for illusionism about color starts from the scientific fact that the physical sphere before you (like every other physical object) is nothing but a collection of colorless particles, reflecting colorless photons (Newton's "corpuscles"). Suppose that we also accept *dissective principle* for color (Goodman 1951: 53): if a surface has a color, then every proper part of the surface must have a color. This principle explains why, if you start with a number of transparent ping-pong balls, then, no matter how you combine them, you will never make a colored object. If the physical sphere is wholly composed of particles, none of which have any color, then the dissective principle implies that the physical sphere cannot be blue, contrary to naïve realists. So the blue object you experience (by the act-object assumption) must instead be a sense datum, a non-physical image that is *not* made up of colorless parts. Every subregion of this image is colored, in conformity to the dissective principle.

In response, naïve realists might just reject the dissective principle. Consider this: prethcoretically, you would not have thought that you could arrange a bunch of non-wet particles and obtain a wet thing. But this is exactly what happens when individual H_2O molecules (none of which is wet) condense to make a water droplet (which is wet). Maybe the dissective principle for color is likewise mistaken even if it is initially compelling. Maybe the right theory of color is something like this. The physical surface of the sphere itself (not a distinct "sense datum") has a primitive, emergent property *blueness* distinct from its ordinary physical properties, even if its smallest parts do not have this property (Campbell 2020). The emergent blueness of the physical sphere depends on the way it reflects light, so it is detectable by your visual system. When your visual system detects it in the right way, you experience the blueness of the physical sphere – not a blue sense datum created by your brain (there is no such thing).

Another old argument for illusionism is based on the surprising finding of variation in color perception among normal perceivers (Locke 1869: II.viii; Kuehni 2004). To illustrate the argument, let us suppose that your friend is looking at the sphere along with you. To you, the sphere looks pure or "true" blue: a shade of blue not tinged with any other hue. To your friend, it might look slightly different in color; it might look greenish-blue. (It's not just that you and your friend use different color labels; you have different color experiences.) This leads to the much-discussed puzzle of true blue (Hardin 1988; Byrne and Hilbert 1997). The naïve realist cannot say that the surface has *both* shades at once – that seems incoherent. And, given that both you and your friend are responding to the sphere in a biologically normal way, it is hard for the naïve realist to say that one of you experiences a true color of the sphere while the other undergoes a (mild) color illusion. The best option may be that the physical sphere has *neither* color. In general, it has no color at all. This is illusionism. Given that you and your friend experience differently-colored objects (the act-object assumption), and the physical sphere itself is without color, those differently-colored objects must be distinct from the physical sphere; they must in fact be non-physical *images*, which you mistake for the physical sphere. As the color scientist Kuehni puts it, "the finding of large individual, repeatable variation [makes it] it appear likely that the brain/mind constructs [colored] images of the world rather than reconstructing them from nature" (2004: 162).

In response, naïve realists might say that the physical sphere does after all have both shades of color (or "color aspects"), pure blue and greenish-blue. Your visual system detects one of them and your friend's visual system detects the other. So you and your friend accurately perceive different but equally real color aspects of the same physical object (Byrne and Hilbert 1997: 273; Shoemaker 2019: 461). Another naïve realist response is to say that the physical sphere has only one of the shades but we will never know exactly what that shade is. Let's pretend that the real color is the pure blue color that you experience. Then, on this view, you experience the real color of the physical sphere – not a sense datum. Your friend perceives the same physical sphere but they experience it as having a color that is slightly different from its actual color – they undergo a mild color illusion (Byrne and Hilbert 2003: 17). This avoids across-the-board sense datum view.

A final argument for illusionism about sensible properties depends on other empirical findings in psychophysics and neuroscience. To illustrate the argument, we will start with pain and smell, and then come back to your experience of the sphere.

Suppose that you experience pains in your body of various intensities due to extreme heat, tissue damage, or whatever. As a matter of empirical fact, the intensities of the pains you experience in your body are very poorly correlated with objective features of the bodily disturbances. By contrast, they are linearly correlated with neural firing rates in the cortex. A natural interpretation of these findings is that, although your brain causes you to experience pain qualities in bodily regions, they do not really inhere in bodily regions. This a kind of illusionism about pain. If we also accept the act-object assumption, there must really exist "objects" (pains) possessing the pain qualities that you experience. It's just that, given illusionism, they are not real, *physical* objects. They are subjective, mental objects dependent on the right kind of neural processing.

Next suppose that you consecutively experience three chemical types. The first two smell slightly different but both smell citrus-like. The third smells minty. As a matter of fact, however, the first and second are chemically very different, while the second and third are chemically very similar. There are actual examples of this kind. Why do the first and second smell similar, while the second and third smell different? The explanation is only to be found in the brain. The first and second, although chemically different, result in similar distributed neural patterns in the olfactory system; and the second and third, although chemically similar, result in very different distributed neural patterns (see Chapter 4 for more discussion and references). A natural interpretation of these findings is that smells qualities are not objective features in the external world that were out there before we evolved. Rather, your brain makes it seem that these qualities fill areas in and around your nose, but they are not physically real. They are just "signs" that help you decide what to eat and what to avoid. This is a kind of illusionism. If we accept the act-object assumption, there must really exist "objects", namely smells, possessing the qualities that you experience. But, given illusionism, they are not real, physical objects. They are subjective objects dependent on the right kind of neural processing.

Finally, turn back your experience of the blue-looking sphere. It seems to you that a blue and round object is right there. We are strongly inclined to be realists about color. The blue color is out there, independent of us. But the empirical argument for illusionism applies to color with the same force with which it applies to smell and pain. To illustrate, suppose that, in addition to viewing the blue-looking sphere, you view a purple-looking grape and a green-looking leaf. Blue is more like purple than green. But, color scientists have found that the light reflected by blue-looking things is not more like the light reflected from purple-looking things than the light reflected from green-looking things (see Figure 4.4 in Chapter 4). In fact, surprisingly, the light reflected by blue-looking things is more like the light reflected by green-looking things. So the physical grape, sphere, and leaf don't have any objective physical properties that line up with the color qualities that you experience. Why do you experience color qualities with a similarity-ordering that doesn't line up with the similarity-ordering of the ways of reflecting light? Neuroscientists (Bohon et al. 2016: 18) have shown that the similarity-ordering of the color qualities you experience very nicely lines up with the similarity-ordering of neural patterns in visual area 4 ("V4"). As in the cases of pain and smell, the simplest interpretation of these findings is that the color qualities you experience when you view the grape, the sphere, and the leaf are not objective features of these physical objects that were out there before humans evolved. It is only because of your neural processing that you experience these qualities. They are "signs" that help you identify objects and talk about them. (For example, the way the poison dart frog reflects light is not objectively associated with a stunning bright red; it only looks that way because of your evolved neural response to it.) Given the act-object assumption, there must exist objects possessing these color qualities that you experience when you view the sphere, the grape, and the leaf. But, given illusionism, these objects must be distinct from the physical objects. They are mental images dependent on the right kind of neural processing.

All of these arguments for illusionism about sensible properties can be questioned. (We will take up the issue again in Sections 4.9 and 5.6.) So one response naïve realists might give to this argument for sense data is simply to reject illusionism.

However, let us concede illusionism for the sake of argument. That is, let's assume step [3] above. The physical sphere is not blue; in general, physical things are without colors. Your experience as of a blue object is an illusion in the sense that no blue physical object is there.

This means we must reject naïve realism. But does it mean we must accept the sense datum view instead? No. Those who wish to avoid sense data have another response available to them. For, the argument from illusionism about sensible properties doesn't just depend on illusionism [3]; like the argument from hallucination, it also crucially depends on the initial act-object assumption [1]. This assumption is crucial because the argument works like this: there exists no round and blue *physical* object in the physical space before you (illusionism), but there does exist *some* kind of round and blue object that you experience (the initial act-object assumption), so this blue and round object must be non-physical (a "sense datum"). Now, we saw that, in the case of a blue-sphere hallucination, we can avoid postulating a non-physical blue and round sense datum by rejecting the act-object assumption and retreating to the seems-gambit. In the same way, even if your present color experience of the sphere is an illusion, and indeed all normal color experience is illusory, we can avoid sense data by just re-deploying the same seems-gambit more generally.

As a warm-up, consider some uncontroversial illusions. For instance, suppose that you look at a colorless ice-cube under blue light, so that it seems blue to you. Or suppose that you stare at a bright red surface for a minute, then look at a grey surface, so that it will seem tinged with green. To make sense of these cases, ordinary people employ the seems-gambit. You experience the ice-cube itself – not a sense datum distinct from it. It's just that it seems other than it is. Likewise, you experience the physical surface. It's just that it seems tinged with green. But it isn't. There is nothing greenish in the situation – not even a sense datum.

The idea is that, if we think science shows that *all* color experience is an illusion, we can just apply the same seems-gambit to all color experience, thereby avoiding sense data. For instance, suppose that the physical sphere before you, like the ice-cube, is without color, but, owing to the operation of your brain, it seems quite blue all over. As in the ice-cube case, we can say that you don't experience a brain-created sense datum distinct from the physical sphere that is blue. You experience the physical sphere and it merely *seems* that it is blue. There is on this view no blue object in the situation distinct from the physical sphere. In general, there are no colored objects whatever – whether physical or mental. There just seem to be colored objects. We will examine in more detail just such an alternative to the sense datum view in Section 4.9.

The seems-gambit is not just our commonsense view of illusions. In Section 1.11, we will see that there are strong theoretical reasons to use it to handle certain puzzle cases. And, once we accept it in some cases, it might be applied to all of our experiences, if it should turn out that color illusionism is correct.

In short, there are two possible responses to the argument from illusionism about sensible properties for sense data. One is to simply reject the illusionism on which it depends. Another is to concede illusionism, but then avoid sense data by applying the seems-gambit to all experiences of sensible properties.

1.6 The sense datum view neatly solves the external-internal puzzle

We have seen that the arguments for the sense datum are not decisive – hardly any arguments in philosophy are. Nevertheless, the sense datum view is undeniably attractive. Here is one way of summarizing the foregoing arguments: the sense datum view provides a neat solution to the puzzle that will be a central focus throughout this book, the puzzle of how experience can be both externally directed and internally dependent.

For instance, take the blue-sphere experience. It is essentially externally directed. Roughly, this means that the act-object assumption at least *seems* true. Necessarily, in having this experience, it *seems* that there is a blue and round object distinct from you. However, as we saw in discussing the argument from hallucination, it can also be internally dependent. This type of experience can occur as a result of aberrant internal neural processing in the absence of a physical round object. Together, these ideas imply that it can vividly seem you as if a blue and round object is right there, even though no physical blue and round object is there. How to explain this?

The puzzle generalizes to normal experience. In the previous section, we reviewed some empirical findings involving the experience of smell, pain, and color. This evidence shows that even normal experience is internally dependent. For instance, as you view the physical sphere, the explanation for why you experience the color blue rather than another color (like the explanation of why you experience certain pains and smells) resides inside the brain, not external sphere. Yet it seems to you that the color blue pervades the surface of a round object distinct from you. How to explain this?

Naïve realism does a great job explaining the externally directed character of normal experience because it accepts the act-object assumption. Why does it seem to you that there is a blue and round object in space? Because there actually is a blue and round object in space, and you experience it! However, as we have seen, naïve realism has difficulty accommodating internal dependence: for instance, internally-generated hallucinations, and the dependence of our experience of color on internal processing.

To accommodate internal dependence as well as external directedness, sense datum theorists retain the same act-object model as naïve realists, but re-locate it within a mental realm created by the brain (compare Figures 1.1 and 1.2). Yes, experience has an act-object structure (explaining externally directedness), but the "objects" are creations of the brain (explaining internal dependence). The perceptual process works in this way: first the world, then the brain, and then a reproduction of the world in the mind. In this way, sense datum theorists explain how experience seems to acquaint us with objects distinct from us while at the same time being modulated by internal processes (Jackson 1977: 128–129).

We are now finished looking at arguments for the sense datum view. In the remaining sections, we are going to switch gears. We are going to look at arguments *against* the sense datum view. We start with arguments that may not be decisive (Sections 1.7 and 1.8). Then we turn to arguments that go to the heart of the sense datum view (in Sections 1.9–1.11). Even though its underlying act-object assumption may be intrinsically plausible, there are strong arguments for rejecting it and accepting the "seems-gambit" instead. If that is right, then the sense datum view, and the arguments for it, collapse.

1.7 The *percipi* problem about pain

We have been focusing on visual experiences. But early sense datum theorists applied the sense datum theory more generally. The first question we will take up is whether this is plausible. For example, can the view be applied to the experience of a tooth-ache?

Here is a simple argument for thinking not. The sense datum view is an act-object theory. Applied to this case, the theory would say that there is you, the subject, and then there is a wholly distinct object, the pain. The pain resides in a kind of private "body space" (in particular, it resides in the "mouth-region" of that space). You stand in the relationship of "experiencing" to the pain. Now, generally, wholly distinct objects can exist apart from each other. So if pains are objects wholly distinct from subjects, as this view maintains, then in principle they should be able to exist apart from subjects. For example, it should be within God's power to cause there to be in a lone pain the room, even though no subject is around to perceive it. However, this appears incoherent: for pains, it is in their essence to be perceived, or, if you prefer Latin, *esse est percipi*. Call this the *percipi* problem (Berkeley 1713; Moore 1942).

The first thing to say about this argument is that it doesn't threaten the sense datum view for other types of experiences. For instance, there is no problem with thinking that visual sense data should exist apart from subjects. Indeed, early on, G. E. Moore (1914: 366) and Bertrand Russell (1913: 79) explicitly held that in *principle* visual sense data could exist unperceived. In that sense, visual sense data, although non-physical, are *mind-independent*. They are objects of mental acts but they are not themselves essentially mental. True, Russell and Moore held that this strange scenario will never in fact happen. For the "psychophysical laws" are such that, whenever a brain causes a visual sense datum to come into existence, it also causes the subject to perceive the sense datum, somewhat as nature guarantees that thunder and lightning go together (see Russell 1913: 79 and Moore 1911: 40 and 1914: 369). But, according to Moore and Russell, it could in principle happen that a round and blue sense datum should come into existence in your backyard, with no one around to perceive it. It would be within God's power to make this happen. The mere claim that this *could* happen doesn't seem to be a problem. In fact, since we are all naïve realists, we think that there are actually lots of blue spheres around without anyone perceiving them.

So one response to the *percipi* problem would be to adopt a mixed view: the sense datum view is right for experiences of mind-independent objects

(visual experiences, auditory experiences, etc.), but it is not right for experiences of pain (Broad 1923: 254–257). Maybe, for instance, the right view
of experiences of pain is something like the internal physical state view to
be discussed in Chapter 2.

In fact, the *percipi* problem may not even undermine the sense datum
view for the experience pain. For instance, some sense datum theorists
have said that sense data are experience-dependent entities (Ayer 1940).
Yes, pains are wholly distinct from subjects. Nevertheless, maybe it is just
in their essence that, if they exist, then they must be accompanied by a
subject who experiences them. Compare: holes (such as the holes in a piece
of cheese) cannot exist unless there is a hole-host (such as a piece of cheese)
for them to exist in.[6]

1.8 Can the sense datum view explain our access to the external world?

If we only really experience short-lived sense data in our private mental
spaces, does it follow that we only can *think about* such sense data, and that
we never think about real physical things, like persisting tomatoes, President Obama, or electrons? Is our *thought* restricted to sense data?

Relatedly, does it follow from the sense datum view that we can only
know about our own sense data, and that we cannot know about real physical things, like tomatoes, President Obama, or electrons? Is our *knowledge*
restricted to sense data? If so, then, for all you know, you and your sense
data could be the only things that exist!

Let's address these issues in turn.

First, it is not at all clear that the sense datum view implies that we only
can think about such sense data, and that we never think about real physical things. To see this, let's engage in fanciful thought-experiment for a
moment. Suppose that, whenever someone is born, we immediately put
goggles on their head, which they can never take off. The goggles display
images of things in the environment. So everyone experiences a high-fidel-
ity virtual model of the environment. Suppose that this has been going on
for 100 years or so. People might not even have any idea that they experience
images on a screen. Their lives are experientially just like our own. They go
around saying much the same things as we do, such as "Obama was a great
president", "there is only one tomato left in the fridge", "electrons explain
the photoelectric effect". Now, if this scenario came to pass, would the
people wearing the goggles be talking about the external physical things

themselves, or only the momentary images that they experience on their private screen? Intuitively, the most charitable – and correct – view is that they would be talking about the physical things. But since this scenario is very similar to actual scenario if the sense datum theory is right, everyone should agree that, if the sense datum theory is actually true, we are likewise normally correctly interpreted as talking about physical things beyond the sense data we experience.

Still, you might wonder, if the sense datum view is true, *how* do we think about anything beyond our sense data? To answer this question, let's forget about the sense datum view for a moment. How do I think about Obama? Even though I've never met the man, there is a causal chain going from Obama to my use of the tag "Obama". Now, this is not enough, since *Obama's outside flesh* and *Obama-images on the TV* are also parts of the causal chain gong to my use of "Obama". I count as thinking about *Obama the man*, and not just his *outside flesh*, or *Obama-images*, because I *intend* to be thinking about the man (Hawthorne and Manley 2012: 18–19). It is not clear why sense datum theorists could not co-opt this same explanation for how it is that I think of *Obama the man*, and not his *flesh*, or *Obama-images on the TV screen*, or *Obama-like sense data images* in my mind.

However, suppose I open the refrigerator, so that a physical tomato is right there before me. Then, attending to the red and round object that fills my visual field, I say "that is a tomato". In this case, I intend to refer to the red and round object that I experience in my visual field. And, on the sense datum view, that red and round object is a non-physical sense datum. So I am referring to a sense datum, but I am mistaking it for a tomato, because I instinctively accept the naïve realist view that the colored objects that fill up my visual field are physical things. But sense datum theorists will say it is understandable that we should make this kind of mistake because it is understandable that we should be fooled into accepting naïve realism.

Sense datum theorists face another question about thought: given that we experience only a limited range of properties, how do we acquire fancy concepts like *refrigerator* and *electrons*, and *mind-independent world* (Campbell and Cassam 2014)? However, even on alternative views such as naïve realism, we only experience a limited range of properties. We don't *experience* something's being a refrigerator, or mind-independent, or an electron. These are just not visible properties in the way that colors and shapes are visible. So naïve realists face the same question. It's not clear that the question is harder for sense datum theorists than for naïve realists.

Finally, even if sense datum theorists can explain how we think about external objects, how do we really know about those things? Are all of our beliefs about the world beyond our sense data just guesses?

This too is a question for everyone. Even if naïve realism is true, we face the question "How do you know that your life is not an elaborate dream or hallucination?"

But you might think that a simple two-step argument shows that sense datum theorists have an especially tough time with this question – indeed that they are committed radical skepticism. To illustrate, suppose you see a refrigerator. First, sense datum theorists are committed to a form of *austere foundationalism* (Russell 1912a). That is, the only things you know "immediately" (without inference) are very simple things about the colors and shapes of the sense data you experience (together with some truths of logic and mathematics). Second, given austere foundationalism, skepticism follows. You do not, and could not, make a good inference from the sense data present in your experience to the existence of an external refrigerator (much less electrons, etc.). So your belief that there is a refrigerator there is not knowledge. It is a "leap in the dark". In fact, you don't even have good *reason* for this belief (but see Russell 1912a; Vogel 1990).

Here is a response. True, many sense datum theorists in fact accepted austere foundationalism. But there is no reason why they couldn't accept a more liberal approach. For instance, Timothy Williamson (2000) says that, if in fact you live in the real world (your life is not just an elaborate dream), you know a lot, because knowing things is easy: it only requires that you have beliefs that are safely or reliably connected to the world. So you know that there is a refrigerator there, even if you don't really infer it from the colors and shapes, because your belief that a refrigerator is there is safely connected to the presence of a refrigerator, thanks to your automatic object-recognition system. Since you know it, it is part of your foundational evidence. So not just things about colors and shapes, but also things about refrigerators, are part of your evidence. (For more on this view, see the Discussion Box in Section 3.5 of Chapter 3.)

Now, Williamson himself is no sense datum theorist. But there is no reason why sense datum theorists could not co-opt his liberal foundationalism and agree that knowledge is pretty easy to achieve. After all, sense datum theorists can agree that when we have experiences we just immediately have beliefs about external things without going through any kind of inference. And they can agree that these beliefs are "safe" and constitute knowledge.[7]

1.9 Do simplicity considerations undermine the sense datum view?

Imagine that you are hallucinating a blue sphere. At the heart of the sense datum view is the act-object assumption. There really exists a blue and round object, and you experience it. But we saw (at the end of Section 1.4) that there is another option. We can employ the seems-gambit. So the sense datum view hangs on the question: act-object assumption or seems-gambit?

Sense datum theorists thought that the act-object assumption is intrinsically plausible. However, in the remaining sections of this chapter, we will look at strong arguments for rejecting it and going with the seems-gambit instead.

To begin with, there is a *simplicity argument* against the act-object assumption. The act-object assumption requires that, in your hallucination, there really and truly exists a blue and round object that you experience. Further, this object must be *non-physical* – a "sense datum". So the act-object assumption requires that we believe in non-physical objects, over and above physical objects.[8] Further, there must be a special, fundamental "psychophysical law" [L] connecting the occurrence of your neural state in the physical realm with the generation of the sense datum in your private mental realm. In fact, there must be a whole swarm of such laws, governing the generation of different kinds of sense data (smells, sounds, etc.).[9] The sense datum view, then, leads to *dualism* about persons. Your brain and behavior are part of the physical realm. The sense data you experience are part of a non-physical realm. The two realms are connected by strange "psychophysical" laws. This is all very complicated. And that complexity provides a reason to reject the act-object assumption.[10]

To avoid such a complex picture of persons, the Australian philosophers U. T. Place (1956) and J. C. Smart (1959) did just that: they rejected the act-object assumption by invoking the seems-gambit. In the hallucination case, there's no mysterious non-physical blue and round object – there merely seems to be one. This allowed Place and Smart to defend a quite different positive theory of experience: the *internal physical state view* (which will be the subject of Chapter 2). This alternative view fits with a *physicalist view* of persons. Physicalists have a dream picture of reality quite different from the theoretical nightmare of dualism. The only things that fundamentally exist are physical particles and fields. The physical laws governing them are the only fundamental laws. We don't know what they are yet, but we can hope that they are so simple that they could be written on the front of a T-shirt (like Schrödinger's law governing the evolution of the quantum wavefunction). If the act-object assumption underlying the sense datum view is incompatible with this physicalist dream picture (see the Discussion Box for more discussion), it must be rejected. Since the 1950s and 1960s, the philosophy of perception has been closely connected to the broader project of understanding the mind in physical terms.

Is this a persuasive argument for rejecting the act-object assumption and adopting the seems-gambit? For a few reasons, the argument is somewhat shaky. (1) Many think that there are persuasive arguments against

Discussion Box: Are sense data compatible with a simple physicalist view of reality?

The simplicity argument says that belief in non-physical "sense data" is incompatible with the attractively simple worldview of *physicalism*. But this might be questioned.

Many philosophers nowadays equate physicalism with "grounding physicalism": roughly, the thesis that all "high level" facts are *metaphysically grounded in* fundamental physical facts. The key idea of "grounding" can best be explained by examples (Fine 2012). Take a piece of Swiss cheese that is, as we would put it, "filled with holes". Some philosophers hold that there really and truly exist holes. They are non-physical objects of a certain kind (Casati and Varzi 1994). But they are grounded entities. A hole is always a hole in something – a hole-host. The existence and character of the hole is fully "grounded in" the existence and nature of the hole-host – for instance, the cavities in the piece of cheese. So even though holes are non-physical entities, they are consistent with grounding physicalism.

In the same way, maybe it is possible to accept the act-object assumption, and believe in sense data, but also accept the attractive worldview of physicalism. For instance, when someone hallucinates a blue sphere, maybe there really exists a blue and round non-physical sense datum (in the same sense in which there exists an electron in an atom), but its existence and character is fully "grounded in" the nature of her brain state. So this view maintains, in contrast to dualism, that there is no possibility in which the brain state, and the experience of a blue and round sense datum, are separated. Here the "grounded" fact (her experiencing a sense datum) and the "grounding fact" (her being in a certain brain state) are very different. Still, this view – call it *physicalist sense datum theory* – is coherent.

However, even if this physicalist sense datum view is a possible view, it may be that the simplicity argument is still effective against it. For though it is a form of physicalism, it is very complicated. It requires special "grounding laws" connecting a person's brain states with her experiencing various sense data. These "grounding laws" would add to the complexity of our theory of the world no less than the "psychophysical laws" of dualism. It may be argued that the simplest form of physicalism is one that entirely does away with the act-object assumption and "sense data" altogether, such as the internal physical state view to be examined in Chapter 2.

physicalism and for dualism quite independent of sense data (see Stoljar 2010 for a summary). So any argument against sense data founded on a simple, physicalist theory of the world is far from decisive. (2) We should favor the simplest theory consistent with our evidence. But hardcore sense datum theorists like Price (1932) thought that the act-object assumption is simply part of our evidence. If you should hallucinate a blue sphere, there is a blue and round *something* there and then. This is just something you know. If it is non-physical, so be it. (3) At the very least, sense datum theorists might say that we have extremely strong reason to accept the act-object assumption. So perhaps we should turn the argument on its head. Since the act-object assumption leads to a complex dualist view of the mind, we should learn to live with it. In fact, Daniel Dennett (although himself a staunch physicalist) concedes, "This is the shortest, sweetest and most convincing argument for dualism I know" (2012: 12:41).

1.10 Where are sense data?

We just saw that a preference for a simple "physicalist" view of reality may not be a decisive reason to reject the act-object assumption that is part of the sense datum view. But in the present section and the next, we will look at some other problems with the act-object assumption that you should find serious even if you are open to dualism.

To begin with, there is a puzzle about where sense data are located (Huemer 2011). There are two main options here: they exist in private mental spaces and they exist in public physical space. But neither option is very good.

Let us start with the traditional view that sense data reside in private "mental spaces" (Broad 1925: 181; Price 1932: 246ff). For example, imagine that you have a complete hallucination in which there is a blue sphere a few feet in front of you in a white empty space. The act-object assumption implies that there exists a blue and round non-physical object. On the private mental space option, it resides in a private mental space or field. This is a three- or two-dimensional space whose parts cannot be located within the three-dimensional region occupied by the brain. Yet it is somehow generated by the brain. The characters in comic books have "thought-bubbles" over their heads. The idea here is that whenever we open our eyes, our brains generate a "perceptual bubble" and it is there that your sense data reside. But the perceptual space is of course not literally above your head. It is like a "parallel universe".

There are many problems with private mental spaces. Let me mention just one. How come sense data wind up in the "right" spaces? For instance, suppose I am put into neural state N, which generates a blue and round sense datum. How come the sense datum winds up in a private mental space, and not in public physical space (as on the view about the location of sense data we will explore presently)? And how come it winds up in my private mental space, and not yours? It is not as if each mental space has its own unique number, and my brain has instructions to generate sense data in the mental space with a particular number.[11]

Some sense datum theorists have taken a different view. They have said that sense data reside in public physical space (Jackson 1977: 77–78, 102–103). Thus, when I hallucinate a blue sphere, my brain causes the coming-into-existence of a blue and round sense datum in the physical space in front of my head (a kind of spooky action-at-a-distance). Only I can experience this ghostly creation proceeding from my brain. No one else can detect it there. Thus, the brain is a kind of a projector, creating holograms in the space in front of it.

One problem with this option is about how to formulate psychophysical laws governing precisely where sense data wind up. For instance, for starters, we might suppose that the law has the following rough form: *if an individual undergoes neural state N, then a sense datum comes into existence three-feet away from the individual in direction D.* But what does "three feet from the individual" mean? Does it mean "three feet from the individual's eyes" or "three-feet from the gravitational center of the individual's brain", or what? The psychophysical laws are now looking even more complex and arbitrary. Or maybe it's "metaphysically indeterminate" which answer is right? But then it will be metaphysically indeterminate precisely where the sense datum comes to be located in physical space – an odd result.

The upshot is that, while the general act-object assumption required by the sense datum view may be very intuitive, the puzzle about location provides a strong countervailing argument against it and for the seems-gambit. If we hold that there really does exist a blue and round "sense datum" when you have your hallucination, we face the question: *just where is it?* If instead we employ the seems-gambit, and hold that there doesn't exist a blue and round sense datum even if it seems to you that there is such a thing, then we avoid the puzzle about where "it" is located. There is no more a puzzle about where "it" is located than there is a puzzle about where the Tooth Fairy is located.

1.11 Hard cases: perceptual imprecision and incompleteness

Finally, perhaps the strongest reason to reject the sense datum view is that it sits very poorly with perceptual imprecision and incompleteness.

Let's start with perceptual imprecision. Fixate on the cross in the figure below, so that you experience the tomato in peripheral vision.

If the tomato is far enough in the periphery, then you will be unable to precisely describe its apparent location, shape, and color. For instance, it will appear to take up space. But there will be no maximally specific shape that it appears to have. If asked to draw its precise apparent shape while fixating on the cross, you would be unable to do so.[12]

Now let us suppose, for the sake of argument, that the sense datum view is right. As you view Figure 1.5, your entire visual field is a non-physical "picture" created by your brain in a private mental arena. So in particular your brain creates a non-physical object in the periphery of your visual field – a kind of copy of the physical tomato. Now, if this object exists, we can inquire about what it is like. Sense datum theorists face a dilemma. They have two options, and neither is at all plausible.

The first option is to say that the peripheral, non-physical sense datum your brain creates is "metaphysically imprecise". It has a roughly round shape. But, for every maximally specific round shape, it determinately lacks that specific round shape. The explanation of perceptual imprecision is that you experience an imprecise object. The trouble with this option is that it is intuitively impossible that there be such an object – whether physical or non-physical.

This leads to the second option. Maybe the peripheral, brain-generated sense datum is precise in every way. It has a maximally precise location, shape, and color. It's just that your awareness of it is incomplete. However, there are a few problems with this option. First, the brain just "doesn't have enough information" to create a sense datum with a precise location, shape, and color. And it would be implausible to reply that, in the absence of sufficient information, your brain, so to speak, just arbitrarily "picks" a precise location, shape, and color. Second, if your brain does indeed go to the trouble of creating a sense datum that is precise in every way,

Figure 1.5 Perceptual imprecision.

G   +   K G P

Figure 1.6 Visual crowding.

why wouldn't your brain also allow you to experience its precise location, shape, and color? Third, if the sense datum has a precise shape but it doesn't seem that way, why not apply the seems-gambit more generally, and avoid the sense datum view?

Therefore, we must reject our initial assumption that the sense datum view applies to this example. It is not the case that, as you view Figure 1.5, your entire visual field is a non-physical "picture" created by your brain in a private mental arena. The "inner picture" model of perception is misguided. To handle perceptual imprecision, we need some other account.[13]

The phenomenology of "visual crowding" creates a similar problem for the sense datum view. Take a look at Figure 1.6.

You will find that, while fixating on the cross, it is easy to identify the G on the left but hard to identify the G on the right. Here is a rough explanation:

> The ease of recognizing the isolated target indicates that crowding is not simply a by-product of reduced visual acuity in the periphery. Instead, it seems that the visual system applies some as-yet-unspecified lossy transformation – perhaps some form of "feature integration", pooling, or averaging to the stimulus, resulting in the subjective experience of mixed-up, jumbled visual features.
>
> (Rosenholtz *et al.* 2012: 1–2)

On the sense datum view, as you view Figure 1.6, your entire visual field is a non-physical "picture" created by your brain in a private mental arena. But what could the sense data in the periphery of your visual field be like, such that their character might constitute the "jumbled" character of your experience? Again, we must reject the sense datum model.

The argument generalizes to the experience of objects in central vision. To see this, let's return to Figure 1.5. Imagine that, as you view Figure 1.5, the tomato slowly moves to the center of your visual field. Even though at the end of the process there is increased perceptual precision, we cannot accept the sense datum view here. For one thing, even here there is not total perceptual precision. For instance, there is no precise answer to the question: what is the apparent ratio of the tomato's height to its width? So we can repeat the same argument against the sense datum view. For another thing, we just argued that, at the start of this process when the tomato is in peripheral vision, it is not the case that your brain is generating a non-physical object for you to experience. It is implausible that, at some point in the process, your brain suddenly does generate such an object. So the sense datum model is wrong even at the end of the process when the tomato is in central vision.

The argument also generalizes to hallucination. Imagine you have a brief, imprecise hallucination of a tomato on a white background. The dilemma above shows that it is not the case that your entire visual field is a non-physical "picture" created by your brain in a private mental arena. There is no round object present at all – whether physical or non-physical. This means that the general act-object assumption is mistaken. H. H. Price was right when he said that the general act-object assumption is intrinsically plausible. But perceptual imprecision creates a strong countervailing argument against it. In the case of hallucination, we must reject the act-object assumption and apply the seems-gambit. This undermines both the sense datum view and the argument from hallucination for that view.

Visual imagery provides another, more indirect argument from perceptual imprecision against the sense datum view. Suppose that you imagine a tomato. Because imagery is very imprecise, the argument from perceptual imprecision shows that it is not the case that your brain creates a non-physical sense datum for you to experience. Further, there is some reason to think that ordinary visual experience and visual imagery belong to the same kind; visual imagery is degraded visual experience (Byrne 2018: 186–189). So if the sense datum view is not right for visual imagery, it is also not right for ordinary visual experience.

Some interesting motion illusions create additional trouble for the sense datum view. Max Wertheimer (1912/2012) successively presented people with a vertical line in different places, A and B. A vertical line would appear at place A, then disappear, and then another would appear at place B. When the interval was very small (near simultaneity), something very odd happened. (You can see for yourself by looking at video demonstrations on the internet.) Here is a nice description:

> If the blank interval was brief enough both straight lines were seen simultaneously; nevertheless, something was perceived as moving from A to B. Line A was not seen to move over to B. Rather it was an objectless movement, or "pure motion" as Wertheimer called it. Without seeing any moving objects or figures, there was a clear impression of motion from one place to another.
>
> (von Fieandt 1966: 263)

In another striking example, identical disks are arranged in a circle. In rapid succession, one disappears while the others remain; and then the next one disappears while the others remain, and so on. The result of viewing the video is that you experience movement in a circle. The movement seems to successively block the disks. Yet you don't seem to experience any well-defined object moving in a circle. For instance, if you are asked, "what is the precise apparent shape of the object moving in a circle?" you cannot give an answer.

The *waterfall illusion* may be related to such experiences of pure movement. In the waterfall illusion, you first look at a waterfall. Then you look at a stationary object, say, a black rock. Then you can get a very strange experience. Different people describe the experience differently. I think that the most apt description is that *there seems to be movement upward but nothing – including the rock – seems to be moving upward.*

There is a more everyday illustration of the experience of pure motion. If something in your peripheral vision moves, you experience movement but you don't experience any object as moving.

You can think of experiences of pure motion as a kind of perceptual incompleteness. Your visual system registers movement but doesn't specify any other features. On the sense datum view, your entire visual field is always a non-physical "picture" created by your brain in a private mental arena. To handle such cases, sense datum theorists would apparently need to say that your brain generates a sense datum that is moving in a certain way, but that has no other properties. For instance, in the waterfall illusion, your brain creates a black and round sense datum that is stationary, and a second sense datum whose *only* property is *moving upward.* It is hard to believe in such an incomplete object. Therefore, experiences of pure motion give us more reason to reject the sense datum model.

If the sense datum view fails, what is the explanation of perceptual imprecision and incompleteness? We will discuss this in more detail in later chapters. In Chapter 3, we will see that proponents of the "representational view" give an especially satisfying explanation. There are also still naïve realists around; in fact, we will see in Chapter 5 that it has made a comeback and become very popular. Naïve realists can give another explanation of perceptual imprecision and incompleteness. We just saw that perceptual imprecision gives us a reason to reject the general act-object assumption (and the sense datum view) for the case of hallucination. Contemporary naïve realists agree – we need some other account of hallucination. But they think that the lesson is not that we should entirely reject the act-object assumption but that we should restrict it to normal experience. On their view, when you have a normal experience of a tomato in peripheral vision, the character of your experience is constituted by your experiencing a very limited set of general features of the physical tomato. In reality the physical object may be perfectly precise, but your awareness of it is incomplete.

Summary

If the sense datum view were true, it would provide a neat solution to a central puzzle about experience. It would explain how experiences can essentially seem to present items in space but also depend on our internal processing.

But there are serious problems with the sense datum view and its underlying general "act-object assumption" about the character of experience. Because of these problems most philosophers today hold that we must reject the sense datum theory and the general act-object assumption. But what's the alternative?

In the rest of the book, we will look at three alternatives to the sense datum view: the *internal physical state view*, the *representational view*, and *contemporary naïve realism*. These theories all deny the strong starting assumption of sense datum theorists that the character of *all* sensory-perceptual experiences (including illusory and hallucinatory ones) consists in the character of the objects that we perceive in having the experience. So they avoid "sense data". But they offer radically different positive accounts of the character of experience.

Further Reading

Jackson (1977) and Robinson (1994) are excellent book-length defenses of the sense datum view. Robinson (1994) also provides invaluable material on the history of the sense datum view. They would be good places to start.

Other, more recent defenses of the sense datum view, or something very much like it, include Brown (2012), Garcia-Carpintero (2001), and Hoffman (2019).

Austin's *Sense and Sensibilia* (1962) is an entertaining critical discussion of the sense datum theory. Place (1956) and Smart (1959) reject the sense datum view on the basis of a "physicalist" view of the world. In her classic (Anscombe 1965) essay, Anscombe argues that the sense datum view fails because it does not recognize the "intentionality" of verbs of perception.

See also Hintikka (1969). Jackson (2004) rejects the sense datum view he had defended in his 1977 book and converts to the representational view to be discussed in Chapter 3.

Notes

1　See Russell (1912a) and Moore (1914, 1957). For recent defenses of the sense datum view, or something very much like it, see Garcia-Carpintero (2001), Brown (2012), and Hoffman (2019).

2　Here and in what follows, I use the ordinary color term "red" to describe the reddish quality of the round image in your visual field (Russell 1912a; Moore 1953/1910: 30; Jackson 1977). Others who defend this kind of view (e.g., Peacocke 2008: 10) call it *red**. Despite the different terminology, they have the same distinctive, familiar quality in mind.

3　Sense datum theorists can also provide a less-than-full-blooded sense in which the physical tomato is red: it normally causes experiences of red sense data (Jackson 1977: 128).

4　This is called a "representative realist" version of the sense datum view because it holds that (at least in respect of spatial properties) sense data are "representative" of physical objects (Locke 1869; Russell 1912a; Moore 1914; Jackson 1977). (This is not to be confused with the representational view to be discussed in Chapter 3.) There is another, "phenomenalist" version (Foster 2000), but I will ignore it. Russell (1912a, 1913) accepted an even more extreme illusionism: physical objects not only lack the colors of our sense data, they even lack the visual *shapes* of our sense data. We will discuss generalized illusionism later on this book in Section 4.10.

5　You might worry that the dispute between those who say "there exist sense data generated by the brain in accordance special psychophysical laws" and those who say "there don't exist sense data – it merely seems that there exist such things" can only be a mere *verbal dispute*. In particular, the disputants don't substantively disagree, because they mean different things by "there exists". However, there are certainly substantive disputes about what exists – for instance, disputes about whether there exist subatomic particles obeying certain laws. So it is not clear why the dispute over sense data cannot be equally substantive.

6　As explained in Section 1.3, sense datum theorists hold that every experience is a relationship between a subject and a sense datum, somewhat as dancing is a relationship between two participants. So they cannot hold that sense data are experience-dependent in the sense that they exist *because* we have experiences of them; this would be like holding that people exist *because* they dance. What is suggested in the main text is that perhaps sense data are experience-dependent in the sense that they must be experienced by some subject. This differs from the problematic claim that they exist *because* they are experienced.

7　Besides Williamson's (2000) *knowledge-based* form of liberal foundationalism, there are *reliabilist* forms of liberal foundationalism. They hold that loads of our beliefs are immediately justified just because they are the outputs of reliable, non-inferential belief-forming mechanisms. This form of liberal foundationalism, too, is perfectly consistent with the sense datum view (Jackson 1977: 152).

8　Peacocke (2008) advocates something like the sense datum theory, but in some hallucination cases he employs the seems-gambit to avoid non-physical sense data: "it is *as if* [i.e. it seems as if – AP] there is something [a visual sense datum] which enjoys the relevant sensational properties, even though there is no such thing" (2008: 14). But if Peacocke allows that the seems-based account is adequate in this kind of hallucination case, why doesn't he advocate it in every case? This would result in the "representational view" to be discussed in Chapter 3.

9   Following Chalmers (1996; 214), sense datum theorists might hope that such laws could be systematized. For problems with this idea, see Adams (1987: 256–257), Chalmers (2012: 279, 341), Prinz (2012: 126–133).

10 Another argument against dualism concerns mental causation: given the "causal closure" of the physical world, dualism leads to "epiphenomenalism" about experience. But, as Smart (1959: 156) noted, the argument against epiphenomenalist dualism depends on the simplicity argument. So the simplicity argument may be the most fundamental argument against dualism.

11 See Kim (2005: chap. 3) for discussion of a similar "pairing problem" involving *souls* rather than non-physical spaces.

12 It is a myth that there is *no color vision at all* in the periphery (Noorlander *et al.* 1983; Tyler 2015). But chromatic detection certainly gets worse with increasing eccentricity (Hansen *et al.* 2009: 1). Spatial vision, too, gets worse in peripheral vision.

13 Price (1959: 461–465), Armstrong (1968: 219–221), and Hardin (1988: 100–101) discuss the argument from perceptual imprecision against the sense datum view. Traditionally, the target of the argument was a principle – called "the phenomenal principle" – stating (roughly) that a visual sense datum is *F* if, and only if, it phenomenally looks *F*. Many consider this to be a commitment of the sense datum view. By contrast, in my formulation of the sense datum view (Section 1.2), I didn't see the need to include any such strict principle. And there are good reasons why sense datum theorists should reject it. For instance, in effect Russell (1914: 144) argues using "phenomenal continua" that sense datum theorists should reject it. And it requires a special "phenomenal" sense of "looks" or "appears", but Byrne (2009: 442) argues that there is no such special sense. So instead of formulating the problem of perceptual imprecision as a problem for the "phenomenal principle", I have formulated it as a general dilemma that arises for sense datum theorists even if they reject that principle.

2

THE INTERNAL PHYSICAL
STATE VIEW:
EXPERIENCES AS INNER MODIFICATIONS

The only properties of conscious experience with which we can make contact are intrinsic [neural] properties of subjects.

—David Papineau (2016)

Visual experience is intrinsically [essentially] spatial ... if we do not use spatial properties in characterizing visual [experience], we omit a subjective feature of experience.

—Christopher Peacocke (2008)

In Chapter 1, we considered the sense datum view of experience. On this view, when you view a scene, the entire space you experience is in fact a private mental arena created by your brain, and the "objects" within this space are very life-like mental images called "sense data". Changes in the character of your experience are changes in the sense data you experience.

By the 1950s and 1960s, everyone wanted to get rid of sense data because they would have to be strange, non-physical objects. But if we reject the sense datum view, what view should we put in its place?

The *internal physical state view* is the first alternative we will consider. Instead of holding that experiences are relations to non-physical sense data created by neural activation states, this view holds that experiences are identical with the neural activation states themselves. Changes in the character of experience *just are* changes in those neural states. After the sense datum view, this is a very natural next choice.

Recent proponents of the internal physical state view include Ned Block (2019), C. L. Hardin (1988), Geoff Lee (2020), Brian McLaughlin (2016a), David Papineau (2014), Thomas Polger (2004), and Hilary Putnam and Hilla Jacobson (2014). Unsurprisingly, it is popular among neuroscientists. For instance, Guillermo Tononi and Christof Koch (2015) have proposed the "integrated information theory" of experience, which is a form of the internal physical state view.

The internal physical state view may seem obvious, almost inevitable. After all, your internal physical state is the common factor between a normal experience of a tomato and a hallucination of one. But we will see that it also faces a problem. How does it accommodate the phenomenological fact of external directedness? For instance, visual experiences are quite different from internal sensations, like headaches. Even if they depend on internal factors, they also essentially involve the seeming presence of objects in space with various spatial features. Is the internal physical state view consistent with this fact?

The plan for this chapter is as follows. In Section 2.1, we will learn more about what the internal physical state view is. In Section 2.2, we will look at a possible argument for the internal physical state view based on a particularly strong version of "internal dependence". In Sections 2.3–2.5, we will consider problems for it concerning whether it can accommodate the essentially externally directed character of some experiences.

2.1 What is the internal physical state view?

Recall that the central question of this book is the *character question*: What is the correct definition of what it is to have an experience with a certain character? What is a sensory experience? What do differences in the character of experience consist in? The internal physical state view gives a simple answer.

Internal physical state view. Every sensory-perceptual experience with a certain character is necessarily identical with an "internal" physical property, as it might be, a distributed neural pattern. This property is an *intrinsic* property of the brain; it is not a relation to anything outside the brain. Differences in the character of experience consist in differences in such intrinsic physical-properties of subjects.

For instance, the vast difference between an experience of color and an experience of smell is just an internal physical-computational difference in the brain, as it might be, a difference in the spatio-temporal pattern of neural firings.

Our go-to example in Chapter 1 was the experience of a humble tomato. To mix things up a bit, in the present chapter, let's consider an experience of an orange. This is a nod to one of the originators of the internal physical state view, J. C. Smart (1959), who used this example.

As we will see in the next section, there is reason to believe that the character of your experience depends in some systematic and regular way on the character of your internal neural activity. In the end, this is what pins down the character of your experience. So if we knew the spatio-temporal pattern of activity in some population of your neurons coding for color, and if we knew the systematic "neural code" for color, we could determine the character of your color experience as you view the orange (see Figure 2.1). Likewise, if we knew the pattern of activity in some other population of your neurons coding for spatial features, and if we knew the systematic "neural code" for shape, we could determine that you have a round-experience rather than a square-experience. As the neuroscientist Stanislas Dehaene writes, "the [neural] code contains a full record of the subject's experience" and "if we could read this code we should gain full

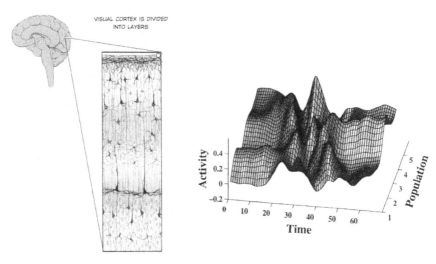

Figure 2.1 *Left.* A system of neurons. *Right.* A neural pattern "shape" generated by combining the temporal pattern of several different neurons in response to a color. From McClurkin *et al.* (1996) with permission.

access to a person's inner world" (2014: 143–145). (See also Prinz 2012: 126–133 for an important discussion of this issue.)

Now if this is right, then a simple and natural hypothesis suggests itself: having an orange-experience (the kind of experience you in fact have when viewing the orange) just is undergoing a unique set of neural patterns in different parts of the brain – in the way that water just is H_2O or lightning just is electrical discharge.

Suppose that the orange appears to change color, from orange to green. Then the pattern of firing in some population of neurons changes (those coding for color), while the pattern in another population of neurons (those coding for shape) stays the same. On the internal physical state view, the change in the character of your experience is just identical with this change in the pattern of firing in your neurons. It is not a change in a "non-physical sense datum" that is "created by" the change in neural pattern; it is just the change in the neural pattern itself. Likewise, if the orange appears to move, the change in the character of your experience just is another change in the neural pattern.[1]

On the internal physical state view, is your experience identical with a biological state of your brain, so that a robot couldn't have it? Or is it identical with a more abstract (but still intrinsic and physical) state of your brain that a robot could be in principle share? There are different versions of the internal physical state view. I will typically focus on a version that holds that different types of experiences are necessarily identical with different types of *patterns of neural activity*, or *neural states* for short.

Now you might think that the internal physical state view is obviously wrong. For instance, when you see an orange, you know that you have an orange-experience. But you don't know that you are undergoing a certain distributed neural pattern. When you inspect your experience, you don't find any neurons firing at all. Furthermore, there is an "explanatory gap": how could the activity of neurons in soggy grey matter constitute technicolor phenomenology?

But these quick arguments are suspect. To see this, consider an analogy. My daughter knows that there is water in the tub. But she doesn't know that there is H_2O in the tub. And when she inspects the water, she doesn't detect individual H_2O molecules. Nevertheless, water is H_2O. In the same way, maybe having an orange-experience is identical with undergoing a certain type of distributed neural process, even though this is not evident to you.

The internal physical state view is the polar opposite of "naïve realism". On naïve realism, the character of your experiences is constituted by the objective character of the external objects you experience. On the internal physical state view, it is entirely constituted by your internal neural processes.

The internal physical state view also differs from sense datum view. To see this, suppose you have a total hallucination. You hallucinate an orange rolling on a table. On the sense datum view, your brain causes an orange and round object to come into existence. It cannot be found within your physical brain but lives in a separate, private mental arena. And you experience this ghostly object. Internal physical state theorists avoid this "act-object" account of your hallucination by invoking the "seems-gambit" (Chapter 1). They hold, while there seems to exist an arena containing an orange and round object, there is no such arena. However, your *experience* exists: you really have an experience in which it seems to you that there is such an object. Your experience is identical with the relevant neural state in your brain.

It would be a mistake to think that the internal physical state view resembles the sense datum view, with the only difference being that it holds that the orange and round object you experience exists *inside your brain* (so that, although you do not know it, you are seeing your own brain). This would still be an act-object theory, but where the "object" is interior to the brain. Internal physical state theorists reject the act-object view entirely. To repeat, their picture is this: your hallucinatory experience is your neural state N, and your neural state N makes it seem as if there is an orange and round thing, but *there is no such thing anywhere* – not even in your brain.[2]

In short, internal physical state theorists allow that the "act-object" view seems true, but they insist that it is totally false. In that sense, they favor an *error theory*. The true nature of experience differs from how it seems.

You might have some residual questions about the internal physical state view. For one thing, I just said that internal physical state theorists invoke the "seems-gambit". But since they deny that descriptions of how things seem are grounded in the literal properties of sense data in a private sense-field, they must give some alternative account of how things seem. What is their alternative account?[3]

Relatedly, you might wonder, what do internal state theorists say about the whereabouts of the sensible properties that are necessarily bound up with the character of experience, such as sensible colors, audible qualities, and pain qualities? For instance, having an orange-experience necessarily involves "being presented with" an orange quality that appears to fill a round region in space. Where in reality is this quality to be found?

Some philosophers and scientists – for instance, Ned Block (2010: 24, 56n2), Semir Zeki (1983: 764), and Stephen Palmer (1999: 97) – seem to hold that this orange quality is actually a neural property of the population of neurons that codes for the chromatic aspect of your experience (as it might be, a unique spatio-temporal pattern of neural firings). The poet Oscar Wilde (1854–1900) puts it this way: "It is in the brain that the poppy is red, that the apple is odorous, that the skylark sings". Maybe internal physical state theorists could take this brain-based view of sensible properties?

This may seem to be a natural combination, but it faces an immediate difficulty, which we can appreciate by contrasting it with the sense datum view. On the sense datum view (e.g., Russell 1912a; Peacocke 2008), when you have the orange-experience, the orange quality is a property of a *literally round* "sense datum". Internal state theorists reject the existence of such a thing, so they cannot take the same view. Instead, the brain-based view holds that this same quality is a neural property of a population of neurons that is *not* round. And now the difficulty is this: if the orange quality that is essentially involved in the orange-experience is really a neural feature of a population of neurons that *isn't* round, how come it *appears* to fill a round region?

In view of these problems, could internal physical state theorists about experience reject the brain-based view of sensible properties? For instance, might they instead accept an extreme version of the *rife illusion view* (Section 1.5)? That is, might they say that experiences are neural states, and undergoing those neural states makes it seem that objects arranged in space "out there" have sensible properties, but in fact nothing has these properties – not sense data (the sense datum view), and not even bits of the brain (the brain-based view)?

These questions are important. The central puzzle of this book concerns how experience can be both externally directed and internally dependent. These questions concern the question of how internal physical state theorists might accommodate the "externally directed character" of experience. As I formulated the internal physical state view above, it is neutral on these questions. So we can understand it without having answers. We will take up the question of whether the internal physical state view comports with the externally directed character of experience later on (Sections 2.4–2.7).

First, we will consider an argument for the internal physical state view based on a particularly strong form of "internal dependence".

2.2 From experiential internalism to the internal physical state view

The argument for the internal physical state view to be examined in this section has two steps. The first step will argue for the general thesis of "experiential internalism": for every sensory-perceptual experience, there is a neural state that is directly and necessarily sufficient for that experience. This eliminates "externalist" theories like naïve realism and moves us to a ballpark of views that includes the sense datum view and the internal physical state view. The second step will use additional considerations to argue that, between these two options, the internal physical state view is to be preferred.

Let's look at these steps in greater detail, and then turn to some problems with the argument.

First step: experiential internalism. Experiential internalism is an especially strong form of "internal dependence". To see this, let N be the distributed neural pattern that underlies your experience of an orange. Experiential internalism goes beyond the generally accepted claim that, if N were reproduced in your brain in the absence of an orange and round thing, you would hallucinate an orange and round thing. It implies something much stronger. For instance, imagine that, in some other "possible world", there happens to be a brain floating in space that popped into existence from out of nowhere, and *purely by chance* it undergoes neural state N. Experiential internalism implies that, even in this "brain in the void", N results in an experience as of an orange and round thing, even though in this scenario N has no history of registering the presence of a round thing.

Sense datum theorists accept experiential internalism because they hold that the neural state N *directly causes* the experience of an orange and round non-physical sense datum. Internal physical state theorists accept it because they hold that the neural state N *just is* the orange-experience. Furthermore, experiential internalism is generally accepted among neuroscientists (Dehaene 2014; Koch and Tononi 2015).

However, you shouldn't get the wrong idea. Not everyone accepts experiential internalism. As we shall see later in this book, "externalist" representationalists (Chapter 4) and contemporary naïve realists (Chapter 5) reject experiential internalism. They think that if we are to explain how experience is "externally directed", then we need to retreat to a weaker form of "internal dependence". The neural state N is not necessarily sufficient all on its own for an experience of a round thing. It needs to have a history of registering the presence of a round thing. So if the "brain in a void" were to undergo neural state N, it would not have such an experience, because in this scenario N does not have a history of registering the presence of a round thing.

Therefore, we need an *argument* for experiential internalism. The best argument for experiential internalism is based on empirical findings. (In Chapter 1, we cited the same empirical findings in support of "illusionism" about the sensible properties.) Start with the experience of pain. Even under normal conditions, there is no simple or systematic relationship between bodily disturbances and sensory pain intensity. By contrast, neuroscience has shown that firing rates in the cortex are "linearly related to subjects' perceived pain intensity" (Coghill et al. 1999: 1936). So, pain intensity is more directly related to internal firing rates. In the domain of smell, similarities and differences in the smell qualities we experience are very poorly correlated with similarities and differences in the molecular-types that we smell. They are only well-correlated with distributed patterns of neural firing in the smell system (Youngentob et al. 2006; Howard et al. 2009). Likewise, in the domain of color, similarities and differences in color experiences fail to line up with similarities and differences in the ways external objects reflect light (MacAdam 1985; Byrne and Hilbert 2003: 13). They only line up with similarities and differences in distributed patterns of neural firing in the color system (Bohon et al. 2016).

These findings support experiential internalism. True, they are limited to the experience of certain sensible properties: pain, smell, and color. But they provide some support for the conjecture that all aspects of our experiences – including spatial and temporal aspects – are completely determined by our neural states (we will discuss this in greater detail in Section 4.8).

Second step: from experiential internalism to the internal physical state view. As noted above, the empirically-supported thesis of experiential internalism is not the same thing as the internal physical state view. For experiential internalism is consistent with the claim of the sense datum view that neural states *cause* our experiences as well as the claim of the internal physical state view that neural states are *identical* with our experiences (Figure 2.2). The second step of the argument uses more "philosophical" considerations to argue that, as between these options, we should favor the internal physical state view.

For one thing, the sense datum view is a dualistic theory that holds that our internal neural states generate non-physical sense data that reside in private mental spaces. This is complicated and mysterious. The internal

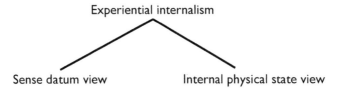

Figure 2.2 If we accept experiential internalism, we have two options.

physical state view eliminates this extra step. It is a "reductive physicalist view" that *directly identifies* experiences with our internal neural states. It is therefore simpler and less mysterious than the sense datum view.

In addition, since the internal physical state view uses the "seems-gambit" to avoid sense data (Chapter 1), it avoids the myriad puzzles attending sense data: the *percipi* puzzle, the puzzle of the location of sense data, and the puzzle of perceptual imprecision. For instance, take the puzzle of perceptual imprecision for the sense datum view (Section 1.11). You view a tomato in the center of your visual field and then in the periphery of your visual field. In one version, the sense datum view holds that the tomato-like sense datum created by your brain becomes metaphysically indeterminate in shape and color – an idea that is difficult to accept. The internal physical state view avoids sense data and therefore avoids indeterminate items. What is going on in this case is that your underlying neural state somehow becomes "degraded".

That, then, is the argument for the internal physical state view. Is it convincing? One potential problem is that its first step, experiential internalism, is an especially strong and controversial form of "internal dependence". However, the empirical case for experiential internalism is quite persuasive. We will develop it in greater detail in Chapter 4. And experiential internalism is generally accepted by neuroscientists, even if it is rejected by some philosophers.

So, for the sake of argument, let us suppose that experiential internalism is right. There is still a big problem with the argument. The problem concerns the second step, which moves from experiential internalism to the internal physical state view. True, between the internal physical state view and the sense datum view, there is some reason to prefer the internal physical state view. But Figure 2.2 is misleading. If we accept experiential internalism, these are not the only options. They are just the only options we have discussed. Many philosophers who accept experiential internalism today favor a third option: "internalist representationalism", which we will discuss in Chapter 4. So we should add this third option to the decision tree. Like the internal physical state view, it fits with experiential internalism and avoids the problematic sense datum view. So, to complete the argument, internal physical state theorists would need to provide additional reasons for accepting the internal physical state view over internalist representationalism. We will return to this issue in Section 4.11.[4]

In any case, the empirical facts cited above provide *some* reason to accept the internal physical state view. If in many cases the structural relations among experiences (similarity and difference, equal intervals, proportion) do not match the structural relations among the complex external physical properties that our brain is responding to, but they do match the structural relations among the internal neural correlates, then this certainly raises the probability of the view that our experiences are just identical with those neural correlates. For instance, maybe pains just are distributed neural states in the "pain matrix", with their intensity constituted by the average firing rate of neurons. Experiences of color and smell just are different distributed neural patterns. The internal physical state view provides a simple and natural answer to the "character question" that is in line with the empirical evidence. It is certainly worth discussing.

So much for the case for the internal physical state view. In the rest of the chapter, we will look at problems for the view. For one thing, many have objected to it on the grounds that it is inconsistent with the so-called "transparency observation" (Section 2.3). For another thing, it is arguably inconsistent with the externally directed character of some experiences (Sections 2.4–2.7).

2.3 Can the internal physical state view accommodate the transparency observation?

When you see an orange and a tomato on a table, you come to know things about the *objects that you experience*, for instance, that there is an orange thing and a red thing there. But you also come to know something about the character of *your experiences themselves*: for instance, that you are having an orange-experience and a tomato-experience.

The "transparency observation" is about the second type of knowledge: it is about how you attain knowledge about what your own experiences are like. It is about "introspective" knowledge.

The transparency observation is one of the most discussed ideas in recent philosophy of perception. Different philosophers formulate it differently.

We will focus on M. G. F. Martin's forceful discussion of the issue in his paper "Setting Things Before the Mind" (1998). In this paper, Martin offers a particular formulation of the transparency observation, and also argues that it rules out the internal physical state view. Following him, we will focus on the case of visual experience.

Here is how Martin formulates the thesis:

> **Transparency observation.** In general, "the way in which we learn what our [visual] experiences are like is by attending to the objects and features [in space] which are presented to us in perception". For instance, if I view an orange, I know what my experience is like by focusing on an orange and round thing in space.

This is called the "transparency" observation because the idea is that your experience itself is "invisible". You cannot attend to it *as distinct from* attending to the objects and features you are presented with.

This thesis fits poorly with the internal physical state view. It fits much better with the kind of "act-object" approach that was our focus in Chapter 1.

To illustrate, suppose you have a normal experience of an orange and then you have a hallucination of an orange (maybe you have "Charles Bonnet syndrome" discussed in Section 1.4). On across-the-board sense datum theory (Chapter 1), the relevant object in both cases is a sense datum created by your brain. On "normal-abnormal naïve realism" (Section 1.3), the object is the physical orange in the first case and an orange and round sense datum created by the brain in the second case. Both of these versions of the act-object model predict the transparency observation: in both cases, you know what your experience is like by attending to the objects and properties you perceive.

But now consider the internal physical state view. This view holds, contrary to the act-object model, that the character of experience is not determined by any colored and shaped objects that you experience. Rather, it is constituted by your internal *neural patterns*. Unlike the act-object model, the internal physical state view would not seem to predict the transparency observation at all. And this counts against it.

That is a first-pass statement of the argument from the transparency observation against the internal physical state view. Is it a good argument?

One problem is that the transparency observation has been much disputed. There are apparent counterexamples (see Chapter 3). For instance, if you look at two dots on a piece of paper and move your attention from one dot to the other, you know that your experience changes. But it seems that you don't know this by focusing on some change in "what you experience". There is no change in *what* you experience. There is only a change in *how* you experience it. Or again, if you take off your glasses so that things look blurry to you, then you know that your experience changes, but it seems that you don't know this by focusing on some change in "what is presented to you". *What* you experience doesn't seem to change; there is only a change in *how* you experience it.

However, here I will set such apparent counterexamples aside and focus instead on what I think is a deeper problem with the transparency observation as Martin formulates it.

The problem I have in mind concerns illusion and especially hallucination. When we formulated the transparency observation, we did not restrict it to veridical experience. It was meant to apply to all visual experience. But consider an actual hallucination. One woman with "Charles Bonnet syndrome" described hallucinating "a colored flag in sharp focus ... it looked exactly like a British flag" (Sacks 2012: 11). She surely knew what her experience was like. Now, the general transparency observation entails that she knew what it was like by attending to some existing *object*. If you attend to something, then it must exist. But since no physical object was present, this would have to be a non-physical object, namely, a flag-like sense datum created by her brain. So, on the face of it, the transparency observation as formulated above requires sense data!

But we have seen that there are very strong reasons to reject sense data. Therefore, the transparency observation as formulated above is very likely *false*, because there are some hallucinations where it is not the case that we know what our experience is like by attending to objects that we experience.

(It may be that we can draw a more general conclusion from cases of illusion and hallucination. If in non-veridical cases attending to objects is not part of what explains the justification we have for our beliefs about our experiences, then it becomes natural to think that in veridical cases too it is not part of what explains our having justification for such beliefs.)

In fact, Martin seems to briefly acknowledge in passing that hallucination undermines the general transparency observation as formulated above. He acknowledges that "even in cases of hallucination, there is a way that one's experience is for one, and one can come to know what one's experience is like, *yet there are no objects [no 'sense data'] of perception for one to attend to*" (my italics).

But if the general transparency observation as formulated above is false, then it cannot be used in a sound argument against the internal physical state view.

At this point, we might try to formulate an alternative version of the transparency observation, one that is not undermined by hallucination. And then perhaps we might use it in a sound argument against the internal physical state view. But what would that be? Martin does not officially offer a revised transparency observation. However, he does write, "In as much as an hallucination may be indistinguishable for one from a genuine perception, it will still *seem to one as* if there is an array of objects there for one to scan and explore" (my italics). This suggests:

> **Seeming transparency.** Whenever you have a visual experience and you know what it is like, then the following things at the very least *seem* true: it seems that there are objects in space for you attend to, and it seems that you know what your experience is like by attending to some objects.

Maybe "seeming transparency" is true. In fact, maybe it is pretheoretically plausible. But now we need to ask whether it also has teeth. That is, can it also be used in a convincing argument against the internal physical state view?

This is not clear. Even though internal state theorists reject the general act-object model of experience, that doesn't automatically forbid them from saying that this assumption at least seems true to us when we reflect on what our experience is like. This is just an extension of the "seems-gambit". They will just say that in this case things are not as they seem. In other words, reflection on our experiences leads us astray about their nature. As I said before, in that sense, they advocate an "error theory". In that case, even if they must reject the transparency observation as initially formulated, they can accept that the transparency observation seems true. That is, they can accept "seeming transparency". At least, we have been given no reason to think otherwise. In short, once we water down the thesis in this way to accommodate hallucinations, it is not clear that it is inconsistent with the internal physical state view.

Maybe internal state theorists can even explain seeming-transparency. Maybe there is seeming-transparency because our most natural way of describing experiences is indirect: our most natural way of describing experiences is in terms of the worldly situations that bring about our internal experiences (Papineau 2014: 24).

Now you might think we shouldn't quite yet give up on the idea that some stronger version of the "transparency observation" (stronger than mere "seeming transparency") *does* undermine the internal physical state view. You might think: we just have to formulate such a stronger version of transparency thesis, one that is (a) pretheoretically plausible and defensible (e.g., compatible with hallucination), *and* (b) at the same time has *bite*, that is, is *inconsistent with* the internal physical state view.

Here we will not attempt to search after such a version of the transparency observation.[5] For, in the remainder of this chapter we will see that, to rule out the internal physical state view, we may not need to rely on any controversial "transparency thesis" about how we come to know things about our experiences. We may be able to rule it out on the basis of a related but much simpler idea, namely the idea that some of our experiences are *essentially* "externally directed". Unlike the transparency observation, this is not a theory concerning the thorny issue of *how we know* what our experiences are like. It is a more modest and defensible claim just concerning *what some experiences are like.*

I will begin by saying more about what essential external directedness amounts to (Section 2.4). Then we will use it to construct a new argument against the internal physical state view (Sections 2.5 and 2.6).

2.4 The externally directed nature of some experiences

Suppose that (for some reason) you have an experience of an orange moving to the right as depicted in Figure 2.3.

Call this type of experience (whether it occurs in normal experience or hallucination) the *orange-experience.*

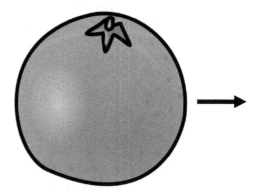

Figure 2.3 An orange moving to the right.

Intuitively, the orange-experience is essentially externally directed in the following sense. It is part of the *essence* of the orange-experience that, if you have it, then it *seems* to you that there is *right there* an orange and round object moving to the right. In that sense, the experience is "directed at" such an object. To put it differently, it is in the essence of the orange-experience that it is an experience *as of* an orange and round object moving to the right. Here "object" is used neutrally – it needn't be a physical object, it could be transitory sense datum.

Why call this essential *external* directedness? Because, if there really is an orange and round object there (a physical object or a sense datum), it presumably exists somewhere external to your physical brain (after all, such an object needn't exist in your physical brain while you are having the experience).

What does the term "directedness" mean? It's a metaphor. Your experience is metaphorically "directed" at an orange object moving to the right. You shouldn't read too much into the metaphor. In particular, the same metaphor of "directedness" is sometimes used to explain the idea of "representation", as when a belief or a sentence "directed at" or "represents" something that may or may not exist. So the metaphor might suggest the representational theory of sensory experience that we will discuss in Chapter 3. But essential external directedness is not equivalent to the representational theory – although the representational theory accommodates it. It is a pretheoretical idea. And, as we shall see, nearly all major theories accommodate it, with the exception of the internal physical state view.

What does it mean to say that the orange-experience "essentially" involves the seeming presence of an orange and round object? Water is *essentially* made up of H_2O: it wouldn't be water if it didn't have this chemical composition. Or again, the number eight is *essentially* the successor of the number seven. In the same way, some facts about our experiences touch on their essence. The fact that the orange-experience is directed at an orange and round object is one of them. Part of *what it is* to have the orange-experience is for there to seem to be an orange and round object moving to the right. This isn't something that just happens to be true. Rather, in *any* possible situation, if any individual has this experience, then they have an experience as of an orange and round thing moving to the right.

This means that, even if someone should have the orange-experience during a hallucination, it seems to them that there is an orange and round object moving to the right. It is just that, in a hallucination case, no such physical object really is present.

I've focused on an ordinary visual experience. Other experiences are essentially externally directed, but not to the same degree as ordinary visual experiences. We do not need to formulate a general thesis. The right thing to say is that we can roughly arrange experiences in a series depending on how externally directed they are. For instance, experiences of after-images are somewhat externally directed, because they present images as located and as having shape; but their content is not as richly spatial as ordinary experiences, since they needn't present the images as being at any determinate distance. Bodily experiences are externally directed: they present qualities in bodily regions. Auditory experiences present sounds as coming from certain directions. However, I will continue to focus on visual experiences.

So here is an initial formulation of essential external directedness:

> **Essential external directedness.** It is part of the essence of some types of visual experiences that in having those visual experiences it seems that there are objects with certain spatial features. They are essentially *as of* such objects. This is so whether they are veridical or hallucinatory. For instance, having the orange-experience essentially involves the seeming-presence of a *round* thing that *moves to the right*.

This formulation uses the term "seems". There are controversies about what "seems" means in ordinary perception-reports (Jackson 1977: chap. 2; Breckenridge 2018). However, I think we can sidestep these controversies by using an alternative, simplified formulation that doesn't use the word "seems" at all:

> **Essential external directedness (simplified).** For many experience-types, a correct definition of them will use certain spatial terms. For instance, a correct definition of what it is to have the orange-experience will somehow include spatial terms such as *round* and *moving to the right*. It will have the form: to have the orange-experience is to [... *round* ... *moves to the right*].

An answer to the character question will be a definition of what it is to have a certain experience-type (Dorr 2016). Essential external directedness is a constraint on a correct definition. As Christopher Peacocke has put it, "visual experience is intrinsically [essentially] spatial ... if we do not use spatial properties in characterizing visual [experience], we omit a subjective feature of experience" (2008: 10).

In Chapter 1, we saw that the starting point of the sense datum view was the act-object assumption. This assumption is very strong. It implies that having the orange-experience essentially involves the real presence of a round object, even in a hallucination case. We saw that there are reasons to doubt this starting point because it leads to problematic sense data.

Essential external directedness doesn't face the same problem. For instance, if you have the orange-experience in a hallucination case, the term *round* might enter into the definition of the experience because it enters into how things "seem" or are "represented" in having the experience, even though no *round* sense datum is present. This is to apply the "seems-gambit". As we shall see in Chapter 3, the representational view is an example of a view that accommodates essential external directedness without sense data.

While essential external directedness is not committed to sense data because of the availability of the seems-gambit, it is compatible with the sense datum view. In fact, the sense datum view implies and explains it (as we discussed in Section 1.6). If the orange-experience essentially involves the actual presence of an orange and round sense datum, this explains why it essentially involves the seeming presence of such an object.

The case for essential external directedness is based on reflection. It just seems to be an obvious description of the phenomenological character of some types of experience. To see this, suppose you have a diffuse headache throughout your whole head. Here is an obvious comment about the phenomenology of this experience: it does *not* essentially involve the seeming presence of a round thing moving to the right. It is an equally obvious comment about the phenomenology of the orange-experience (in both normal experience and hallucination) that it *does* essentially involve the seeming presence of a round object moving to the right. It is part of the essence of the orange-experience that it is an experience as of a certain specific apparent *scene*. And this apparent scene can only be adequately characterized by using the terms *round* and *moving to the right*, where these terms are used with their normal meanings to express genuine spatial properties.

Here is another argument for essential external directedness. The following conditional claim is very plausible: if any individual (even a "brain-in-a-void" to be discussed in Section 2.6) were to have all the same visual experiences as you, then they could have concepts of shapes and beliefs about the shapes of things. This requires that it is *built-in* to visual experiences that they involve the seeming presence of things with those shapes.

So even if, owing to hallucination, we deny the act-object assumption that in every case of having the orange-experience there must really be an orange and round object present ("sense data"), we should retreat to the weaker claim that in every case there at least seems to be such an object. That is why this book started in the introduction with essential external directedness, and not the stronger and more controversial act-object assumption.

The assertion that some visual experiences are necessarily externally directed is neutral on many questions. For instance, one question is: when you view a tilted penny, is the type of experience you have necessarily as of a thing that is elliptical, or of a thing that is tilted and round, or as of a thing that is "elliptical-from-here" (the viewpoint-relative but objective property of having a shape that would be occluded by an ellipse placed in a plane perpendicular to the line of sight)? Or are multiple answers correct? The arguments to follow are neutral on this issue.

Essential external directedness is quite minimal in another way. It is not committed to the claim that, necessarily, whenever someone has the orange-experience, it seems to them that there is a "mind-independent" orange and round object – an object whose existence and character are independent of you. That is good because this stronger "mind-independence" version of essential external directedness is problematic. Imagine that you have just come into the world and your first experience is the orange-experience. In accordance with my simplified form of essential external directedness, it is correct to say that there is ostensibly an orange and round item in your visual field moving to the right. But, since this is your first experience and you know nothing of the objective world, it doesn't yet seem "mind-independent" to you. For all you know, it is a transitory mind-dependent sense datum. So the stronger "mind-independence" version of essential external directedness is mistaken (Farkas 2013; Byrne 2013).

The thesis of essential external directedness differs from the transparency thesis in a couple of respects. First of all, the transparency thesis is a controversial and general claim about *how we know* what *all* visual experiences are like. We saw that there are potential counterexamples involving attention shifts and blurry vision. We also saw that it faces a problem about hallucinations. By contrast, essential external directedness is only a claim about what *some* experiences are like. So attention shifts and visual blur are not problems. And hallucination is not a problem either, as we have seen.

Second, the transparency observation (at least the form discussed in the previous section) is not obviously inconsistent with the internal physical state view. By contrast, essential external directedness is apparently inconsistent with the internal physical state view, as we shall now see.

2.5 The argument from essential external directedness against the internal physical state view

The argument from essential external directedness against the internal physical state view uses a simple logical rule called *Leibniz's law*. This rule states that if what is true of *A* is not true of B, then *A* ≠ B. The argument says that different things are true of types of experiences and types of neural states, so they cannot be literally one and the same:

(1) A correct definition of what it is to have the orange-experience will include the spatial terms *round* and *moves to the right.*

(2) This is not true of the underlying neural state *N*. It is not the case that a correct definition of neural state *N* will include the spatial terms *round* and *moves to the right.*

(3) Therefore, having the orange-experience is not identical with the underlying neural state *N*, even if it may be dependent on that neural state.

To appreciate the argument, look at Figure 2.3 illustrating the orange-experience. Premise 1 says that a definition of what it is to have the orange-experience will include the spatial terms *round* and *moves to the right.* This is just our "simplified" formulation of essential external directedness. It is pretheoretically very plausible. Now look at Figure 2.1 illustrating neural pattern N. Premise 2 says that neural pattern N is different. No definition of what it is to undergo the neural pattern N will include the spatial terms *round* and *moves to the right.*[6] Because different things are true of them, having the orange-experience cannot be *identical with* undergoing neural pattern N, even if they are intimately connected. Because it concerns spatial features, we might also call this the *spatial argument* against the internal physical state view.

At this point, the internal state theorist might respond as follows:

I want to agree with premise 1. But what is the case for premise 2? Why can't I just reject it? Of course, undergoing the neural pattern *N* doesn't involve the real existence of a round thing *in the brain* moving to the right. But why can't I say – contrary to Premise 2 – that part of the essence of undergoing the neural pattern is that it involves there *seeming to be* a round thing moving to the right? In that case, the argument collapses. The internal physical state view is totally consistent with essential external directedness.

Here is the reason why the internal physical state theorists cannot make this response. Look again at Figure 2.1. What it is to undergo the neural pattern can be completely described in terms of *types of neurons* and the *times, directions, and intensities* at which they fire. This is just what it is to be a neural pattern. Therefore, in accordance with premise 2, the definition of what it is to undergo the neural pattern can be given without mentioning spatial terms *round* or *moves to the left*. (It is true that states can have hidden essences but we know that the essence of the neural pattern doesn't involve these spatial features.) This rules out the response that it is part of the definition of undergoing the neural pattern that it involves the seeming-presence of a *round thing moving to the right*.

The argument from essential external directedness against the internal physical state view is analogous to an argument that all will accept:

> (1) A definition of what it is to *think* that something is *round* and *moving to the right* will mention *round* and *moving to the right*; for to think this is to attribute *round* and *moving to the right* to something.

> (2) This is not true of making the noise "something is round and moving to the right"; this noise can be fully characterized without mentioning the spatial features *round* and *moving to the right*.

> (3) So to think that something is round and moving is not just to make the noise "something is round and moving"; it might sometimes *involve* making this noise, but it is *something more* than making this noise.

Suppose we accept the argument from essential external directedness against the internal physical state view. What alternative view might we accept? What views are consistent with essential external directedness?

In fact, all the other views we discuss in this book endorse the argument and its conclusion:

Sense datum view. To have the orange-experience is to experience a sense datum that is *orange, round,* and *moving to the right*, in accordance with essential external directedness. By contrast, neural states can be defined entirely in terms of types of neurons and the times, directions, and intensities at which they fire. So, on the sense datum view, to have the orange-experience is not just to have a neural state, since they have different definitions. The orange-experience is dependent on a neural state, but it is something more than a neural state.

Representational view. To have the orange-experience is to "experientially represent" that something is *orange, round,* and *moving to the right*. (If someone has the orange-experience in a hallucination, there is in fact no such object – not even a "sense datum".) So spatial terms enter into a definition of what it is to have the orange-experience. This is not true of any neural pattern. So, on representationalism, to have the orange-experience is not just to have some neural state. The orange-experience may be dependent on a neural state, but it is something more than a neural state. To define what it is to have this experience, neural terminology is insufficient. We must mention that the neural state enables one to "experientially represent" a *round* thing that is *moving to the right*.

Contemporary naïve realism. To have the orange-experience is to *either* really experience an external physical thing that is *orange, round,* and *moving to the right* (in normal perception) *or* to be in a state that is indiscriminable from experiencing such a thing (in illusion or hallucination). Since this is not the definition of any neural state, to have the orange-experience is not just to undergo a neural state. The orange-experience is something more than a neural state.

All these views endorse essential external directedness because the terms *round* and *moves to the right* show up in their definitions of what it is to have the orange-experience. Notice that the "representational view" rejects the act-object assumption. Contemporary naïve realism also rejects the act-object assumption in the case of hallucination. This reinforces the point (made in the previous section) that essential external directedness is not committed to the general act-object assumption.

Let me conclude with some comments.

First comment. There is a long history of Leibniz's law arguments against the identification of experience-types with internal neural-types (Smart 1959). For instance, suppose that you smell some mint tea. Against the internal physical state theory, it might be argued that your sensation involves the smell quality *minty*, but your underlying neural state S doesn't involve this smell quality (just neuronal firings), so they cannot be one and the same. But the "spatial" Leibniz's law argument above is superior to this traditional kind of Leibniz's law argument. For in response to this traditional Leibniz's law argument, the internal physical state theorist can say that the neural state S *does* essentially involve a minty smell quality, because that smell quality itself *just is* a neural pattern involved in S (even if this is not evident to you). By contrast, a parallel response to the spatial Leibniz's law argument above is not possible. For no one thinks that the spatial features *round* and *moving to the right* involved in the orange-experience turn out to be neural properties involved in the underlying neural state N!

Second comment. The argument from essential external directedness is only supposed to rule out the internal physical state view, which makes the strong claim that all experience-types are *identical with* neural-types. By this argument, experiences and neural states have different natures. So even if neural states are sufficient for experiences, experiences cannot be identical with neural states.

The argument from essential external directedness is not meant to rule out experiential internalism – the weaker claim that, for every experience-type, there is an internal neural-type that is necessarily *sufficient for* it. In fact, it doesn't rule out experiential internalism. This is good, because experiential internalism is a popular idea.

To see that the argument from essential external directedness does not rule out experiential internalism, notice that there are views that accommodate experiential internalism but that are not ruled out by essential external directedness. One such view is the sense datum theory (see especially Box 1.1 in Chapter 1). On this view, the orange-experience depends on a neural pattern but it has a different nature from the neural pattern: it is a relation to a round and moving sense datum. So, unlike the underlying neural pattern, the experience is essentially externally directed.

Another such view is "internalist representationalism". We already mentioned this view in passing in Section 2.2 and will consider it in detail in Chapter 4. On this view, too, the orange-experience depends on the neural pattern, but it has a different nature from the neural pattern: it consists in *experientially representing* a round and moving thing. So, unlike the underlying neural pattern, the experience is essentially externally directed. In this way, unlike the internal physical state view, internalist representationalism allows us to hold that experience is both internally dependent in a strong sense *and* essentially externally directed.

Third comment. It may be that the *only* way for internal physical state theorists to save their view in the face of this argument would be to deny premise 1. If this is right, then the internal physical state view requires that it is *not* the case that spatial terms like *round* and *moving to the left* enter into a correct definition of what it is to have the orange-experience (because they don't enter into a definition of what it is to have the neural pattern with which this type of experience is identical). It is worth pausing for a moment to appreciate what this would amount to.

Return to an example we have already used before: having a diffuse headache. Clearly, you can define what it is to have an experience with this character without using the spatial terms *round* and *moving to the right*. So if the internal physical state view implies the rejection of premise 1, then what it implies is that having the orange-experience (Figure 2.3) is like having a headache in this respect. And this amounts to saying that the experience "really" has a character other than the character it seems to have. For it certainly seems to have a character radically different from the character of a headache, a character that can only be defined by using spatial terms like round and moving to the right.[7]

In Section 2.7, we will explore the question of whether internal physical state theorists might block the argument by denying essential external directedness. However, let us first put another argument on the table.

2.6 Could a brain-in-the-void have a favorite shape?

The argument of the previous section, if sound, shows that essential external directedness and the internal physical state view are inconsistent. If the orange-experience is essentially externally directed (premise 1), but the neural pattern is not (premise 2), the orange-experience cannot be identical with the neural pattern. Now we will sketch a further argument for thinking that the internal physical state view and essential external directedness are in tension. The argument concerns our ability to be *mentally related* to *properties* – for instance, our ability to think about shapes.

Let me first explain the idea of a property (van Inwagen 2004; Yi 2018). A property is a *way things might be*. For instance, purple is a way things might be. Properties – ways things might be – are more abstract than ordinary things (somewhat as numbers are). For instance, a specific shade of purple cannot be located in any particular place; if it is anywhere, it is wherever there is a thing with that shade. Properties are not created by the mind, any more than numbers are created by the mind. They are "objective". Even before minds came on the scene, external objects were certain ways: they had certain shapes, distances, orientations, and so on. There are properties that nothing has. For instance, in usual circumstances people can hallucinate novel colors that nothing has (see Section 5.5); those colors still exist because they are ways things *might* be.

By having experiences, we become *mentally related* to properties in various ways. We mentally represent them. For example, when you see an orange, you believe it is round. You mentally attribute the property of being round to the orange. You can think about its round shape.

How do you become mentally related to properties in such ways? Can these mental relationships be identified with some kind of physical relationships? Or are they spooky non-physical relationships?

Here is one natural idea. The round shape presented to you is a real property of the orange detected by your visual system (via the light coming from the orange). There is presumably a pattern of firing in your cognitive

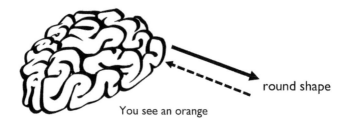

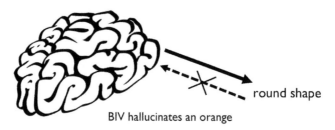

Figure 2.4 You and your BIV counterpart.

system that has the function of detecting round things in the world (see Figure 2.4, top). So maybe your *mentally representing* roundness (the solid arrow in Figure 2.4) can be identified with a complex "detective" relationship to roundness (the dotted arrow). Analogy: a thermometer's representing temperatures is a matter of its levels of mercury having the function of detecting those temperatures in the world. Different versions of this approach have been developed by Fodor (1992), Dretske (1995), and Neander (2017).

But if we accept the internal physical state view and essential external directedness (McLaughlin 2016a: 856–857), then we must reject the idea that your mentally representing roundness can be identified with your detecting roundness. Indeed, then we must accept that it is a spooky, non-physical relationship.

To see this, let's forget about you for a moment. Imagine that, in some other "possible world", there happens to be nothing but a brain floating in space that popped into existence from out of nowhere, and *purely by chance* it undergoes the same neural activity as your own brain (Figure 2.4, bottom). Internal physical state theorists must say that this brain-in-a-void (BIV) has exactly the same experiences as you, because it has the same neural states. It's just that all of its experiences are hallucinatory. And, supposing for the sake of argument that they also accept essential external directedness, in having those experiences it seems to the BIV that there are variously-shaped things in space. For instance, if you have an experience as of a round orange on a table, then the BIV has the same experience as of a round orange on a table. So, like you, the BIV can mentally represent the shape *round* (the solid arrow in the figure). In fact, the BIV could have a favorite shape just like you do. True, the BIV may not see any objects (physical objects or even "sense data") that possess the shape *round*. But the shape *property* still exists – it is a way things might be – and the BIV is mentally related to it.

But, of course, the BIV doesn't undergo a neural state that has the function of detecting the occurrence of roundness in the world (the dotted arrow is eliminated). Indeed, the BIV is in every way cut off from *any* relevant physical relations to roundness. So if both the internal physical state view and essential external directedness are correct, then the *mentally represents* relationship that the BIV bears to roundness cannot be identified with any *physical* relationship between the BIV and roundness.

If all this is right, then your *mentally representing* the shape *round* (the solid arrow in Figure 2.4, top) cannot be *identified with* a physical relationship, such as a relationship of causal detection (the dotted arrow in Figure 2.4, bottom). For even if you do in fact causally detect roundness, the BIV thought-experiment shows that you *could* have an experience of roundness and mentally represent it, *without* detecting it. This means that your mentally representing roundness cannot be *the same thing* as detecting it.

As Jeff Speaks (2015: 272) says, the combination of the internal physical state view and essential external directedness "would have as a surprising (and presumably unwelcome) consequence the irreducibility of [representational] relations". Likewise, Ned Block says, "it may be right that we internalists should acknowledge an irreducible representation relation" (2019: 426). That is to say, the internal physical state view and essential external directedness together entail that brains simply have an innate, intrinsic capacity to mentally represent shapes and other perceptible properties. And here mental representation cannot be identified with more a basic physical relationship; it cannot, for instance, be identified with a causal-informational relation (the dotted line in Figure 2.4, top). This is somewhat mysterious.

If this is correct, it means that the internal physical state view and essential external directedness do not sit together very well. Part of the argument for the internal physical state view is that it provides an attractively simple "reductive physicalist" theory of *experience* (Section 2.1). But now we see that, if it is combined with essential external directedness, it implies a somewhat mysterious "non-reductive" theory of *mental representation*. This result will be unwelcome to internal physical state theorists (e.g., McLaughlin 2016a and Papineau 2014) who want to entirely reduce the mind to more basic physical elements.

We have been considering the question of whether internal physical state theorists can accept essential external directedness. We now have two reasons to think that they cannot. In the previous section, we saw that, given essential external directedness, the internal physical state view can be ruled out by a Leibniz's law argument. In the present section, we saw that, if internal physical state theorists accept essential external directedness, they must accept a strange, non-reductive theory of the mental representation of shapes and other perceptible properties – one that is quite antithetical to their reductive theory of experience.

For these reasons, proponents of the internal physical state view are under pressure to reject essential external directedness.[8]

2.7 Papineau's reply: rejecting essential external directedness

David Papineau (2014, 2016) is a proponent of the internal physical state view who does exactly that: he rejects essential external directedness (personal discussion). In this way, he avoids the problems raised in the previous sections for the internal physical state view based on external directedness.

For instance, take the argument from essential external directedness (Section 2.5). Papineau accepts premise (2): neural patterns don't essentially involve spatial features like round and moving to the right in any way (they don't essentially involve the seeming presence of objects with these spatial features, and they are not essentially "as of" objects with these spatial features). To block the argument, he denies premise (1), that is, essential external directedness (or "essential spatial character"): he denies that such spatial features essentially enter into the characterization of our visual experiences (they don't essentially involve the seeming presence of objects with these spatial features, and they are not essentially "as of" objects with these spatial features). That is, he thinks that visual experiences are like neural patterns in that spatial features like round and moving to the right do not essentially enter into their characterization. If so, there is no good "Leibniz's law" argument for thinking that visual experiences are distinct from neural patterns.

Likewise, Papineau's response to the BIV argument (Section 2.6) is to deny essential external directedness. So, while he accepts that a BIV could indeed have the same rich visual and other experiences as you (including the orange-experience represented in Figure 2.3), he denies that the BIV would thereby be mentally related to external shape properties. Even though it has all the same rich visual experiences as you, BIV cannot think about any shapes (and so cannot have a favorite shape).

In the introduction, I started off with two initial assumptions: essential external directedness and some form of internal dependence. I said that the traditional puzzles in the philosophy of perception can be summed up in this way: how can both of these things be true? Papineau is saying that one of our initial assumptions – essential external directedness – turns out to be mistaken. We should accept internal dependence but not essential external directedness. And the view that best explains internal dependence is the internal physical state view.

Papineau doesn't just reject essential external directedness and leave the matter there. Although he denies essential external directedness, he suggests a few points that might be thought to soften the blow of this denial.

(1) Papineau says (2016: 340) that internal physical state theorists can be "quite happy to agree with" the following "alternative" to essential external directedness: necessarily, many of our visual experiences contain "phenomenal objects" with various shapes* and colors*. For instance, the orange-experience (Figure 2.3) essentially "contains" a round* phenomenal object. So, necessarily, if a thinker has this experience, she is in a position to refer to and think about the property being round*. Call this Papineau's replacement thesis.

Papineau seems to be thinking along the following lines: "We internal physical state theorists must deny the initially plausible thesis of essential external directedness, but at least we can accept a replacement thesis that comes close to accommodating essential external directedness". In that case, rejecting essential external directedness comes to appear more acceptable.

But does Papineau's replacement thesis really come close to accommodating essential external directedness, making his rejection of that thesis more acceptable?

To answer this question, we first need to understand Papineau's replacement thesis. On the face of it, it does look close to essential external directedness. For, to formulate it, he uses similar-looking spatial vocabulary, such as "round*". But whether it is close to essential external directedness depends on what Papineau means by this vocabulary. What in the world does he mean by a "phenomenal object" and "round*", and so on? In fact, Papineau doesn't say. So we need to try to figure that out on our own.

One interpretation is a *sense datum interpretation*. Let N be the neural state that, on the internal physical state view, the orange-experience is identical with. On the sense datum interpretation, Papineau holds that undergoing N necessarily causes the coming-into-existence of an orange and round non-physical sense datum or "visual field region" (Peacocke 2008). This non-physical sense datum is literally *round*: it has *edges that are equidistant from a common point*. And this is what Papineau means by a "phenomenal object": it is just another word for a sense datum or Peacocke-style visual-field region.

But, of course, this cannot be Papineau's idea, because it is inconsistent with the internal physical state view and its motivations. It is the sense datum theory, which the internal physical state view was meant to avoid. Further, if this were Papineau's idea, he would not need to reject essential external directedness and move to his replacement claim in the first place, because the sense datum theory fully accommodates essential external directedness (as noted in Section 1.6).

Evidently, by "phenomenal object", Papineau must mean some kind of physical object, since the whole point of the internal physical state view is to avoid non-physical sense data. But what kind of physical object? One clue is provided by the fact that Papineau says that a visual experience "contains" a phenomenal object. Now Papineau holds that a visual experience is just a type of a neural state, N. So he must think that a phenomenal object is some kind of physical object that is "contained in" neural state N. What could this be?

One possibility is that Papineau has in mind something like a *population of neurons*. Let us adopt this interpretation.

Now we can also figure out what Papineau means by his starred vocabulary, such as *round**. He uses this expression to characterize the phenomenal object contained within a visual experience. We have just seen that for Papineau such a phenomenal object must be something like a population of neurons. So, round* must refer to a property that characterizes such a population of neurons, as it might be, the property *firing in pattern Z*. That is, for Papineau, "is round*" doesn't literally mean *being round*, that is, *having edges equidistant from a common point*. It refers to a radically different kind of property.

It follows that Papineau's use of spatial vocabulary like "round*" is somewhat misleading. He is not using it to pick out properties with a spatial structure, like *having edges equidistant from a common point*. So even if he packages his replacement claim in vocabulary that looks similar to that used to formulate essential external directedness, it is a radically different thesis.

In the end, here is what Papineau's replacement thesis amounts to:

Papineau's replacement thesis. Necessarily, the orange-experience is nothing but a neural state N that "contains" a *neuro-computational* object with internal physical properties P_1, P_2, ... (as it might be, *firing in pattern Z*). So having this experience only gives thinkers the capacity to think about these neural properties. This is true even when a BIV has the experience.

Now that we have clarified Papineau's replacement thesis, we are ready to answer our question: does Papineau's replacement thesis make his rejection of essential external directedness any more acceptable? Does it allow the internal physical state theorist to say that there is *a sense* in which having the orange-experience essentially involves the feature *round?*

According to essential external directedness, having the orange-experience necessarily involves the seeming presence of an object that *is round, that is, has edges roughly equidistant from a common point.* Here, in describing how things seem, "round" picks out a genuine spatial feature – it certainly doesn't pick out a neural property.

As we saw in Section 2.4, essential external directedness just seems obvious. It just seems to be an obvious commentary on what the orange-experience is like. It is also needed to explain things we all accept. For instance, we are all inclined to accept the following conditional (if-then) claims: if a BIV had all the same experiences as you, but no objects with shapes were present, its experiences would be non-veridical. If we accept essential external directedness, we can explain this: it would seem to the BIV that there are objects out there with various shapes when this is not so. Further, if a BIV had *all* the same experiences as you, it could think and know about shapes. For instance, it could know Euclidean geometry. And it could have a *favorite shape.* These conditional (if-then) claims are hard to deny. But they presuppose essential external directedness. So internal physical state theorists like Papineau who reject essential external directedness must deny them.

There is, then, some reason to think that Papineau's replacement claim may not make the denial essential external directedness any more acceptable. It doesn't change the fact that it requires the denial of these obvious-seeming truths. The replacement claim just adds: "instead, having the orange-experience only necessarily involves a neural object with neural properties P_1, P_2, ..." Because this replacement thesis is not very similar to essential external directedness – it is not a close replacement to the real thing – it doesn't make the denial of essential external directedness any more palatable.

(2) Here is a second point of Papineau's which might seem to soften the blow of his rejection of essential external directedness: he notes that internal physical state theorists can at least happily accept what we might call "*inessential* external directedness" (2014: 24).

For instance, let N be the neural pattern that is necessarily identical with the orange-experience, on Papineau's view. Papineau can say that the neural pattern N (and hence the orange-experience) is "as of" a round object, and involves there seeming to be a round thing, in the sense that it is normally caused by the presence of a round thing. So he can say that N (and hence the orange-experience) is connected to the shape *round*, but in a way that doesn't touch on its essential nature.

Here is an analogy. Suppose some aliens live on another planet with sudden hailstorms. They get a distinctive head pain when and only when a round hail pellet hits their heads. When the aliens have this head pain, there is a sense in which they have an experience as of a round thing, and they are experiencing as if a round thing is present: for they are then having the kind of experience that normally goes with the presence of a round thing hitting their head. Papineau's point is that internal physical state theorists can at least accept that visual experiences are contingently connected to spatial features, in the way that that the aliens' head pain is. So we can indirectly or obliquely describe experiences by referring to spatial properties.

However, accepting inessential external directedness may not help internal physical state theorists very much. For the fact remains that they still must reject *essential* external directedness. And this is a problem because essential external directedness seems obviously right. As we have noted, visual experiences differ from head pains in the following respect: while spatial features (*round, moving to the right*) don't *essentially* enter into the characterization of a head pain, they do *essentially* enter into the characterization of a normal visual experience. If visual experiences really were purely internal states akin to head pains, then we should be no more inclined to think that spatial features essentially enter into their characterization than the aliens in the above example are inclined to think that they enter essentially into the characterization of head pains.

(3) I said that Papineau thinks that the only possible response to the argument from essential external directedness against the internal physical state view is to reject essential external directedness. However, in his work, he gives the impression that internal physical state theorists only need to reject the controversial *representational view* of experience. We will look at this

theory in detail in Chapter 3. Briefly, on this theory, having the orange-experience essentially involves "representing" the presence of a round thing. Papineau also associates this theory with the somewhat obscure claim that experiences "lay claim" to the world (2016: 341).

If essential external directedness is equated with a controversial and obscure theoretical claim about experience, then it would no longer look so bad if internal physical state theorists must reject it.

But it would be wrong to equate essential external directedness with representationalism or any other theoretical claim. It just says that having the orange-experience essentially involves the seeming presence of a round object moving to the right. This is not a theory; it is a pretheoretical claim formulated in non-theoretical language that is compatible with a number of theories: the sense datum theory, the versions of naïve realism, and all the versions of the representational view.

We have critically evaluated three points of Papineau's that might seem to soften the blow of his rejection of essential external directedness. In fact, they don't seem to much soften the blow.

But what if internalist state theorists like Papineau still decided to reject it? For instance, what if they said, contrary to essential external directedness, that the orange-experience (Figure 2.3) is like a head pain in the following respect: since it is just a neural pattern, its essential nature can be fully characterized without mentioning spatial features like *round* and *moving to the right?*

Against this, it will seem obvious to many that this is incorrect. It is also worth emphasizing again that, in the history of philosophy, nearly all major theories of experience (naïve realism, the British empiricists' "theory of ideas", sense datum view, Peacocke's related visual field view, representationalism, multiple relation theory) have accommodated essential external directedness, even if they have provided different theoretical accounts of it.[9] In fact, while Papineau rejects it, other internal physical state theorists such as McLaughlin (2016a: 856–857) are favorable toward it (even if the previous two sections brought out problems with combining the internal physical state view with essential external directedness). The widespread acceptance of essential external directedness further testifies to its truth.

Maybe it would be reasonable to accept the internal physical state view and reject essential external directedness if there were decisive problems with all the alternative views that vindicate essential external directedness: the sense datum view, the representational view, the theory of appearing, naïve realism, and so on. Papineau (2014, 2016) thinks that the representational view, in particular, faces debilitating problems. We will address the representational view, and the problems for it, in Chapters 3 and 4.

Summary

The sense datum view (Chapter 1) provided a neat solution to the puzzle of how experiences can be essentially externally directed and also dependent on internal processing. But it required strange non-physical objects, sense data. The desire to avoid sense data led naturally to the internal physical state view examined in the present chapter. Rather than holding that experiences are relations to non-physical sense data created by neural states, the internal physical state view holds that experiences should be directly identified with neural states themselves. It nicely explains experiential internalism, an especially strong form of "internal dependence". It is also in line with the worldview of "physicalism" and has the virtue of simplicity. However, there is one major rub: it is inconsistent with the essentially externally directed character of some types of experiences.

Therefore, we are still without a totally satisfying solution to the puzzle of perception that started off this book. What we need is a theory that simultaneously accommodates the role of internal factors as well as the essentially externally directed character of experience, while avoiding "sense data".

While we do not have a solution, we have made significant progress. In the present chapter, we emphasized essential external directedness. For instance, having the orange-experience essentially involves the seeming presence of a round thing moving to the right. In Chapter 1, we learned that, in some cases, even if it seems to you that a round object is present, no such object really is present – not even a "mental image" or "sense datum". Putting these lessons together, we arrive at the result that *some experiences essentially involve the seeming presence of an F object, even if they do not essentially involve the real presence of an F object*. As Fred Dretske (2003) puts it, "there needn't be anything orange or pumpkin-shaped in (or outside) the head at the time the experience is occurring in order for us to have an experience as of an orange pumpkin".

Now here is something interesting: this is a feature that perceptual experience shares with *mental representation*, as when you represent the world to be a certain way in thought. For instance, the thought that there is a ghost in the next room is essentially "about" a ghost in the next room, but needn't involve the real presence of a ghost in the next room.

This suggests an intriguing idea: perhaps perceptual experience should be understood as a species of mental representation. This would explain how it can be directed at things that need not exist.

In this way, our discussion so far naturally leads to a "representational" view of experience. It will be the subject of Chapters 3 and 4.

Further Reading

For recent defenses of the internal physical state view, see Papineau (2014) and (2016), McLaughlin (2016a), and Block (2019). The view derives from Place (1956) and Smart (1959). It is associated with an "adverbialist" account of our descriptions of experience (see notes 3 and 9 in this chapter). For a recent defense of adverbialism, see Breckenridge (2018).

In this chapter, we looked at the much-discussed "transparency observation". It comes in many different versions. Some sources are Moore (1903: 449–450), Price (1932: 5), Geach (1957: 126–128), Armstrong (1981: 85), and Harman (1990: 39). For some recent defenses of different versions, see Tye (2000) and Byrne (2018). For criticism, see Kind (2003).

Notes

1 Here is another example. Suppose you experience a blue square above a red circle and then a red square above a blue circle. There is some change in how your neural patterns coding for shape and color are "bound" together in the brain. The change in your experience *just is* this change in your total neural state, according to the internal physical state view. So, internal physical state theorists have a simple answer to the "many-property problem" (Jackson 1977).

2 Russell (1927: chap. 26) said that we don't know about the intrinsic nature of the physical world, including our own brains. See also Strawson (2020). But we know enough to know that there is not an orange and round thing in your brain moving to the right, fully constituted by neuronal firings!

3 Internal physical state theorists can combine their view with an "adverbialist" semantic theory about the meaning sentences like "it is *as if* I'm seeing a round thing, but I'm not seeing a round thing". Roughly, on this semantics, this sentence means that you are sensing in a "way" that *generically* goes with seeing a round thing, but in this case you are *not* seeing a round thing. Notice that, whereas the internal physical state view is about the metaphysical structure of experience itself, "adverbialism" in this sense is a *semantic theory* about the meanings of *sentences* describing experiences. In fact, adverbialism in this sense is totally quiet about the metaphysical structure of experience. So it is not only compatible with the internal physical state view; it is compatible with all the other theories about the metaphysical structure of experience discussed in this book (Breckenridge 2018: 7).

4 The argument for the internal physical state view based on experiential internalism presented in the text has a significant empirical component. Papineau (2014, 2016) gives a different, more philosophical argument for the internal physical state

view. In particular, he thinks that its only viable rival is representationalism. But he thinks that representationalism is ruled out by reflection on the nature of experience. We will examine Papineau's arguments against representationalism in Sections 3.6 and 3.7 of Chapter 3.

5   Another alternative formulation of the transparency observation, which avoids commitment to sense data, implies that when someone hallucinates the British flag they know what their experience is like by becoming aware of, and attending to, an abstract "property-complex" (a way things *might* be) even if there exists nothing that instantiates that property-complex (not even an array of sense data). For discussion of this kind of idea, see Tye (2000: 48) and (2019), Dretske (2003: 73–74), Johnston (2004: 134ff), Watzl (2017: 236–237), Schellenberg (2018: 145ff), and Sethi (2019: 2). But this is hardly a pretheoretical idea. And since property-complexes are abstract items that don't take up space (like numbers), it is hard to see how the hallucinator could be aware of them and attend to them. In general, it is difficult to formulate a version of the transparency observation that is both pretheoretically plausible (e.g., compatible with hallucination) and rules out the internal physical state view (Pautz 2007).

6   Some philosophers, for instance Russell (1913: 79) and Chalmers (2010: 443; 2012: 296–297), accept essential external directedness but then go on to argue on the basis of physics that experienced spatial features are not really instantiated by physical objects (just as many argue that color qualities are not really instantiated by physical objects). We will discuss this "illusion" view in Section 4.10. Even if it is correct, the argument from essential directedness against the internal physical state view is sound. Even if the relevant spatial features are uninstantiated, if *they enter into the definition of experience-types but not neural types*, it follows that experience-types are distinct from neural-types. That is the key point.

7   Of course, internal physical state theorists who reject essential external directedness don't have to say that the orange-experience is like a head-pain in *every way*. For instance, they can say that the orange-experience is a neural pattern with *more complexity* than the neural pattern that they identify with the pain. But they do have to say that the orange-experience is like a head-pain in this respect: its essential nature can be fully characterized without mentioning spatial features like *round* and *moving to the right*.

8   For more detailed discussion of the BIV argument and the Leibniz's law argument for thinking that the internal physical state view and essential external directedness are incompatible, see Pautz (2010a: 265ff) and (2010b: 335ff); Speaks (2015: 271–272); and Block (2019).

9   It might be thought that there are figures in the history of the philosophy who did reject essential external directedness. One candidate is Thomas Reid (1785). But while it is true that Reid thought that the character of an experience is partly determined by a "sensation", which is not essentially externally directed, he held that it is also determined by a "conception", which is essentially external directed. See van Cleve (2005: 468). So, given Reid's view, it is natural to take "the orange-experience" to refer to a hybrid state involving a color sensation and a conception. In that case, it is essentially directed at a round thing. Another candidate is Chisholm (1957). Chisholm is often called a proponent of "adverbialism" or the "multiple relation theory" (see Jackson 1977: 63, 90). But Chisholm's main point was to reject "the sense datum fallacy" (1957: 151). He denied that having the orange-experience essentially involves the presence of a round sense datum. He nowhere explicitly denied essential external directedness: that it essentially involves there *seeming* to be a round object. (Thanks to James van Cleve for discussion of these matters.)

3

THE REPRESENTATIONAL VIEW:
EXPERIENCING AS REPRESENTING

One can sense the condition that something colored red is surrounded by something blue quite independently of whether there actually is something colored red surrounded by something blue.

—George Bealer (1982)

Nothing needs to have the properties we experience. There needn't be anything orange or pumpkin-shaped in (or outside) the head at the time the experience is occurring in order for us to have an experience as of an orange pumpkin.

—Fred Dretske (2003)

Imagine that you see a pumpkin. The representational view holds that for you to have this experience is for you to "experientially represent" that an orange and pumpkin-shaped thing is there. Put differently, for you to have this experience is just for it to "experientially seem" to you that an orange and pumpkin-shaped thing is there. If you should later hallucinate a pumpkin, there needn't exist a spooky non-physical "sense datum" or "picture" of a pumpkin created by your brain for you to experience (as the sense datum view examined in Chapter 1 would have it). It merely seems to you as if there is such a thing; that is, you merely experientially misrepresent that there is such a thing. In general, the phenomenological character of your experience is not constituted by the intrinsic character of the underlying internal neural state (as the "internal physical state view" examined in Chapter 2 would have it). Rather, it is constituted by how you experientially represent the external world to be, as a result of being in that neural state.

The central puzzle in the philosophy of perception can be summed up in this way: how is experience both essentially externally directed and internally dependent? How can it be that your experience of things as "out there" depends on internal neural processing going on "in here"? The representational view may be able to solve the puzzle. The idea is that experiencing consists in representing qualities in space but in some cases what qualities we experientially represent is due to our own internal processing, rather than to the character of the world itself.

Since the representational view is a very large topic, our discussion of it will be divided into two chapters. In this chapter, we will mostly focus on the basic idea and how it explains the externally directed character of experience. In Chapter 4, we will be more concerned with the question of how it might accommodate internal dependence.

The plan for the present chapter is as follows. In Section 3.1, we will take some time to understand the representational view. In Section 3.2, we will consider an "inference to the best explanation" argument for it. In Sections 3.3–3.7, we will consider several questions and problems faced by representationalists.

3.1 What is the representational view?

To explain the representational view, I will focus on an actual example. People with "Charles Bonnet syndrome" (CBS) have impaired eyesight. However, due to spontaneous internal neural activity, they often have hallucinations that are so vivid and detailed that they cannot tell them apart from real life. In their essay "I See Purple Flowers Everywhere", Mogk and Mogk (2003) include fascinating descriptions of the hallucinations of people with CBS. One of them was Buddy Burmester, who often hallucinated amazingly vivid and detailed purple flowers. He could even draw them. Below is a drawing of one of the unreal flowers proceeding from his brain (Figure 3.1).

Let's imagine that Buddy has a total hallucination. He hallucinates nothing but a flower in empty space, even though in fact he is in a room filled with objects. How to account for Buddy's hallucination?

Representationalists combine two ideas familiar from Chapters 1 and 2. First, essential external directedness: having this experience essentially

Figure 3.1 A drawing of a flower Buddy Burmester hallucinated.

involves the seeming presence of a purple, flower-shaped object before
him. Second, the seems-gambit: though it vividly seems to Buddy that there
is a purple, flower-shaped object in empty space, none of it exists. Against
the sense datum view, there does not even exist an "image" or "picture" of
a flower in a private visual field – it just seems to Buddy that all this exists.
In this sense, experience is existence-neutral.

Representationalists go beyond these ideas. On their view, we shouldn't
think that Buddy first has a hallucinatory experience and then this explains
why it seems to him that there is a purple and flower-shaped object before
him (a "dual component" theory). Rather, Buddy's experience is nothing but
this seeming-state. There is nothing more to the experience. His experience is real, but the reality of the experience completely consists in something seeming real.

Representationalists have a special terminology: they say that for Buddy
to have his experience is just for him to "experientially represent" that
there is before him a purple and flower-shaped thing in empty space, as a
result of his aberrant neural activity. This is not something he does inten-
tionally; it is involuntary and passive.

The reason why representationalists use the terminology of "representation" is that they hold that experiences are in one respect like
"representational" mental states such as beliefs. In particular, they hold

that experiences, like beliefs, are *existence-neutral*. In belief, you can represent the Tooth Fairy, even though there doesn't exist such a thing. Similarly, in Buddy's hallucination, it seems to him that there is a flower in empty space, even though there doesn't exist such a thing.

However, you should not read too much into the terminology of "representation" here. Representationalists do not think that experiences are in every way like beliefs and other mental states in which you represent the world. If you believe in the Tooth Fairy, that doesn't make it seem to you that the Tooth Fairy is right there before you in vivid detail. By contrast, when Buddy hallucinates a flower, it seems to be present *right there* and in vivid detail.

In fact, even though the view is called the "representational" view, it could be described without using the terminology of "representation" at all. Instead of saying that Buddy "experientially represents" that there is a purple and flower-shaped thing before him, we could say that it "experientially seems" to Buddy that there is a purple and flower-shaped thing before him. And we could call it the "seeming theory" instead of the "representational theory".

Now suppose that Buddy's friend "Barry" views a real flower in empty space. The scene looks just like the one that Buddy hallucinates. Then Barry and Buddy "have exactly the type of same experience", even though Barry is seeing and Buddy is hallucinating. Call this maximally-specific experience *the flower-experience*.

Representationalists hold that, quite generally, for a person to have the flower-experience just is for the person to "experientially represent" that there is a purple, flower-shaped thing in empty space. Thus for Barry no less than Buddy, his experience is constituted by his experientially representing such a thing. True, there is a physical flower before his body. But there is a sense in which the physical flower doesn't matter. Even if the flower is annihilated, there might be no change in the nature of Barry's experience as long as he continues to experientially represent that there is a purple, flower-shaped thing in empty space. The only difference between Buddy and Barry is that, while Buddy's representational state occurs "off-line", Barry's representational state is controlled by the impact of an actual flower on his visual system. When Barry has the flower-experience, the way he experientially represents the world to be (the way the world experientially seems to him) happens to coincide with the way the world really is.

Likewise, as you read these words right now, your own present total visual experience is nothing but a super-complex seeming-state in which it seems to you that there are many items filling your visual field. In principle, if your current neural processing were artificially reproduced, you would be in the same seeming-state, even if there is really nothing at all before you.

The representational view as we have formulated it is not the view that you experience the world by first experiencing a literal "picture" or "representation" generated by the brain. That would be the sense datum view examined in Chapter 1. The whole point of the representational view is to avoid a screen of "sense data" interposed between you and the world. When you believe that there is an evil presence behind you, there is no such thing there (hopefully). Similarly, when Buddy hallucinates a flower, he experientially represents that there is a purple and flower-shaped thing, so that it seems to him that a purple and flower-shaped "sense datum" is present, but no such item is really present. In the normal case, where there is a physical flower in front of Buddy, there is once again no mental image or sense datum "between" Buddy and the physical flower. All that is going on is that he experientially represents that a flower-shaped object is there (it experientially seems to him that such an object is there), and there is one: the physical flower itself.

On the representational view, when Buddy hallucinates the flower, he does of course undergo a neural state – a pattern of neuronal activity – in his visual system. This is what enables him to experientially represent that a flower-shaped object is there, so that it seems to him that such an object is there. Dretske (1995) calls this neural state the "representation-vehicle". To make it vivid, we might fancifully imagine that a kind of "sentence" occurs in Buddy's brain, written in the brain's language of synaptic interconnections and neural spikes. The neural sentence means *that there is a flower-shaped thing in front of me*. (In fact, the representation-vehicle for experience is more likely "iconic" and "analog" in format; see Section 3.8.) Now, when you read written English, you have access to both the representation-vehicles (the sentences on the page) and their representational contents (what the sentences mean). But, according to representationalists, experiential representation is very different. Buddy has no access at all to the neurally-realized representation-vehicle. He only has access to the representational content – the way the world seems to him as a result of his neural state.

To better understand the representational view, it will be helpful to appeal to the idea of a *property* (an idea we briefly encountered in Section 2.6). Suppose you believe that a certain flower is *purple* and *flower-shaped*. You are "mentally attributing" two properties to the flower: the property of being purple and the property of being flower-shaped.

A property is a *way things might be*. For instance, purple is a way things might be. Properties – ways things might be – are more abstract than ordinary things (somewhat as numbers are). For instance, a specific shade of purple cannot be located in any particular place; if it is anywhere, it is wherever there is a thing with that shade. Properties are not created by the mind, any more than numbers are created by the mind. They are "objective". Even before minds came on the scene, external objects were certain ways: they had certain shapes, distances, orientations, and so on. There are properties that nothing has. For instance, in usual circumstances people can hallucinate novel colors that nothing has (see Section 5.5); those colors still exist because they are ways things *might* be. Properties – ways things might be – can be complex. For instance, there is the complex property of simultaneously being purple, flower-shaped, and three-feet away. Here I will simply assume the existence of properties, without presenting reasons to accept this assumption (but see van Inwagen 2004 and Yi 2018).

Now we can restate the representational view: having a flower-like experience is nothing but experientially representing that something has the complex property of being purple, flower-shaped, and three-feet away. In the case of Buddy's hallucination, there exists nothing that has this complex property; but Buddy's brain still "tells him" that something has the property.

In what follows, I will often drop mention of represented things and simply say that people "experientially represent properties" or "experientially attribute properties". You can take this as shorthand for saying that people experientially represent *that things have properties*. That is, it experientially seems to people that things have properties.

Representationalists do not think that Buddy *sees* the property of being flower-shaped and purple when he has his hallucination (but see Dretske 2003 and Tye 2019). Indeed, he sees absolutely nothing. All that is going on is that Buddy experientially represents that something has the property of being purple and flower-shaped. There is no such thing there for Buddy to see; it just seems that there is. Buddy also doesn't see the property of being purple and flower-shaped (a property which in this case nothing before him has), because this property is merely an abstract *way things might be*, not something Buddy can see. Rather, Buddy's mental relationship to the property is that he experientially represents that something has the property; it seems to him that something has the property. The property characterizes how it seems to him.

Of course, representationalists hold that, in normal experience, you count as seeing physical objects, states, and events. To return to the example above, Buddy's friend Barry counts as seeing a real flower, because the flower causes his experience in the normal way and the properties he experientially represents sufficiently match those of the flower (Jackson 2012: 203–205).

Representationalists hold that experientially representing a property gives you cognitive access to that property. It "puts you in touch" with the property. If you experientially represent a property at a time, then at that time you thereby can have thoughts according to which a thing has that property and can know what that property is like. So experiential representation plays an explanatory role in grounding cognition. It plays a role in the representational theory that is similar to the role played by experiential acquaintance in other theories (sense datum theory, naïve realist theory).

Here, then, is an initial formulation of the representationalist answer to the "character question", the question of what it is to have an experience with a certain character:

> **Representational view.** Having an experience with a certain character is identical with *experientially representing* a complex array of perceptible properties (shapes, distances, colors, and so on). All differences in the character of experience are differences in what complexes of perceptible properties one experientially represents – roughly, what your brain is "telling you" about the world. Experiential representation provides cognitive access to those perceptible properties.

Representationalists generalize their view beyond vision. For instance, in phantom pain, a person experientially represents that there is pain "in" the region where they used to have a leg. In fact, it is a misrepresentation; things aren't the way they seem. For their leg has been amputated. Likewise, having a smell experience consists in experientially representing that a smell quality (minty, citrus-like, etc.) is in a certain diffuse location. In a smell hallucination (phantosmia), the relevant quality is not really there (Batty 2010).

There is a problem with our initial formulation. It contains a made-up technical term, namely "experientially represents". To really understand the theory, we need to explain this term. You might think this is easy: to say that you experientially represent that something is F (e.g., purple, flower-shaped) is just say that that it seems to you that something is F. But, while this is a helpful initial gloss, we cannot explain "experientially represents" in terms of the ordinary English term "seems". If you are stuck at a traffic light, it seems to you that you will be late. But, according to the representational theory, you do not experientially represent that you will be late. You experientially represent more basic things, and infer you will be late.

The best solution is to treat "experientially represents" as a new theoretical term akin to the theoretical terms of science, and then apply the general *Ramsey-Lewis method* (Lewis 1970) for defining new theoretical terms.

To illustrate, according to Ramsey-Lewis, the cosmological theory of "dark energy" can first be formulated without using this term. Fundamentally, it just says that there is some invisible stuff in the universe that explains certain observable phenomena (e.g., that the expansion of the universe is accelerating). Then we can introduce "dark energy" to refer to whatever in reality plays this role.

Likewise, representationalists postulate the mental relationship of experiential representation playing a certain explanatory role. Most importantly, it plays a *character*-role: the hypothesis is that having an experience with a certain character consists in nothing but experientially representing a certain array of perceptible properties (ways things might be), so that differences in character are always differences in the array of perceptible properties. In addition, representationalists say that experiential representation plays the *cognitive-access* role. That is, if a thinker experientially represents a perceptible property at a time, then at that time they thereby can have thoughts according to which a thing has that property and can know what that property is like. According to representationalists, another key feature of the experiential representational relation is that, like other representational relations, it is *existence-neutral*: one can experientially represent a property (e.g., being purple and flower-shaped), so that it *seems* that there exists something with the property, even if in actuality there exists nothing that has that property.

So by using the Ramsey-Lewis idea, we can eliminate from our formulation of the representational view the distracting technical term "experientially represents":

> **Representational view.** All sensory-perceptual experiences consist in a basic mental relationship R between *subjects* and *ways things might be* such that: R plays the cognitive-access role, R is existence-neutral, and R plays the character-role.[1]

Then we can introduce the theoretical term "experientially representing" to mean the unique relation R (if there is one) that has the postulated features.

But, as I said above, you shouldn't get too caught up in terminology; we could also call R the "seeming relation" or the "appearing relation".[2]

I have formulated the representational view in terms of properties (like Dretske in the opening quote). But you will also often encounter formulations of the representational view in terms of possible states of affairs (or what Bealer calls "conditions" in the opening quote). The idea is that there are possible states of affairs that do not obtain as well as states of affairs that do obtain (Plantinga 1974). Philosophers sometimes call these sorts of things "propositions" or "contents" that can be true or false. For instance, there exists a possible state of affairs in which Hilary Clinton became the US president, but it doesn't obtain. On this way of thinking about the representational view, if Buddy should see a flower and then have an identical hallucination of one, in each case he experientially represents (or, as Bealer says, "senses") a state of affairs (or possible scene) in which there is a purple and flower-shaped thing before him, so that it seems real to him; in the first case the state of affairs obtains and in the second case it doesn't.

Finally, we must make sure we understand the difference between the representational view and the views examined in Chapters 1 and 2.

On the sense datum view, in both the normal case and the hallucination case, Buddy's brain creates a life-like image (a kind of mental field) for him to experience, an image that has the properties of being purple and being flower-shaped. By contrast, on the representational view, the brain never creates any images or mental objects for you to experience; it just causes it to seem to you that some objects exist. For example, due to Buddy's aberrant neural processing, it experientially seems to him that there is something before him with the properties of being purple and being flower-shaped. In this hallucination case, no such thing does exist. His brain also doesn't create the properties: these are objective, abstract ways things that might be. Analogy: when the schizophrenic's brain causes him to believe that there is a demon with the property of being evil, it doesn't cause anything new to come into existence.

As for the internal physical state view, it holds that the essence of experience is to be found entirely in the neural patterns that realize experience. Representationalists think that this is a big mistake. The essence of experience is not to be found in the internal neural patterns that enable us to experientially represent the world, but in the external properties (flower-shaped, purple, etc.) that we experientially represent. In the same way, it would be a mistake to think that the essence of a story is to be found in the patterns of marks on the pages of a book. It is to be found in what the patterns of marks represent.

Our basic Ramsey-Lewis formulation of the representational view is schematic. It leaves many questions open. It says that there is a mental relationship, experiential representation, that plays a certain theoretical role. But it doesn't say anything about the nature of this mental relationship (just as the theory of dark energy doesn't say much about its nature). For instance, can what it is for you to experientially represent that something has a certain perceptible property (what it is for it to experientially seem to you that something has a certain property) be reduced to something more basic? In addition, our formulation of the representational view leaves open the nature and status of the perceptible properties.

One version of the representational view holds that physical things had perceptible properties before sentient creatures like ourselves evolved. For instance, things were purple before we came on the scene. Then we came to experientially represent the color purple by virtue of having visual systems that detect its occurrence in the world (in the way that a thermometer represents a preexisting temperature). On another version of the representational view, before we evolved, physical objects merely reflected colorless photons, and didn't intrinsically possess any colors. Our brains are inventive: they somehow enabled us to experientially represent wholly chimerical color properties (the apparent purple of flowers, the apparent bright red of a tomato, etc.) that had never occurred in the world, in order to help us identify and keep track of objects. In normal perception as in hallucination, the experience of the color purple is internally generated.

We will look at these different versions of the representational view in Chapter 4. The present chapter is about the basic theory.[3] Now that we understand the basic theory, we can ask why we should believe it.

3.2 The argument for the representational view: an inference to the best explanation

The standard arguments for the representational view are based on the "transparency observation" (Section 2.3), the desire to have a physicalist theory that avoids non-physical sense data (Section 1.8), or the analysis of statements describing how things look or seem. However, many think now that these standard arguments fall short.[4]

Therefore, we will develop an alternative *inference to the best explanation argument* for the representational view. I will begin with a brief summary of the argument, so that you can get the general idea. Then I will develop the argument in more detail.

In short, the argument is that the representational view may better explain the facts of perception than rival views. It has many explanatory virtues. Let me briefly list some of them.

First, the representational view is in line with the pretheoretical datum of essential external directedness. This is an advantage of the representational view over the internal physical state view, which is apparently incompatible with essential external directedness (Chapter 2). For instance, it is in the essence of typical visual experiences that when you have those experiences it seems to you that there are things arranged in space. As a result, experience is a source of externally directed cognition. The representational view explains this in the simplest way possible: it holds that for you to have visual experiences *just is* for it to seem to you that there are things arranged in space – that is, for you to "experientially represent" that there are things arranged in space. This explanation of essential external directedness has the added advantage of avoiding the problematic sense datum view. Just as you can believe that there is a sphere in the next room even if there isn't one, so you can hallucinate a sphere in front of you even if there isn't (a physical or mental) sphere in front of you.

Second, the representational view nicely explains another important fact about the phenomenology of experience. Experiences vary in precision and completeness. For instance, when you view an object in front of you, there may be imprecision in how distant it appears to be, if depth cues are absent. If an object is moved from central vision to peripheral vision, there is a gradual reduction in perceptual precision. If you then close your eyes and imagine the object, you have a kind of visual experience, but it is even more imprecise and degraded. An example of perceptual incompleteness is the experience of "pure motion", in which you experience movement separately from all other features (see Section 1.11). The representational view elegantly explains and predicts these facts. Representational states in general vary in precision and completeness. For instance, as more evidence comes in, a detective can form more and more specific beliefs about a murderer. And if someone tells you that something in the next room fell down, but tells you nothing else about it, you represent its movement but you attribute no other properties to it. So if experiences are also a special kind of representational states, we would expect that they too can vary in precision and completeness. No other view so neatly predicts these facts.[5]

Third, internal dependence. There are internally-generated illusions and hallucinations. There is also evidence that, even in normal experience, your experience of "sensible properties" (pain qualities, smell qualities, color qualities) is more dependent on your neural responses than on the objective character of external items. The representational view can explain internal dependence as well. Experiencing consists in representing things and qualities in space, but in some cases how we experientially represent the external world is due to our own internal processing, rather than to the character of the world itself. In Chapter 4, we will take up the issue of how this is so. In Chapter 5, we will see that contemporary naïve realism has trouble with internal dependence.

So much for our brief summary of the best explanation argument for the representational view. I will now develop a more detailed form of the argument. For purpose of illustration, I will continue to focus on the example introduced in Section 3.1 in which Buddy hallucinates a purple flower and Barry has an identical experience of a real flower.

But first some preliminaries. To begin with, in the case of the flower-experience, *essential external directedness* is the claim that it is part of the essence of having the flower-experience that when a person has this experience it seems to them that there is something there that is shaped f_{17} and colored purple$_{42}$ – you have an experience as of such an object. Here f_{17} is the specific, irregular apparent shape that appears to Buddy and Barry when they have their experience – the one depicted in Figure 3.1. (Imagine that we assign a number to different specific flower-shapes, and that this shape is f_{17}.) And purple$_{42}$ is the specific apparent color.

Because the flower-experience is essentially externally directed, it can explain *externally directed cognition*. Necessarily, if a thinker has this experience, then they thereby can have a thought that is true just in case something before them is shaped f_{17} and colored purple$_{42}$.

Now for another preliminary point. Given the existence of *properties* (Section 3.1), essential external directedness implies something a bit stronger and more theoretical: having the flower-experience, in both veridical and hallucinatory cases, provides "cognitive access" to the external properties of having shape f_{17} and having color purple$_{42}$. These properties are "external" in the sense that they needn't be instantiated in a person's brain when they have the experience.

For instance, consider Barry again. Barry enters a room and actually sees a flower just like the one Buddy hallucinates. By having the flower-experience, Barry can now think that something is f_{17}. He can think this by thinking that something is *shaped that way*. Before entering the room and having this experience, he didn't have this specific cognitive capacity. True, using language, he could think, for instance, that "something in the next room is roughly flower-shaped". But, unaided by experience, he couldn't think that something is *precisely* f_{17}. For he had no way of mentally singling out precisely this shape. It is only by entering the room and having his present experience that he can now attribute this shape to something in thought. His experience offers up an ostensible example of this precise shape.

The same points apply to Buddy. Even though it is hallucinatory, Buddy's flower-experience enables him to wonder whether there actually is something before him that is f_{17} – something he cannot do unaided by experience. It does this by offering up an ostensible example of this precise, idiosyncratic shape. Furthermore, in both veridical and hallucinatory cases, the flower-experience provides cognitive access to the color $purple_{42}$.

With the preliminaries out of the way, we can formulate an argument for the representational view. Recall that, according to our final "Ramsey-Lewis" formulation of the representational view, it amounts to this: sensory-perceptual experiences consist in a basic mental relationship R between *subjects* and *ways things might be* such that: R plays the cognitive-access role, R is existence-neutral, and R plays the character-role. The argument will establish these tenets of the representational view one-by-one in a series of steps. I will first list the steps; afterward I will explain them.

(1) To explain how the flower-experience provides cognitive access to the external properties of having shape f_{17} and having color $purple_{42}$, in both veridical and hallucinatory cases, we should hold that having this experience essentially involves standing in some *relation R* to these properties. This relation plays the *cognitive-access role*. Therefore, contrary to the internal physical state view, the flower-experience is more than a neural state.

(2) To explain perceptual imprecision, we should hold that this relation R to the external properties of having shape f_{17} and having color $purple_{42}$ is *existence-neutral* rather than *existence-dependent*: in a hallucination case, there exists no object ("sense datum") having the properties. This rules out the sense datum view.

(3) Once we go this far and accept that having the flower-experience *necessarily involves* standing in an existence-neutral "representational" relation R to the external properties of being f_{17} and being $purple_{42}$, the simplest theory becomes that the flower-experience is *nothing but* standing in this representational relation to these perceptible properties.

(4) The previous steps can be repeated for other experiences with different characters: the relation is the same, and only the array of represented properties differs. Therefore, the hypothesized "representational" relation R plays the *character-role*.

(5) In addition, the representational view can accommodate internal dependence, by holding that in some cases what properties a person is R-related to depend on their internal physical state. This is an advantage of the representational view over naïve realism.

(6) *Conclusion.* The representational view follows: all sensory-perceptual experiences consist in a basic relationship R between *subjects* and *arrays of perceptible properties* such that: R plays the cognitive-access role (step 1), R is existence-neutral (step 2), and R plays the character-role (steps 3 and 4).

Now let us go through these steps.

Step 1. This step claims that, in order to explain how the flower-experience provides cognitive access to the external properties of having shape f_{17} and having color $purple_{42}$ in both veridical and hallucinatory cases, we should hold that having this experience essentially involves standing in some *relation* R to these properties.

How to prove this? G. E. Moore (1903: 450) famously said, "when we try to introspect the sensation of blue, all we can see is the blue: the other element [the mental relation we bear to blue] is as if it were diaphanous [invisible]". Even if he was right, we can support step 1 by a theoretical inference.

First, consider Buddy's flower-like hallucination. Having this experience *must* involve his standing in a basic perceptual relationship to the properties of being f_{17} and being $purple_{42}$ – a relationship that is more basic than cognition. For, if this were not the case, how might his experience *explain* his cognitive access to *these specific properties*, rather than some other properties?

(In Section 5.5, we will see that proponents of the "indiscriminability" theory of hallucination deny any such positive characterization of Buddy's hallucination, but they face a problem concerning how hallucination explains cognitive access to novel properties.)

Now turn to Barry's flower-like experience in a veridical case. The same point applies. And there is reason to think that the relevant relation, R, to the properties of being f_{17} and being $purple_{42}$ is the same in Barry's case and in the case of Buddy's hallucination. This is the simplest view; and it is supported by the finding that the underlying neural processing is similar across the cases (ffytche 2013).[6]

Step 2. This step says that, in order to explain perceptual imprecision, we should hold that the hypothesized perceptual relation R that Barry bears to the properties of being f_{17} and being purple$_{42}$ is *existence-neutral* rather than *existence-dependent*.

To see this, suppose instead that we accept existence-dependence about our postulated mental relation R rather than existence-neutrality. This assumption means that, when Buddy has his hallucination and is R-related to the properties of being f_{17} and being purple$_{42}$, then there must exist before him a spooky non-physical image ("sense datum") that possesses these properties. In general, whenever you have a visual experience, the entire space you experience is in fact a private mental arena.

In Chapter 1, we saw that the sense datum view is seductive. H. H. Price (1932: 3, 63) noted that it just seems obvious that there exist colored objects in all visual experience, even hallucinatory visual experience. However, we also saw that its many problems outweigh its initial appeal. Those problems support existence-neutrality.

For one thing, if there exists a flower-like sense datum that Buddy experiences, *where is it?* Is it in the physical space before Buddy, but only visible to him? Is it in a private mental space, like a non-physical ghost in another realm? Existence-neutrality allows us to entirely avoid the question. Buddy is R-related to the properties of being f_{17} and being purple$_{42}$, so that it *seems* to him that something has these properties, but in reality there exists no such spooky thing. If it doesn't exist, we don't have to worry about its location, just as we don't have to worry about the location of the Tooth Fairy.

For another thing, existence-dependence fits poorly with perceptual imprecision (as we discussed in Section 1.11). To see this, take a different case. Imagine that Buddy has a very degraded and imprecise hallucination of a purple flower – more like visual imagination. We can explain this by supposing that Buddy can be R-related to unspecific properties (e.g., being roughly purple, being roughly flower-shaped, having many pedals), without being R-related to more specific properties (e.g., having shape f_{17}, being purple$_{42}$, having exactly 17 pedals). Given existence-dependence, there would have to exist a "sense datum" experienced by Buddy that has unspecific properties without any specific properties. It would have to have many pedals but no specific number of pedals. This is incoherent. If, on the other hand, we hold that our postulated perceptual relation R is existence-neutral, then we can avoid this result.

Sense datum theorists like Russell (1912a: 101–102) claimed that visual experience necessarily relates us to ("puts us in touch with") both objects and properties; in fact, experience relates us to properties by relating us to objects ("sense data") that actually exemplify the properties. The lesson of the argument so far is that we should keep their claim when it comes to properties but reject it when it comes to objects. For instance, having the flower-experience necessarily relates you to the properties of being f_{17} and being purple$_{42}$ but it doesn't necessarily relate you to an actual object (physical or non-physical) having these color and shape properties. In hallucination, it only seems that this is the case. So the "common factor" running through all cases of the flower-experience is not the presentation of the same kind of existing *object* (e.g., a sense datum) but the presentation of the same *properties*. The common factor is not a relationship to a *thing* but rather a relationship to a *way things might be*.

In sum, the best view is that our hypothesized R relation to the properties is existence-neutral. For this reason, it is fitting to call it a "representational" relation, where inaccurate as well as accurate representation is possible. So we can say that both Buddy and Barry "represent" the complex property of being f_{17} and purple$_{42}$.

Step 3. This step says that, once we think that having the flower-experience *necessarily involves* standing in an existence-neutral, representation relation R to the property of being f_{17} and purple$_{42}$, the simplest view becomes that the flower-experience is nothing but standing in this special relation to this complex property. The relation is an *experiential* representation relation. If you stand in this special relation to the complex property, in a way that gives you cognitive access to it, then this is enough for you to have the flower-experience in which it seems to you that something is present with this complex property. Nothing more is required. The experience is a pure representational state, or a pure seeming-state.

Some will resist this step. They will say that, in addition, the flower-experience involves underlying "sensations" or "qualia", which somehow "ground" or are a "vehicle for" the representation of being f_{17} and purple$_{42}$ (e.g., Peacocke 2008). But representationalists will object that this "dual component" view may lead back to the sense datum view (Chapter 1), and that it is unmotivated and obscure.

Step 4. This step says that the previous steps can be repeated for other experiences with different characters: the relation is the same, and only the array of represented properties differs. Therefore, the hypothesized "representational" relation R plays the *character-role*.

In particular, the steps 1–3 apply equally to other types of visual experiences. Different types of visual experiences provide cognitive access to different arrays of perceptible properties. Steps 1–3 show that the best explanation is that they consist in nothing but standing in the same existence-neutral "representational" relation R to these different arrays of perceptible properties.

Further, steps 1–3 extend beyond vision. Take bodily sensations. Bodily sensations give you cognitive access to properties that need not be located where they seem to be located. For example, you can have an experience of a *stabbing pain* in your forearm as being *closer* to an *itch* in your elbow than another *stabbing* pain in the same forearm. These sensible properties needn't be instantiated in this spatial pattern anywhere in the physical world or in your brain (they could be phantom sensations). Nor should we posit non-physical sense data arranged in some kind of non-physical "body space" to account for this case. The best account is that your experience consists in your standing in the same representational relation R to certain sensible properties and spatial properties – the same representational relation involved in visual experience.[7]

Still, you might wonder how do we know that there aren't some counterexamples: cases of differences in the character of experience that cannot be said to consist in differences in the properties to which we are R-related? Shouldn't we address this question on a case-by-case basis?

We will look at several hard cases in the next section. For now, we can give the following argument that there cannot be decisive counterexamples to our very schematic "Ramsey-Lewis" version of the representational view. To begin with, if you have reason to believe that there is a difference in character between two of your experiences, then you must notice a difference, or an apparent difference. Otherwise, why believe that there is a difference? But a difference is just a difference in properties. Now, our Ramsey-Lewis formulation of the representational view doesn't come with any "rule" concerning what properties we can experientially represent (see note 2 of the present chapter). It places no restriction here. So it will always be possible for representationalists to say that the relevant difference in character consists in a difference in what properties you bear relation R to. Further, considerations of uniformity and simplicity will favor generalizing the representational view in this way. In the next section, we will apply this strategy to a number of cases.

Step 5. In addition, the representational view can accommodate internal dependence, by holding that in some cases what properties a person is R-related to depend on their internal physical state. This will be taken up in Chapter 4; and in Chapter 5, we will see that naïve realism has difficulty with internal dependence.

Summary and Conclusion. The representational view follows from these steps: all sensory-perceptual experiences consist in a basic relationship R between subjects and arrays of perceptible properties such that: R plays the cognitive-access role (step 1), R is existence-neutral (step 2), and R plays the character-role (steps 3 and 4).

This concludes our discussion of the best explanation argument for the representational view of sensory experience. In Sections 3.3–3.7, we will consider several questions that all representationalists face. Some of these questions may call this argument into doubt.

3.3 Can the representational view explain all sensory-perceptual experiences?

The best explanation argument for the representational view initially focused on the flower-experience (steps 1–3) and then argued that it will always be possible and indeed desirable to extend the representational view to other types of experiences (step 4). But you still might wonder exactly how the representational view applies to certain hard cases. We will address impoverished experiences, blur, and gestalt switches.

Impoverished visual experiences. Christopher Peacocke argues that the representational view fails for impoverished visual experiences:

> When you close your eyes and point your head in the direction of the noonday sun, you have a visual experience in which there are colours and shapes, and usually some motion, in your visual field. It does not thereby look as if there are objects or events in your spatio-temporal environment. The visual experience in this example [therefore] has no representational content concerning the subject's environment.
>
> (Peacocke 2008: 8–9)

Peacocke's argument here assumes that you experientially represent property P only if it looks to you as if some ordinary (physical) object or event in your environment has property P (see also Boghossian and Velleman 1989).

But, as noted in step 4 of the best explanation argument for the representational view, our final Ramsey-Lewis formulation of the representational view is not committed to any such general, hard-and-fast rule. It merely says that experience consists in bearing some relation R to properties, where the relation plays a certain theoretical role. It places no constraints on what those properties might be. In particular, the properties needn't always seem to qualify some physical object. Some forms of experiential representation may not take the form of attributing properties to physical things. This calls into question Peacocke's stated reason for there being no representational content in his noonday sun case.

Representationalists still need an account of the case. But this is not far to seek: they might simply say that you experientially represent that some shapes and colors are "in" some region, even though this is not the case.

This co-opts Peacocke's own account. Peacocke (2018) develops an account resembling the sense datum view. He believes that all visual experience involves a kind of mental screen or visual field. In his example, the screen is very boring; as he says, you just experience a few colors and shapes "in" visual field regions. The above representationalist account agrees with Peacocke's characterization of the state of affairs you experience; the only difference is that it holds that the state of affairs doesn't obtain. So it doesn't require the real existence of a peculiar mental screen where the colors and shapes reside. Such a screen doesn't exist anymore than Buddy's hallucinated flower does. (See also note 8 of Chapter 1.)

Blurry vision. Another common argument against the representational view involves blurry vision. You look at a red tomato on a white table with your glasses on. Then you take your glasses off. The character of your experience changes. Yet, to a mature perceiver, it doesn't look as if there is any real difference in the tomato itself. As A. D. Smith puts it, "Blurriness is not a way that things in the world themselves seem to be" and "blurriness is not taken to be a feature or apparent feature of the object seen" (2008: 200–201). Therefore, you might conclude, there is no difference in what you experientially represent, contrary to the representational view.

The reason offered here for the assertion that there is no representational difference is questionable, just like the reason Peacocke offered for there being no representational content at all in his noonday sun case. The fact that it doesn't look as if any physical thing is different doesn't mean there is no representational difference at all. No such restriction is part of the representational view.

Still, representationalists will want some positive account of blur. Two main representationalist accounts have been proposed. On Michael Tye's (2000: 79–83) *under-representation* account, when you take off your glasses, you continue to experientially represent the color and shape of the tomato in a pretty determinate way, but you no longer experientially represent precisely where the boundary is between the red tomato and the white table. Your visual system represents that it is *somewhere* in a certain range (e.g., between points A and B), but not exactly where. Since the boundary is in fact within the range, the representational content of the experience is accurate. Tye claims that this kind of under-representation constitutes the experience of the blurry "halo" around the tomato. Keith Allen (2013) rejects this account; he surmises that such under-representation, if it were to happen, would be phenomenally different from our actual experience of the blurry halo. So he offers a different account: the *over-representation* account. It is as if the visual system thinks along these lines: "I know that the boundary between the tomato and the table is roughly between places A and B, but I don't know precisely where the boundary is between A and B, and so, rather than taking a stand, I will just represent it as being at *every* point in this range!" On this view, blurry vision is an extreme illusion: you visually (mis)represent an impossible state of affairs. According to Allen, this is what is needed to explain the experience of blurry "haloes" around the tomato. On both views, there is a representational difference, even though it is also correct to say "it doesn't seem to you that there is a real difference in the tomato itself" because you know that there isn't one.

For the sake of discussion, suppose both accounts fail. Would that mean that the representational view fails in the case of blurry vision and we should instead accept a non-representational account?

This is not obvious. Often opponents of the representational view who use the example of blur (e.g., Burge 2003) do not offer their own illuminating account of it. But when they do, it can just be co-opted by the representationalists.

For example, Boghossian and Velleman (1989: 96) offer an account of blur that presupposes something like a general "sense datum" theory of experience. When you see a tomato, what you take to be public space is in fact your private mental arena. A region within this mental arena has the properties of being reddish and being round. When you take off your glasses, this region acquires a third property: being blurry. Boghossian and Velleman do not say anything about this property, except that it is a property of visual field regions and not physical objects.

Representationalists could co-opt this account. They can say that you experientially represent that there is before you something, round, and blurry. (Or maybe it is more phenomenologically apt to say you experientially represent that blurriness resides "in" or "around" the region of the red and round thing without being attributed to that thing.) But they will add that, while regions appear "blurred" because of the operation of the visual system, this is a property that nothing in reality ever possesses. This representationalist account agrees with Boghossian and Velleman's description of what you experience; it just adds that what you experience is unreal. So it is hard to see how it could be inferior to Boghossian and Velleman's visual field theory. In fact, it is superior because it avoids the postulation of a peculiar mental screen where blurriness resides.

We have just looked at alleged problem-cases for the representational view in which the qualities we experience don't seem to us qualify any physical objects that we perceive. It is worth mentioning that the responses we have considered generalize to other cases of this kind: pain, brain grey, ganzfeld, highlights, shadows, and so on. The representational view places no restrictions on what we can experientially represent. Take the anti-representationalists' most phenomenologically acute account of what you experience in such cases. Representationalists might co-opt their account, but then add that what you experience may not be real.

Gestalt switches. Some have suggested that certain "gestalt" (form or pattern) switches make trouble for the representational view (Peacocke 1983; Macpherson 2006).

Let's start with a simple example. You are liable to experience the triangles in the top row (Figure 3.2) as pointed to the left, and the triangles in the bottom row as pointed to the top right. In fact, you can also see a solitary triangle as "pointed to the left" or as "pointed to the top right". Between these cases, there is a clear shift in the character of your experience of the solitary triangle. How might representationalists explain this change in your experience of the solitary triangle? At first blush, this is easy: in the first case, you experientially represent the solitary triangle as pointing to the left, whereas in the second case you experientially represent it as pointing to the top right.

The problem is that this is extremely obscure. What does "being pointed to the left" mean? What would it be for triangle – or another object – to actually have this alleged property of "being pointed to the left"?

Here is an idea. Think of a school of fish; we experience them as "pointed" in a certain direction, and this plausibly means they have a propensity to move in that direction. Likewise, we experience a lion about to pounce as having a propensity to move in a certain direction. It makes evolutionary sense that the visual system should have a tendency, given certain cues, to represent natural objects as having such propensities of movement. When we experience the "school" of triangles in a row, maybe the visual system

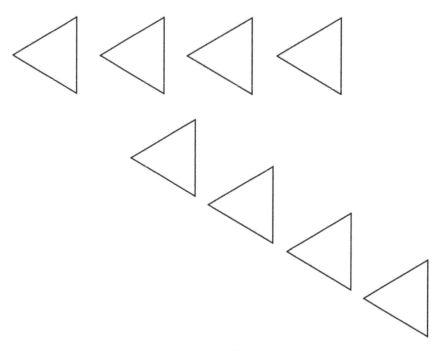

Figure 3.2 A triangle can be seen as pointed in different directions.

overgeneralizes, so that we experientially represent them as "pointed" in a certain direction, in the sense of having a propensity move in that direction, even though they are static lines on a page. Likewise, when we view a solitary triangle, we can experientially represent it as having a propensity to move in various directions.

Now let us turn to another case. You can experience the Figure 3.3 as a tilted kite or as a distorted square (Macpherson 2006). There is a change in the character of your experience between the two cases. This is another "gestalt switch". Given the representational view, you must experientially represent different properties. What might they be?

Vision scientists (Rock 1997; Palmer 1999) say that in such a case the visual system imposes on the figure different "object-centered perceptual reference frames". When you experience the figure as a tilted kite, you represent one axis as the "up-down" direction (below). When you experience it as a distorted square, you represent a different axis as the "up-down" direction (above).

However, as it stands, this account is obscure. What would it be for an axis to really have the property "being the up-down axis"? That is, when

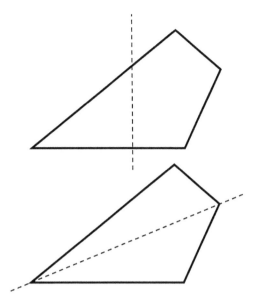

Figure 3.3 You can see this figure as tilted kite or as a distorted square.

you experientially represent one axis as the up-down axis, how would the world need to be in order for your experience to be veridical?

Many natural objects – trees and people, and so on – have an axis that is normally aligned with gravity. So one idea is that, when you represent the sideways direction of the figure as the top-bottom direction, what this means is that you represent it as the axis that is *normally aligned with gravity*. That is, you represent it as *tilted from its normal orientation*. Now, unlike a tree or a person, this is a non-natural object with no privileged normal orientation. So your experience is non-veridical.

But what is it for an axis to be *normally* aligned with gravity? Also, it is a bit hard to believe that the visual system represents these very sophisticated properties about objects' normal orientations.

Here is another account of this case. We just saw that we may experientially represent, at a very basic level, the propensities of objects to move in certain directions. Maybe, when we experience the figure as a kite, we experientially represent it as *unstable*, that is, as having a propensity to fall in a certain direction (for relevant research see Battaglia *et al.* 2013). By contrast, when we experience the figure as a distorted square, we experience it as *stable* – as sitting solidly on its base.

A final point. We have seen that it is unclear how exactly representationalists might account for certain gestalt shifts. Should this cause us to doubt the representational view? Maybe not. For we can apply to gestalt switches the general point made in step 4 of the best explanation argument: since in undergoing the gestalt switch you notice an ostensible difference, it is always open for representationalists to simply rest content with saying that the difference – whatever it may be – is represented, remaining neutral on the difficult issue of how it is to be characterized. No plausible non-representationalist account of the cases has been offered that could not be co-opted by representationalists.[8]

3.4 How rich is the content of experience?

Suppose we land on another planet and interact with aliens for the first time. Unlike us, the aliens haven't seen anything like our human faces and don't have a recognitional capacity for them. If you and an alien look at a human face, it will look totally different to the alien than it does to you. In fact, the human face will look downright weird to the alien.

How should representationalists account for this kind of difference in the character of visual experience? One idea (Siewert 1998; Siegel 2010) is that you and the alien experientially represent the same local colors and shapes, but you also experientially represent the face as a *human face* whereas the alien doesn't. This is a *biological property* in the sense that it is only a property of living things. For instance, in the relevant sense, a statue of a human head doesn't have a human face – it just resembles a human face.

Recently, philosophers of perception have put forward more and more extravagant and attention-grabbing hypotheses about what properties are represented at the level of experience, for instance: *being angry, being a pine tree, being a computer, being mind-independent, being edible, being morally right*. Should we say that the representational content of sensory-perceptual experience is very rich and sophisticated in this way? Or is it relatively "thin" or "low-level", involving only colors, shapes, distances, and motions? This debate may be important. For instance, if it is very rich, the question arises: how does the visual system manage to represent very sophisticated properties (see note 9 of the present chapter).

Before we tackle the rich-thin question, we must better understand it. It is uncontroversial that it *seems to us* that something is a face, and that we *see* that something is a face. So if the issue is to be interesting, it had better not concern such ordinary-language descriptions. Susanna Siegel (2010: 78) says that the issue concerns what properties are "presented to us" in experience. But "property P is presented to person *A*" is a technical locution. What does it mean?

The Ramsey-Lewis approach to understanding "experiential representation" can help us understand the issue. To say that we "experientially represent" a property is to say that we bear to it a relation that plays a certain explanatory role, most importantly, the *character-role*. Then the issue is: what are the properties the representation of which constitutes the character of our experience? For example, do they include the biological property *being a human face?* We will consider two arguments for a negative answer.

First, the *argument from parsimony-uniformity*. To illustrate the argument, consider a fanciful example. Return to the aliens. But now suppose that we never meet them, and so they never come face-to-face with human faces. But suppose that an inventor designs robots that, by a remarkable fluke, look just like humans. At first, the facial expressions of the human-like robots look totally weird to the aliens. But soon the aliens learn to effortlessly recognize them and their facial expressions. So there is a "gestalt switch" in their experience of the faces. Evidently, the explanation of the gestalt difference cannot be that they begin to experientially represent the biological kind *being a human face.* They have never encountered instances of this biological kind. The robot faces do not have this property. Instead, they have a broader property: the property of having a *human-face-like-shape* (or a smiley-face-shape, or any angry-face-shape). This is a complex, disjunctive, and hard-to-specify shape property that is common to both human faces and look-alikes like robots, statues, and so on. Roughly, it encodes a range of low-level visible cues of the kind by which we recognize human faces.

Here is another example due to Alex Byrne (Siegel and Byrne 2017: 71–72). Consider "greebles" (Figure 3.4). They are invented stimuli that are used to study object recognition.

You can learn to recognize greebles as such, as falling into certain greeble-types; after you learn how to recognize them, the character of your experience changes. You do not come to experientially represent greebles as having any new *biological* property – greebles are not living things. Rather, you come to experientially represent a new complex low-level property, the property of having certain shaped parts spatially arranged in a certain way.

Although the examples about the aliens and the greebles don't *prove* that we don't experientially represent the biological kind *being a human face*, they do suggest an alternative: when we look at a human face, we experientially represent the broader complex property *having so-and-so face shape* (for

Figure 3.4 A greeble. By Scott Yu, I. Gauthier, M. J. Tarr. CNBC Wiki at https://commons. wikimedia.org.

details see Chang and Tsao 2017). This would be the same kind of non-biological "gestalt" property that the aliens experientially represent when they encounter robot "faces" and that we experientially represent after we have learned to recognize greebles.

This explanation is not only available; for a couple of reasons, it is superior to the hypothesis that we experientially represent the biological property of being a human face. First, it is more uniform, because it applies the same explanation to all the cases. Second, it is more parsimonious, since the greebles case shows that the visual system already has the capacity to experientially represent such non-biological gestalt properties. Why not then account for the phenomena of face recognition in terms of this capacity we know the visual system already has?

In general, whenever someone proposes that we experientially represent a biological or social category P (being an angry face, being a tea-cup, etc.), it may always be better to hold that we instead experientially represent a more basic, non-biological, non-social property P*, where P* is a complex constellation of the lower-level visible properties ("cues") by which we recognize P.

There is a second argument for doubting that we experientially represent biological and social kinds: the *argument from false predictions*. Here is Alex Byrne:

> Imagine that lemons grown on Island *A* look like normal lemons, and that lemons grown on Island *B* look like cucumbers (due to the strange soil and climate). One develops a recognitional disposition for the fruit on Island *A*, and similarly for the fruit on Island *B* (but does not know that the fruits are identical). If [the rich view is right], then if one sees an *A* fruit and a *B* fruit side by side, they will both be visually represented *as lemons*. Presumably, then, *they will appear more visually similar after one has learned to recognize them by sight than they did before*. [This is] not borne out.
>
> (Byrne 2009: 449–450)

Here is an elaboration of Byrne's argument. The "rich" theorist says that, after the learning period, you will experientially represent both the island-*A* lemons and the cucumber-like island-*B* lemons as belonging to the biological kind *being a lemon*, and this will contribute to the allegedly new phenomenology of each experience. Now the following principle is plausible: if, after the learning period, both the experience of the ordinary lemon and the experience of the cucumber-looking lemon represent those fruits as *being a lemon*, and this contributes to what each experience is like, then there will be a new respect of experiential similarity between the experiences. The trouble, as Byrne says, is that this prediction is not borne out. The island-*A* lemons and the cucumber-like island-*B* lemons will continue to look totally different. This suggests that only lower level properties, like colors and shapes, contribute to phenomenology, and that biological properties like *being a lemon* do not.[9]

Finally, let us briefly consider a quite different debate about the contents of our visual experiences (for recent discussion, see Speaks 2015, 2017; Schellenberg 2018). Suppose you look at a tomato, then you look away, then the tomato is replaced by a distinct but indiscriminable tomato, and then you look back. It looks exactly the same to you. Call the first tomato *Harold* and the second one *Maud*. Here are two views. First, *singularism* says that the representational contents of your experiences differ in the two cases, even though you cannot tell a difference. You first experientially represent that *Harold* is red and round and in front of you, and then you experientially represent that *Maud* is red and round and in front of you. On singularism, then, your experiences, so to speak, encode the identities of the objects you experience, and not just the way they look. By contrast, *generalism* says that the representational content of your experiences is exactly the same in the two cases. In both cases, you experientially represent (roughly) that *something or other* is red and round and in front of you. Your experience doesn't encode the identity of the object.

How might we resolve this debate? And why does it matter? To begin with, everyone will agree with the weak claim that in the two cases your two experiences can be *associated with* different "singular" representational contents, namely *that Harold is red and round* and *that Maud is red and round*. Even generalists can agree that there is a sense in which you "represent" these different singular contents. First Harold looks red and round to you and then Maud looks red and round to you. So what is the issue?

Suppose we take the issue to be whether the *character of your experiences* is constituted or grounded by different singular contents or the same general content. This is congruent with our Ramsey-Lewis formulation in Section 3.1.

In that case, there is a real question about how we could resolve the issue. Would the character of our experiences differ depending on whether singularism or generalism were true? For instance, for the sake of argument, suppose that in fact singularism is true. Presumably, it's possible that generalism should have been true instead. (See Section 3.8 for a general discussion on what kinds of experiences are possible.) Would the character of your experiences of the tomato have been noticeably different, had generalism been true instead? Arguably not. To see this, consider a group of twin humans, and let's stipulate that generalism is true of them. When a twin human looks at the tomato, it would seem to her that something or other is red and round and in front of her. So it would look to her just as it looks to you in the actual situation. There would be no visible difference.

So if we formulate singularism and generalism so that they concern what grounds the character of our experiences, and if which view is true makes no (noticeable) difference to the character of our experience, then it's hard to see how we could determine which view is correct.

3.5 The question of skepticism and the dogmatist answer

Imagine a far-fetched scenario. In the 22nd century, simulation technology (like "virtual reality") has reached an advanced state. Some computer scientists decide to have some fun. They create a brain and put it in a vat in a laboratory. They create a computer program that simulates a world (a world where a guy named "Donald Trump" gets to be president, where there is global warming, etc.). The brain is hooked up to a computer running the simulation. The simulation determines which inputs the brain receives. When the brain produces outputs, these are fed back into the simulation. So this brain would have experiences as rich and convincing as your own, only they would all be hallucinatory. The computer scientists think this is hilarious.

Now here is a mind-bending question. How do you know that *you* are not a brain in a vat (BIV) living in a simulated reality? How do you rule out the *BIV hypothesis?* You think it is early in the 21st century, but maybe in reality you are a BIV in a computer simulation very late in the 22nd century. All your friends and family, all the objects you think are around you, all the world's events, are false creations, proceeding form your computer-stimulated brain. All that you see or seem to see is but a dream. The idea is preposterous, but how do you *know* it is not the case? If you reach out and touch something, you will have the same tactile experiences the BIV would have.

There are two questions here. First, how do you *know* that there really exist things with shapes and colors in space out there, as against BIV hypothesis? Second, how do you so much as have a *good reason* for thinking this?

These are difficult questions for everyone. They even arise for "naïve realists" (see Section 1.8). But the representational view makes them salient. If our experiences are just representations, how do we know that they are not all inaccurate representations?

One traditional answer appeals to an inference to the best explanation (Russell 1912; Vogel 1990). The BIV hypothesis is weird and complicated. A better explanation of why it seems that there are objects out there is that there really are objects out there. So, you might infer that the BIV hypothesis is probably false, and probably things are just as they seem. On this view, ordinary things are theoretical posits no less than electrons.

However, all this seems pretty shaky. Also, ordinary people don't in fact carry out such an elaborate inference. Instead, they immediately believe that there is a real world.

This leads to a quite different response to the skeptic, the *dogmatist* answer (e.g., Pryor 2000). Suppose you experientially represent that before you is something with flower-shape f and the color purple. Dogmatists say that you consequently have a strong reason to believe that an f-shaped and purple thing is really there, contrary to the BIV hypothesis. Dogmatists deny that the reason is based on an inference. Instead, it's just in the essence of "experientially representing" that some object is F that it automatically gives you an "immediate" reason to believe that some object is F, a reason that doesn't depend on your reason to believe anything else. (This is related to idea that the act-object assumption is "intrinsically plausible".) True, Buddy Burmester (or a hypothetical BIV) experientially represents that something before him is f-shaped and purple, even though in this case there is no such thing there. Still, even his experience gives him some reason to believe that such a thing is there. It's just that the reason is defeasible.

Here is an analogy. It's in the essence of some experiences – pains and pleasures, taste experiences, and so on – to give you some reason to *desire* that they stop or continue. So why can't it be in the essence of experientially representing that some object is F to give you a reason to *believe* that something is F?

The dogmatic response to radical skepticism has some plausibility. But it also faces several problems. Let us look at a few.

(1) Dogmatism only addresses the question of how you have a *reason* to believe (for instance) that there really is an f-shaped thing there and to reject the BIV hypothesis. But how can you *know* this? After all, if your reason is your experience, and if you could have the same experience in a hallucination case, your reason isn't conclusive.

In response, dogmatists can deny that knowing something requires a conclusive reason to believe that thing. For instance, they can say (roughly) that you count as knowing that an f-shaped thing is there just in case you have a good (but not necessarily conclusive) reason to believe that an f-shaped thing is there, you believe it on the basis of this reason, and your belief is safely true. So, when you experientially represent that an f-shape thing is there, if you are lucky and really do live in the real world (rather than being a constantly hallucinating BIV), you automatically count as knowing that there is such a thing there, without having to carry out an inference.

(2) Another problem concerns the ability of dogmatism to answer skepticism (Schiffer 2004: 177). We saw that dogmatists hold that when you experientially represent that something has property F, then you automatically have a reason to believe that something has property F, and "inference to the best explanation" is not involved. But, in Section 3.4, we also saw that there are reasons for thinking that the properties we experientially represent are pretty "thin": they include *being f-shaped*, *being purple*, *having a propensity to move left*, but not *being a human face*, *being a flower*, *being a house*, and so on. In that case, dogmatism implies we only have immediate, experience-based reason to believe things about the colors, shapes, and movements of things around us.

However, the vast bulk of our beliefs go beyond this. We believe that the things around us are people, flowers, houses, and so on. We also believe in distant planets and subatomic particles. Dogmatists need a story about the source of our reasons to believe all these other things. For instance, what is the source of your reason to believe that the thing before you is a flower, rather than a fake-flower?

More generally, what is the source of your reason to reject the *fake-world hypothesis*: the hypothesis that you are correct about the colors, shapes, and movements of things in your immediate environment, but everything else is "fake" or "staged" (like in the movie *The Truman Show*)?

To explain how we have reasons to believe all these things going beyond perceptually basic properties, dogmatists may after all need to say that that we make heavy use of "inference to the best explanation". But that is exactly what they wanted to avoid.

(3) We will end with an interesting problem of detail. The problem is generated by two ideas:

(1) *Degree:* Our immediate experience-based reasons come in varying degrees.

(2) *Binary:* Experiential representation does not come in degrees: either you experientially represent a state of affairs or you don't.

(3) Therefore, contrary to dogmatism, facts about what we experientially represent cannot fully explain the facts about our experience-based reasons.[10]

To illustrate, consider your experience of the shades *a*, *b*, and *c* in Figure 3.5.

When you experience the three shades here, it strongly strikes you that shades *a* and *b* are distinct. So you have a strong immediate reason to believe that they are. By contrast, it only *kind of* appears to you that shades *b* and *b'* are distinct. (In fact, shades *b* and *b'* barely differ.) So you have less reason to believe that shades *b* and *b'* are distinct than you have to believe that shades *a* and *b* are distinct.

Now suppose that experiential representation doesn't come in degrees. Either you experientially represent that shades *b* and *b'* are distinct, or you don't. If so, then dogmatists cannot explain why our experience-based

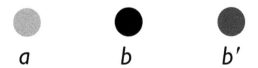

Figure 3.5 Degreed perceptual justification.

reasons vary in degree by appealing to facts about experiential representation alone.

In response to this problem, dogmatists could reject Binary and instead accept *degreed representationalism*. On this view, experiential representation does come in degrees. For instance, you experientially represent that *shades a and b differ* with more "phenomenal force" than you experientially represent that *shades b and b' differ*. This is part of the character of your experience. And dogmatists could put forward a general principle: the strength of your experience-based reasons to believe that a state of affairs obtains is proportional to the "phenomenal force" with which you experientially represent that state of affairs.

There are however problems with degreed representationalism. Let me just mention one. Can degrees of "phenomenal force" vary independently of the representational content of experience? For instance, could the following situation happen? You experientially represent the very same fine-grained shades shown above. In every detail, all the contents of your experience are exactly the same as in the actual situation. In the hypothetical situation, there is only variation in the "phenomenal force" with which you experientially represent the relevant contents. In particular, oddly, you represent *that shades b and b' differ* with much more "phenomenal force" than you represent *that shades a and b differ*. This is so even though the perceived shades b and b' *barely differ* while a and b differ *greatly*. Or take a simpler example: suppose you look at a tomato on a table right before you. Could you experientially represent exactly the same bright color, bulgy shape, and other details, but with much less "phenomenal force" than you actually do? The problem is that it is hard to get a grip on these hypothetical experiences. How would the character of the hypothetical experiences differ from the character of your actual experiences? But if you could not have such experiences, the proponent of the degreed representationalism needs to explain why not.

So degreed representationalism faces a challenge. It remains unclear how to explain the degrees of our immediate experience-based reasons.

One last point. Dogmatism says that experientially representing plays a reason-grounding role: experientially representing a state of affairs grounds your having an immediate reason to believe that the state of affairs obtains. David Lewis (1994: 427–429) has defended another idea: a "reasons-responsive theory" of belief, according to which beliefs are essentially responsive to reasons. The reason-grounding role of experiential representation, together with a reasons-responsive theory of belief, would explain the cognitive-access role of experiential representation (which was part of our formulation of the representational view in Section 3.1): if you experientially represent a state of affairs, you automatically have a capacity to believe that the state of affairs obtains. In fact, these ideas together entail

Discussion Box: Knowledge-first rather than experience-first?

The dogmatist view of the source of our reasons for perceptual beliefs is an *experience-based*, or *experience-first*, view. When you view a tomato, you know that there is a red and round thing there because you first have good-enough reason to believe it – a reason provided by your experience. The picture, then, is this: experience → reasons → knowledge. Recently a quite different, *knowledge-first* picture has become popular (Williamson 2000: 198–199; 2005: 468–470). (For an intermediate view see Schellenberg 2018.) On this view, when you have the experience, you first immediately know that there is a red and round thing there: you just *see* that there is such a thing. Because you know that there is such a thing there, you have a really good reason to believe it. The picture, then, is this: experience → knowledge → reasons. Further, on this approach, knowing things comes easy: roughly, it just requires having beliefs that are in fact reliably (safely) true. Given this standard, we know a lot; skepticism is avoided.

Representationalists could go in for the knowledge-first view rather than the dogmatist, experience-first view. However, it faces a problem. It seems that your reasons are more closely connected to your experiences than to what you know. We can illustrate this with a science-fiction example of a "seamless transition". (Johnston 2004 introduced this example to illustrate a different point.) Suppose that you go into a dining room and scientists in control of your brain cause you to hallucinate a tomato on a table. However, you have no idea; to you, everything is normal, and from the start you're convinced a tomato is there. Then your hallucination stops, but at the same time a tomato is placed on the table, so that (unknown to you) your belief that a red and round thing is there goes from being false to being safely true. Imagine that your hallucination and your "veridical" experience are indistinguishable and the transition between them is seamless. Now, according to the knowledge-first view, though your tomato-experience doesn't change at all in character, at the transition point, you go from being deceived to *knowing* that a red and round thing is there. So the knowledge-first view implies that, at first, you have little or no reason to believe a red and round thing is there; then, at the transition point, you suddenly have extremely strong (indeed conclusive) reason to believe this. So (although you don't know it) at the transition point you should increase your confidence. This is so even though you have the same vivid experience as of a red and round thing throughout and have no idea anything is amiss. The dogmatist, experience-first view avoids these odd implications of the knowledge-first view. On this view, having the reason just requires having the experience. Since your experience remains the same throughout the process, this view delivers the intuitively correct verdict that throughout the process (even when hallucinating) you have the *same reason* to believe that a red and round thing is present (Pautz 2016: 923; Smithies 2019: 99).

that, if you experientially represent a state of affairs, then you automatically have a disposition to believe that the state of affairs obtains. For instance, if your experientially representing that there is a reddish and round thing before you grounds your having a strong reason to believe that there is such a thing there (dogmatism), and if beliefs are essentially responsive to reasons (a reasons-responsive theory of belief), then your experientially representing a reddish and round thing is before you will necessarily dispose you to believe that there is such a thing there. This result is somewhat plausible (Smith 2001; Byrne 2009).[11]

3.6 Does the representational view explain perceptual presence?

The argument for the representational view is that it best explains the central facts about experience. But some have said that one thing the representational view doesn't explain is "perceptual presence". Here John Campbell pressing this objection:

> The color red itself is there in a visual experience of redness ... The presence of the color red in a visual experience of redness is hard to explain on any view that takes your color experience to be a matter of your representing the colors in experience.
>
> (Campbell 2020: 406)

But what does Campbell mean when he says that "the color red itself is there in a visual experience of redness"? (See also Levine 2019: 295–296.) We need to understand what this idea means before we can ask whether representationalists can accommodate it.

On one interpretation, he means that, in any visual experience of redness, a red object is actually present, and you experience it.

But, on this strong interpretation, the claim is false, and therefore no threat to the representational view. It is false because it requires a red sense datum in a hallucination. For suppose Buddy Burmester hallucinates a red flower. He then has "a visual experience of redness". But no red and flower-shaped physical object is present. So if a red and flower-shaped object is present, it would have to be a mysterious non-physical "sense datum" in a private mental space. But in Chapter 1 we saw that the sense datum theory of hallucination faces serious problems. Campbell himself rejects it (see Section 5.5). Instead, the right thing to say that, in his visual experience of redness, it merely vividly seems to Buddy that a red object is present right there.

This naturally suggests a retreat to a weaker interpretation of Campbell's claim that "the color red itself is there in a visual experience of redness". Maybe he only means that, in any visual experience of redness, it vividly seems that a red object is actually present then and there. In fact, elsewhere Campbell himself opts for this weaker formulation: "redness itself *seems to be* present in an experience of redness" (Campbell 2016: 112; my italics).

On this weak "seems" interpretation, Campbell's presence claim may be true – hallucination and illusion are no longer counterexamples. But it is certainly no threat to the representational view. In fact, we saw in Section 3.1 that the representational view could be formulated in terms of the idiom of "experientially seems" instead of "experientially represents". So, truth be told, it doesn't go far beyond the claim that to experience red is for it to vividly seem to you that a red object is present. Therefore, it can hardly be at odds with that claim.[12]

Let's briefly consider another objection to the representational view in the same vicinity that does not use the obscure notion of "presentation". Campbell (2016: 112; 2020: 407) often notes that experiences are just *fundamentally different* from standard representational states. He mentions beliefs (e.g., the belief a red thing is in the next room) and the unconscious representations of individuals with "blindsight" (for details see Weiskrantz 1986). The objection is that the representational view does not accommodate this "fundamental difference" claim, because the representational view holds that experiences are representational states akin to beliefs and other representational states.

But representationalists can respect the "fundamental difference" claim a way that parallels the way in which naïve realists like Campbell do so.

Naïve realists (like sense datum theorists) hold that there is a special experiencing relation; having experiences consists in bearing this relation to *things* (Chapters 1 and 5). According to them, this relation is fundamentally different from the believing relation and any mere "causal detection" relations a blindsight individual bears to objects in their blind field. There is no other relationship like it in nature.

There is no reason why representationalists cannot say similar things. In particular, they hold that there is a special experience relation that we bear to *ways things might be*; having experiences consists in bearing this relation to ways thing might be. True, they often call it "experientially representing", and this may suggest that it is similar to the kind of representing that is done by beliefs and by blindsight subjects. But you shouldn't be misled by the label. Representationalists could also call it "experientially seeming", and entirely refrain from using "representation" in describing their view. (Indeed, the Ramsey-Lewis formulation in Section 3.1 totally eliminates the distracting term "representation".) And they can say that the relevant relation is fundamentally different from the belief relation and any mere causal detection relation a blindsight individual bears to objects in their blind field.

In this way, on the representational view as well as on naïve realism, experiences are fundamentally different from beliefs and unconscious representations in blindsight (for more on this see Section 5.4).

3.7 Is the representational view intrinsically implausible?

Our final formulation of the representational view in Section 3.1 appealed to *properties*, or "ways things might be". Properties are "abstract items". For instance, to have the flower-experience is to experientially represent the properties of being f_{17} and being purple$_{42}$. When Buddy hallucinates, these properties aren't located or instantiated before him. I also noted that the representational view could be formulated in terms of *states of affairs* that can obtain or fail to obtain. These, too, are abstract items. These are forms of *abstract-items representationalism* (Bourget 2019).

You might find abstract-items representationalism intrinsically implausible on the face of it. How can the flower-experience – an experience in which it vividly seems that an extended object is *right there* – consist in nothing but standing in a mental relationship to a complex of properties – abstract items that don't take up space, may have no location, and cannot be seen? Isn't that an obviously absurd identification – like identifying the color red with the number two? This would undercut the best explanation argument for the representational view developed in Section 3.2.

On one way of developing this objection, it depends on a more general claim, namely *concretism* about experience: the definition of what it is to have the flower-experience will only mention concrete items. No abstract items – such as properties or possible states of affairs – enter into the constitution of experience. Maybe *believing* is a relationship to concepts and propositions that are abstract. But that can't be right for experiencing. Experiencing is a wholly here-and-now, concrete affair, involving you (a concrete thing) and concrete things in your brain or immediate environment. Most views respect this: naïve realism, the sense datum theory (sense data are concrete even if mental), the internal physical state view. But abstract-items representationalism does not.[13]

Representationalists can dodge this form of the objection. Although I formulated the representational view in terms of abstract items, it can also be formulated without mention of abstract items. We can simply formulate the representational view as the view that for Buddy to have a flower-like experience is for him to experientially represent that something is flower-shaped and purple. That is, for Buddy to have his experience is for it to experientially seem to him that there is such a thing. This doesn't say that for him to have this experience is for him to be related to properties, abstract "ways thing might be". True, it uses the expressions "is flower-shaped" and "is purple". But, as Quine (1948) pointed out, such expressions can be meaningful without having to refer to special abstract items, "properties", that exist separately from things. In fact, this form of the representational view might be combined with the "ontological" claim that only concrete things exist. Call it *concrete representationalism* (see Prior 1968: 93; Perkins and Bayne 2013: 73). Opponents of the representational view cannot object to concrete representationalism on the grounds that "I find it difficult to understand the claim abstract items should enter into the constitution of experience" (Papineau 2016: 317). For concrete representationalists reject this claim. In fact, they reject abstract items in general.

However, you might even find concrete representationalism intrinsically implausible. In fact, you might go further: as we discussed in Chapter 1, in the past, philosophers such as Price (1932) insisted that the only view that is intrinsically plausible is an across-the-board act-object theory. It's just obvious that to have the flower-experience, in both normal cases and hallucination cases, is to experience the purple color and flower-shape of some actually existing object. Nothing less will do. Since the representational view denies the act-object theory, it cannot be right. In this form, the objection from intrinsic implausibility becomes a strong form of the objection from "perceptual presence" discussed in the previous section.

Do considerations of "intrinsic plausibility" strongly support rejecting the representational view in favor of some alternative?

Let's start with the question of whether intrinsic plausibility supports an across-the-board act-object view (Chapter 1) over the representational view. I think it must be admitted that it provides *some* support for an across-the-board act-object view. But step 2 of the best explanation argument

(Section 3.2) noted that there are countervailing arguments against an across-the-board act-object view and for the representational view concerning perceptual imprecision and incompleteness in hallucination.

Turn next to the question of whether intrinsic plausibility supports the internal physical state view (Chapter 2) over the representational view. The problem is that this view (Papineau 2014, 2016) is not more "intrinsically plausible" than the representational view. It is not at all plausible that having an experience with technicolor phenomenology consists in nothing but undergoing an internal physical-computational state realized in soggy grey matter in the brain. In fact, it may be *less* "intrinsically plausible" than the representational view, since (as we saw in Chapter 2) it denies the externally directed character of visual experience whereas the representational view accommodates it.

In Chapter 5, we will see that some contemporary naïve realists give a "negative" theory of hallucination on which the presence of phenomenology in hallucination is constituted by the *lack* of a certain ability – namely, the ability to tell your situation apart from one of seeing. This is not more "intrinsically plausible" than the representational view.

In sum, considerations of intrinsic plausibility do not seem to strongly support rejecting the representational view in favor of any alternative since the alternatives are intrinsically implausible in their own ways.

3.8 Can the representational view explain the laws of appearance?

Representationalists hold that experiences are representational states. In that respect, they are like beliefs. But there is a big difference. There are few if any restrictions on the weird *beliefs* people can have. Philosophers nicely illustrate the point. For instance, some philosophers – "Meinongians" – believe that there are round squares and things that are pure red and pure green all over but you just cannot interact with them. By contrast, there seem to be some restrictions on what *experiences* people can have. We can call them *laws of appearance*.

For example, you can experientially represent a surface as pure red. And you can experientially represent a different surface as pure green. Could you experientially represent the *same* surface as both pure red and pure green at the same time? Given the representational view, this would mean that your experience of the same region would at the same time have a "pure reddish" character and a "pure greenish" character. It seems to be a law of appearance that no such experience is possible. Likewise, it is a law of appearance that you cannot experientially represent the same object as round and square. So we have:

> **Exclusion law.** An individual cannot experientially represent that a single surface has two distinct pure colors, such as pure red and pure green. Likewise, an individual cannot experientially represent that the same object has distinct shapes, such as round and square.

Although I will focus on the exclusion law in what follows, there are many such laws:

> **Berkeley's law.** (1) An individual cannot experientially represent that something has a color without also experientially representing that it takes up space in some way. (2) Conversely, an individual cannot experientially represent that something takes up space in some way (e.g., being circular) without also experientially representing a qualitative difference (e.g., a *white* circle on a *black* background). See Berkeley (1713: 7).
>
> **No logical structure.** For example, an individual cannot experientially represent merely *that there is either a red square in front or a green sphere on the right*, without experientially representing anything more specific. What would that be like?
>
> **No radical incompleteness.** We have seen that experiences can be imprecise and incomplete. One of the virtues of the representational view is that it explains this (Section 3.2). But there are limits. For instance, an individual cannot merely experientially represent *that there is something in front of me that takes up space*, without experientially representing anything more specific.
>
> **Perspectival law.** An individual cannot experientially represent merely *that there is a cube somewhere in reality*, without any "perspectival content" about its location and apparent shape from "here".
>
> **Property restriction.** An individual cannot *experientially* represent merely abstract properties or state of affairs, such as *justice is a virtue*, or *the republicans will win the election*. Such things can be represented in thought but they are not perceivable.

Now we can all agree that these laws (or some of them) are generally true. However, there is a question about their "strength". There are two options. One option is *necessitism*: at least *some* of the laws of appearance are *metaphysically necessary* truths about experiences. This means that they are necessary in the strongest possible sense. They would be true no matter what else happens. It's not just that they are true of humans' actual experiences;

they are true of the experiences of *any possible creature*. In this regard, they are like truths of mathematics. A second option is *contingentism*: all the laws of appearance are *contingent laws*, where *contingent* means "true but not metaphysically necessary". They might be false for other possible creatures' experiences.

Should representationalists accept necessitism or contingentism about the laws of appearance? Either way, they face problems.

First, necessitism. Maybe some of the laws of appearance are contingent laws about human experience and could fail for other possible creatures, although it is very hard to imagine such failures. However, there is good reason to think that at least some of them are metaphysically necessary. For instance, it is "intrinsically plausible" that the exclusion law is metaphysically necessary. No possible individual could experientially represent the same object as round and square. For, given the representational view, this would require that an individual have an experience of an object that has both a round-character and a square-character. And this is not possible. In the absence of sufficiently strong countervailing arguments, we should accept that the exclusion law is metaphysically necessary.

If some laws of appearance are metaphysically necessary, we want to know *why*. Why cannot they be violated in any possible experiencer? If people can believe that there are round squares, why cannot they have experiences as of round squares? It would be nice to have some kind of systematic, simple explanation here.

But representationalists have special difficulty with providing such an explanation. This threatens the best explanation argument for the representational view developed in Section 3.2. To appreciate the difficulty, contrast the representational view with the sense datum view (Chapter 1). On the sense datum view, if it visually appears to someone that something is F, then there must exist in reality a sense datum that is F. So if nothing – not even a sense datum – can be round and square, then we have an explanation of why it can never visually appear that something is round and square. The exclusion law poses no problem for the sense datum view. But representationalists reject the sense datum view and accept existence-neutrality. So they cannot accept this attractive explanation of the metaphysical necessity of the exclusion law. They hold that, if your brain on the blink, you can hallucinate a flower-shaped thing, even if there exists no flower-shaped thing. So why not a round and square thing?

At this point, representationalists might look for an explanation in terms of the "iconic" or "analog" format of experiential representation in the human brain (Lycan 2019b; Tye 2020). This idea deserves a detailed discussion. But, briefly, such an explanation seems unlikely for a general reason. When you view a moving blue thing, your hidden, subpersonal neural representations of color and movement, which might be located in separate brain areas, are "bound" together, where this is some kind of functional-computational relation. Why couldn't there be possible experiencers whose subpersonal representations of distinct colors (or distinct shapes) could be "bound together" in this way, just as our subpersonal representations of color and motion can be bound together? So if we only look at the neural states and processes underlying our experiences, we cannot explain why it is metaphysically impossible that an individual should experientially represent distinct colors (or distinct shapes) as bound together.

In view of the difficulties with explaining why the laws of appearance should be metaphysically necessary, representationalists may turn to the contingentist option: all of them are merely contingent rather than metaphysically necessary. For instance, Ned Block (2020) says "my view is that [the above-listed] 'laws' are not [metaphysically necessary] truths." And Jeff Speaks (2017: 495) says "I am tempted to doubt whether the laws of perception really are (metaphysically) necessary." On this view, all of the laws of appearance could be violated in hypothetical individuals whose visual systems work differently. True, we cannot imagine what it would be like. But there are possible experiences we cannot imagine.

If contingentism is right for all the laws of appearance, then they pose no serious problem for the representational view. Necessitism sets a very high bar: it means that there must be explanations of why the laws hold in all possible individuals. By contrast, Contingentism would mean there only need to be explanations of why they hold in actual humans. And we know in advance that there must be some such explanations – presumably, neurocomputational explanations.

Now there is reason to accept contingentism about *some* of the above laws of appearance. For instance, although Berkeley's law is generally true, there is some reason to think it is violated by the experiences of a particular brain-damaged patient called "MS" (see Kentridge *et al.* 2004).

The problem is that representationalists cannot plausibly maintain contingentism when it comes to other laws of appearance. Take the exclusion law. As I said above, it's plausibly metaphysically necessary that no individual should experientially represent that something is round and square, just as it is metaphysically necessary that no object should actually be round and square. Unlike in the case of Berkeley's law, we have no reason to believe that there are actual cases where it is violated.[14] True, we cannot now explain the exclusion law. But there are many metaphysical necessities we cannot currently explain in more basic terms. In this situation, it may not be reasonable to outright assert it's possible that an individual should experientially represent that something is round and square.

In sum, representationalists have reason to think that at least some laws of appearance are metaphysically necessary. But so far we have no explanation of why this should be so.

Finally, let us consider a radical solution to this puzzle. It involves giving up the representational view as formulated in Section 3.1 and moving to a quite different view that I will call *sensa representationalism*.

To understand sensa representationalism, you first need to understand the idea of an *ontologically dependent* entity. Consider the holes in a piece of Swiss cheese. They exist by virtue of the fact that there exists a "hole host" (the piece of cheese) with hollowed-out parts. They couldn't exist on their own. Or consider fictional individuals like Sherlock Holmes and Madame Bovary. They exist by virtue of the representational activities of authors (Thomasson 1999).

Likewise, sensa representationalism posits ontologically dependent entities we will call *sensa*. It holds that, in general, if someone experientially represents that something is F, then this experience grounds the coming-in-to-existence of a sensum that really is F. That is the only way for a sensum to come into existence. Thus, if you should have a hallucination of a tomato in which you experientially represent that something before you is reddish and round, this brings into existence a red and round sensum. This sensum is "present to your mind". Even when you see a real tomato, your experience brings into existence a red and round sensum that is distinct from the physical tomato. Thus, there is always a veil of sensa between you and the world. Sensa are ontologically dependent on experiences in the same way holes are ontologically dependent on hole-hosts.

Our original formulation of the representational view in Section 3.1 included a commitment to existence-neutrality. By contrast, sensa representationalism is a form of *actualism*: when you experientially represent the world to be a certain way, there is an actual sensum that is that way. In this way it resembles the sense datum view (Chapter 1). But it also differs from the sense datum view. The sense datum view holds that sense data are among the fundamental elements of reality. By contrast, sensa representationalism holds that sensa "come for free" with the right kinds of experiences, somewhat as holes "come for free" with the right arrangements of matter.

Sensa representationalism may seem strange. But it might explain the metaphysical necessity of the exclusion law. For example, why is it metaphysically necessary that no one should experientially represent that something is round and square? Because, given sensa representationalism, this would require the coming-into-existence of a sensum that is round and square. But nothing – not even a "sensum" – could be round and square.

As a bonus, sensa representationalism would provide a novel answer to the objection from perceptual presence that we discussed in Section 3.6. For, on this form of the representational view, experience is essentially presentational as well as essentially representational. In this way, experience is fundamentally different from other representational states such as beliefs.

In any case, there are two problems with the idea that sensa representationalism might solve the puzzle of the laws of appearance. First, although it may explain the metaphysical necessity of the exclusion law, it is not clear whether it explains the metaphysical necessity of all the other laws of appearance.

Second, the explanation of the exclusion law offered by sensa representationalism depends on the claim that a sensum cannot be round and square. But it's not clear whether sensum representationalists are entitled to this claim. After all, sensa would need to be very peculiar – just like the sense data of the traditional sense datum view. For instance, if you experientially represent that there is something in the periphery of your visual field that is located in a certain region but there no specific location that you experientially represent it to be in, then there must exist a sensum with the property *having a location in rough region* r and also the property *not having any specific location in* r (see Section 1.11). But those properties are intuitively incompatible. Once we have gone this far, why cannot there exist a sensum that has the property *being round* and the property *being square*, even though those properties are intuitively incompatible? Why draw the line there?

The puzzle of the laws of appearance poses a serious unresolved challenge to the representational view.

Summary

The lessons of our first two chapters led naturally to the representationalist explanation of essential external directedness that was the topic of the present chapter. First of all, unlike the internal physical state view

(Chapter 2), the representational view allows us to accept that experiences essentially enable us to grasp external ways things might be, like *flower-shaped*. Second, unlike the sense datum view (Chapter 1), the representational view allows us to say that experiences essentially enable us to grasp ways things might be, even if we do not perceive any objects ("sense data") that really are those ways. In this chapter, we have focused on the basic idea.

But an important task remains. To show that the representational view can fully solve the puzzle of perception, we must not only show that it can accommodate essential external directedness; we must show that it can accommodate "internal dependence", the fact that the brain plays a big role in determining how things appear. How does the brain enable us to experientially represent the world at all, and how does it enable us to represent the world as filled with specific sensible properties, like sensible colors, audible properties, smell properties, and so on? This will be the subject of Chapter 4.

Further Reading

Important sources for the representational view include Armstrong (1968, 1981), Bealer (1982), Hintikka (1969), and Anscombe (1965). The "multiple relation theory" broached by Moore (1918: 23–25) can be seen as an early version. For more on the multiple relation theory see Chapter 5.

More recent defenses include Byrne (2009), Chalmers (2010), Dretske (1995), Hill (2009), Horgan (2014), Jackson (2004), Lycan (2019a), Mendelovici (2018), Speaks (2015), and Tye (1995). Schellenberg (2018) defends a novel form of the representational view based on capacities of discrimination.

For discussion of the laws of appearance, see Speaks (2017), Lycan (2019b), Tye (2020), Block 2020, Duncan 2020, and Green 2020.

Much of the philosophy of perception focuses on experiences of static objects, such as the purple flower discussed in this chapter. But, of course, the perceptual world is filled with change. For discussion of how representationalists might explain this, see Lee (2014, 2017) and Dainton (2018).

Another issue we were not able to discuss is how representationalists might account for how our experiences of objects' spatial properties change (and yet remain the same) due to changes in perspective. See Hill (2009), McLaughlin (2016b), Schellenberg (2018), Green and Schellenberg (2018), and Green 2020.

Notes

1 See Speaks (2017: 492–493) for a discussion of this way of clarifying the representational view and debates about the representational content of experience.

2 Travis (2004: 85, 92) and Brewer (2017: sect. 2.3) object to the representational view on the grounds that it requires – what they think cannot be supplied – a general algorithm (e.g., in terms of "looks"-reports or in terms of underlying facts about causal-covariation) for determining the representational content of any given experience. Against this, the availability of the present Ramsey-Lewis formulation of the representational view shows that talk of the representational content of experience can be perfectly intelligible even in the absence of such an algorithm.

3 For defenses of various forms of the representational view, see, for example, Armstrong (1968), Bealer (1982), Byrne (2009), Chalmers (2010), Dretske (1995), Hill (2009), Horgan (2014), Jackson (2004), Lycan (2019a), Mendelovici (2018), Schellenberg (2018), Speaks (2015), and Tye (1995).

4 For an argument for the representational view based on transparency, see Tye (2000: chap. 3). For problems with transparency, see Section 2.3 of this book. For an argument based on "seems", see Byrne (2001). For problems with Byrne's argument, see Byrne (2001: 225–226), van Cleve (2015: 469), and Lycan (2019b: sect. 3.4). For different forms of the "best explanation" argument, see Byrne (2009) and Pautz (2010a).

5 Here we are saying that it is a virtue of the representational view that it predicts and explains perceptual imprecision. However, it must be noted that Block (2015) gives a complex argument for the opposite claim: that the representational view cannot adequately accommodate perceptual imprecision.

6 For discussion related to step 1, see Russell (1912a: chap. X), Johnston (2004: 130–131), Hellie (2010: fn.5), Brewer (2011: 112–113), Alford-Duguid and Arsenault (2017), Gupta (2019: 175–177), and Tye (2019).

7 Speaks (2015: 177–188) argues on the basis of cross-modal binding that the relevant relation is the same across the board. See also O'Callaghan (2020a).

8 See Green (2016) for other examples of "gestalt switches" and how representationalists might explain them.

9 There is another potential problem for a form of the "rich" view that holds that the visual system enables us to experientially represent "high-level" properties like *being a pine tree* or *being a computer,* in addition to more basic visible properties. In particular, the claim that we experientially represent such fancy properties may be at odds with plausible general theories of *how* we experientially represent properties. See Green (2017) for discussion.

10 For this epistemological puzzle, see Pautz (2016) and Munton (2016). For related discussion, see Morrison (2016).

11 Suppose that we define "having a concept of *F*" as "having the ability to think that something is *F*". In that case, the claim arrived at in the text – that an experience that something is *F entails* the ability and indeed the disposition to believe that the thing is *F* (e.g., red, round) – amounts to a form of "conceptualism" about experience on which having such an experience requires "having a concept of *F*" (Speaks 2020). It is worth noting that conceptualism about experience in this sense is quite consistent with the empiricist idea that experience *explains* our having certain concepts. Speaks (2020: 64) puts this well when he asks, "why should the fact that something *entails* an ability be inconsistent with its *explaining* that ability?" Speaks helps to clear up many ambiguities and confusions in the debate over "conceptualism" about experience.

12   Papineau (2016: 336–337) raises a different objection from Campbell's. He sug-
     gests that representationalists are committed to a *false* claim about perceptual
     presence, namely, that in a hallucination of redness, you are "presented with" (i.e.,
     aware of) the free-floating, abstract universal *redness* even if nothing in your vicin-
     ity is actually red. But, while some few representationalists accept this peculiar
     claim (e.g., Dretske 2003 and Tye 2019), most representationalists do not. Most
     hold that in hallucination there exists *nothing* you are aware of or "presented with",
     as we discussed in Section 3.1. It only seems that you are presented with some-
     thing (Pautz 2007).

13   For this kind of objection to the representational view, see Pautz (2010a: 293ff),
     Kriegel (2011: 141ff), Papineau (2014, 2016), Mendelovici (2018: chap. 9), Langsam
     (2018), and Sundström (2018). Papineau (in forthcoming work) argues for concre-
     tism and against the representational view on the grounds that experiences are
     "causes and effects", which he thinks is at odds with the representational view.
     For replies to this general type of problem, see Schiffer (2003: 333ff) and Dretske
     (1995: 151ff).

14   One might think that, in the waterfall illusion (Section 3.2), you experientially rep-
     resent the impossible state of affairs *that a black rock moves and stands still*. If
     you can experientially represent *some* metaphysically impossible states of affairs,
     shouldn't it be possible in principle that some perceiver should experientially
     represent others, for instance, *that something is round and square*, in agreement
     with contingentism? But, on one natural account of the waterfall illusion, what
     you experientially represent is *that a black rock is remaining in the same place and
     something in the vicinity is moving upward*, which is not impossible. There are also
     plausible accounts of the experiences of "impossible figures" on which their con-
     tents are not in fact impossible (Bayne 2010: 53–58).

4

HOW DOES EXPERIENCE REPRESENT THE WORLD?

Acquaintance with a property involves standing in a certain representational relation to the property; the externalist claims that the relevant relation brings in external conditions.

—Michael Tye (2009)

There are cases in which representing a property crucially depends on causal contact with external instances of it, but there are also many cases of representation that do not work like this.

—David Chalmers (2010)

On the representational view of experience, for you to have an experience of a blue sphere is for you to "experientially represent" (that is, for it to experientially seem to you) that something has the properties *being bluish*, *being round*, and *being in front of oneself*. Likewise, having an olfactory experience of mint is just a matter of experientially representing the co-occurrence of the properties *being minty* and *being in a certain diffuse region in front of oneself*. Even bodily sensations like pain represent qualities as occurring in bodily regions. In illusion and hallucination, the way you experientially represent the world to be (the way it experientially seems to be) doesn't correspond to the way it really is.

In the previous chapter, we looked at the basic representational approach. We were mainly concerned with how it might explain the externally directed character of experience.

In this chapter, we will look at some more developed versions of the representational view, which explain in different ways how we manage to experientially represent the world. And we will be mostly concerned with the following question:

> What version of the representational view best explains internal dependence as well as external directedness?

This fits with the central puzzle of this book. We know from first-person reflection on what experience is like that it is essentially externally directed. But then we discovered from science that it is also internally dependent. How can both of these things be true? For representationalists, the puzzle concerns how soggy grey matter "in here" enables us to experientially represent a variety of colors, shapes, and other perceptible properties as occurring "out there" in external space. In illusion and hallucination, such representations are internally generated and occur in the absence of real objects having those properties, but they are still externally directed. And, as we shall see, there is evidence that, even when you have a totally normal experience of a blue ball, the explanation of why you experience a bluish quality and not some other quality most directly resides in your neural processing, not anything in the external world. Yet you still experientially represent that quality as occurring "out there". How is this possible?

4.1 Two questions for representationalists

I said that in this chapter we will look at different versions of the representational view. They differ in how they answer two questions facing representationalists.

On the representational view, every experience has two elements. In particular, every experience involves *experientially representing* an array of *perceptible properties*. For example, your experience of a blue sphere is depicted in Figure 4.1.

The character of the experience is fully determined by the perceptible properties that you experientially represent. So representationalists face the following two questions.

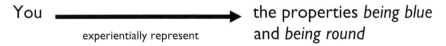

You ⟶ the properties *being blue*
experientially represent and *being round*

Figure 4.1 On the representational view, every experience has two elements.

First, the *perceptible properties question*. In previous chapters, we have been especially interested in the sensible properties. The term *sensible properties* refers to certain distinctive families of qualities presented to us in experience over and above spatial and temporal properties: for example, sensible colors, audible qualities, smell qualities, pain qualities. The term *perceptible properties* is a more general, catch-all term referring to all of the properties presented to us in experience. On the representational view, they include all the properties we experientially represent (the properties that the arrow in Figure 4.1 is directed at). The perceptible properties question is: what is the nature of these properties? When you view a blue sphere, it is natural to think that the spatial property *being round* that you experientially represent is a mind-independent, physical property of the ball, so that your representation of its shape is accurate. But what about the sensible property of being bluish that you experientially represent? Should representationalists follow naïve realists and say that it is also a mind-independent, physical property of the ball – for instance, a property constituted by the way the ball reflects light? Or should they perhaps say that the ball's way of reflecting light is not the same as the bluish quality you experience, that the ball is in fact intrinsically colorless, but that your brain nevertheless experientially represents it as bluish because this helps you to identify the ball – a helpful illusion? This would be akin to the sense datum view (Chapter 1).

Second, there is the *representation question*. In addition to a theory of the nature of perceptible properties, representationalists need to say something about the nature of the experiential representation relation that we bear to these properties (depicted by the arrow in Figure 4.1). For instance, suppose a representationalist thinks that the apparent blue quality of the ball is just a way of reflecting light. She still faces the further question: what is it for you to *experientially represent* this property? In other terminology, can she explain in more basic terms what it is for it to *experientially seem* to you that something has this property, so that it is ostensibly *present to* your mind? Or must she take this as basic and not to be further analyzed?

In this chapter, we will consider three varieties of the representational view (see Figure 4.2). We will see that they give quite different answers to the perceptible properties question and the representation question.

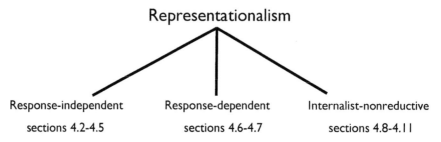

Figure 4.2 Varieties of the representational view.

4.2 Response-independent representationalism

We start with *response-independent representationalism*. We can introduce this view by analogy. Let's pretend that a mercury thermometer experiences temperatures. According to a response-independent representationalist theory of those experiences, temperatures are levels of mean molecular kinetic energy, which are independent of thermometers. Further, the mercury thermometer "experiences" particular temperatures by representing them. And it represents them because its mercury levels have the function of detecting them. It doesn't experience its own internal mercury levels; it only experiences the external temperatures that they represent. According to response-independent representationalism, the qualitative characters of the mercury thermometer's imaginary "experiences" are entirely fixed by what external temperatures it detects and thereby represents. So there is a sense in which its internal states don't matter. For instance, a "thermoelectric" thermometer that detects the same temperatures by way of producing a temperature-dependent voltage has the very same experiences, despite its very different internal states.

Response-independent representationalists provide a parallel account of your experiences. Look back at Figure 4.1. In answer to the perceptible properties question (about the properties the "arrow" is pointed to), they hold such properties are reducible to response-independent physical properties of items in your environment. In answer to the representation question (about the nature of the "arrow"), they hold that you experientially represent these properties because the hidden neural states (patterns of neuronal activity) of your sensory systems have the function of detecting them.[1]

For example, color qualities are identical with reflectance properties (tendencies to reflect varying amounts at light at different wavelengths), odor qualities are identical with chemical properties, audible qualities are identical with complex physical properties, and so on. True, these qualities don't seem to be identical with complex physical properties. Still, on this view, that is what they are. (Compare: water doesn't seem to be H_2O, but that is what it is.) They are *response-independent* in the sense that they do not depend on how sentient creatures respond to them. For instance, the reflectances of ripe fruits and those of background foliage objectively constitute vivid, highly contrasting colors – this is not just a matter of how we evolved to experience them.

So this view tells the following origin story for experience. Even before sentient creatures evolved, the sky was blue. And, if a tree fell in a forest, it made a sound with loudness, pitch, and timbre (O'Callaghan 2007). Then sentient creatures like you and me evolved. We have sensory systems with the biological function of detecting the occurrence of these pre-existing properties, just like thermometers have the function of detecting pre-existing temperatures. For you to experientially represent that something has a certain perceptible property (for it to experientially seem to you that something has a certain perceptible property) is for you to be in an internal physical state that has the function of detecting that something has the perceptible property *and* for that internal state to be directly available to a cognitive system. On this view, then, the following identity holds: the mental relationship *x experientially represents property y* is identical with the complex physical relationship *x is in an internal physical (e.g., neural) state that is available to a cognitive system and that has the biological function of detecting y*. Call this complex physical relationship the *detection relation* for short.[2]

For example, suppose that you view a blue-looking sphere a few feet in front of you. You undergo neural states with the function of detecting the spatial properties *round* and *three-feet away*. You also undergo a neural state with the function of detecting the "blue" reflectance, which on this view constitutes the quality *blue* that you experience. These internal neural states are "bound together" in your brain. This constitutes your experientially representing that there is something before you that is round, three-feet away, and blue. So it vividly seems to you that there is such a thing. To be clear, the idea is not that you experience your own internal neural states. You experience the world; your internal neural states enable you to do so.

Response-independent representationalism may seem similar to "naïve realism", which also holds that the brain plays an enabling role. But it is still a representationalist view. The character of your experience is grounded in how you experientially represent the world to be, not the actual state of the world (see Section 5.2 for more on the difference).

Response-independent representationalism is a radically "externalist" account of the character of experience. Michael Tye, a proponent of this approach, puts it in a slogan:

> Peer as long as you like at the detailed functioning of the brain. That is not where phenomenal character is to be found. Neuroscientists are looking in the wrong place (Tye 1995: 162–163) ... *Phenomenal character is in the world* (Tye 2009: 119, my italics).

For example, suppose you smell a cloud of R-limonene molecules. It will smell citrus-like to you. On response-independent representationalism, the citrus-like quality that you experience *just is* this *chemical-type*, and you experience ("experientially represent") it by undergoing a neural state that normally detects it. This implies that any possible creature that undergoes a state that detects the same chemical-type must experience the same citrus-like quality, no matter what its internal neural processing is like. If we discover an alien that has an internal state with the function to detect the same chemical type, then it will experience the same citrus-like quality, even if that internal state is very different from your own. The phenomenal (experiential) character of the experience is pinned down by the chemical-type, not the nature of the neural state.

On response-independent representationalism, then, we can be conscious of olfactory qualities, color qualities, and so on, only because these qualities are in the world, and our brains are connected to them in the right way — our internal states have a history of detecting them. Our brains do not generate qualities but just enable us to perceive the qualities that were already there. The brain needs help from the world to generate the consciousness of qualities; it cannot do it all on its own.

To illustrate, imagine that, as by magic, a duplicate of your brain forms purely by chance in an otherwise empty universe (a brain-in-the-void, or BIV for short), and by chance undergoes the same neural states that you actually undergo when you see a blue sphere and smell a citrus-like smell. (We considered this example in Section 2.6.) On this view, even though it undergoes the same neural states as you, the BIV would not have any experiences of (would not "experientially represent") any perceptible properties. This is because in the BIV those neural states don't have the historical, biological function of detecting anything. They don't "mean" anything. Compare an insect crawling in the sand on another planet and, purely by chance, leaving a trace in the sand that looks like our word "round". This trace in the sand wouldn't mean *round* or anything else.

That, in a nutshell, is response-independent representationalism. Why believe it? Perhaps the strongest motivation takes the form of a "generalization argument". To illustrate, suppose that you have an experience of a blue-looking sphere. The whole issue of color is a vexed one in philosophy (as we saw in Chapter 1). Is the color blue in the world, or is it "in the mind"? So the argument starts with the experience of the apparent round shape of the sphere, which most people think is a response-independent property of the sphere. Then the argument generalizes to the experience of the blue color:

(1) The shape *round* is a real, response-independent property of the sphere that we experientially represent because we undergo a neural state that has the function of detecting its occurrence in the external world.

(2) If that is so, then it is reasonable to think that the color blue is also a response-independent property of the sphere that we experientially represent because we undergo a neural state that has the function of detecting its occurrence in the external world.

Step 1 of this generalization argument is plausible. Nearly everyone accepts that the perceived roundness is a real, response-independent property of the physical sphere. The sphere might have had this property even before humans evolved. Our visual system detects the occurrence of this property by means of light. So it is very natural to hold that you came to experientially represent it because you undergo a state that has the function to detect it, in the same way that thermometers came to represent temperatures. The details are disputable (Byrne and Hilbert 2003: 8), but something like this is very natural. In fact, the neuroscientists Hubel and Wiesel (1959) discovered that specialized neurons in the visual cortex respond to specific features of an image such as angles, lines, curves, and movement.

Now turn to step 2 of the generalization argument. Step 1 suggests the general hypothesis that the experiential representation relation just is the detection relation. And this requires generalizing response-independent representationalism to the experience of other perceptible properties. For instance, if representation is detection, we must say that the blue quality that you experience is the property your visual system has the function of detecting. It is standardly assumed that your visual system has the function of detecting ("recovering") response-independent "reflectance properties". So, given the detection theory of representation, the quality blue that you experience must be a response-independent reflectance property of the sphere. You experientially represent the color and shape in the same way:

your visual system has the function of detecting these properties. The result is an attractively uniform view.

Let me address several questions you may have about response-independent representationalism.

First, since thermometers detect temperatures, how can response-independent representationalists avoid the absurd result that thermometers experientially represent temperatures – that they have experiences? They answer that a system *experientially* represents properties only when the system undergoes states that have the *biological* function of detecting those properties and these states are *poised to feed into a cognitive system*. We satisfy these conditions but thermometers do not.

Second, you may be wondering whether response-independent representationalism can be generalized to all sensory-perceptual experiences. For instance, pain qualities are intuitively not response-independent properties of disturbances in the body that could exist apart from experience. Despite this intuition, many response-independent representationalists have extended their approach to pain. They say that a pain in your hand has a sensory dimension (e.g., throbbing, intense) and an affective dimension (it bothers you). The sensory aspect of your pain is to be explained in terms of your experientially representing (by way of detection) response-independent properties of the disturbance in your hand.

Third, because response-independent representationalists locate the explanation of experience in the world, you may wonder how they can accommodate different experiences of that world. For instance, dog-fish experience magnetic fields, and pigeons experience ultraviolet (UV) reflectance-types. To explain this, response-independent representationalists hold that magnetic fields and UV reflectances constitute alien qualities that we cannot imagine. Generalizing, for every physical property, it is identical with some quality (although we cannot grasp the alien qualities). When the dogfish detects a magnetic field, it experiences some alien quality constituted by that field. When the pigeon detects UV light, it experiences an alien color constituted by that light. That is, objects have a plurality of different colors, and the visual systems of humans and pigeons "select" different colors for us to be conscious of. This is called a *selectionist* account of variation.

There are also examples of experiential variation among humans. For instance, the same color chip might look pure blue to Jane and green-blue to John. Here response-independent representationalists might invoke either the selectionist account or the illusion account. On a selectionist account, the chip has both colors, where those colors are identical with distinct but overlapping ranges of reflectances. John's visual system detects one of them and Jane's visual system detects the other (Byrne and Hilbert 1997: 272–273). On an illusion account, one detects the "true" color of the chip, while the other represents a slightly different color that the chip does not possess – a mild illusion (Byrne and Hilbert 2003: 17).

Finally, how does response-independent representationalism accommodate illusion and hallucination? For example, suppose that you stare at a bright red surface for a minute and then you look at a grey surface. It will appear tinged with green. On response-independent representationalism, the explanation is that this causes your visual system to malfunction, so that you are put into a neural state that normally has the function of detecting a green reflectance (which on this view just is the quality green), even though a green reflectance is not present in this case. So you experientially represent green even though nothing green is there. An analogy: if a thermometer is on the blink, it might read "60" even though it is really 50 degrees out. The same account applies to hallucinations.

In sum, response-independent representationalism is appealing. It accommodates the *externally directed* character of experience. It also accommodates *internal dependence* in illusion and hallucination. And it makes experiential representation no more mysterious than thermometer representation. For these reasons, it has been the most popular variety of representationalism. Might it be the correct solution to the puzzle of perception?

The plan for the rest of the chapter is as follows. In Section 4.3, we will start with so-called "armchair" arguments against response-independent representationalism. They are so-called because they are based on "intuitions" you can have while sitting in an armchair, without needing to consult the empirical findings about sensory experience. We will find that armchair arguments are somewhat questionable.

This will lead us to look at whether response-independent representationalism fits with empirical findings in Sections 4.4 and 4.5. We will find that there is reason to think not. In particular, in many cases, it may not after all fully accommodate the empirically-determined role of internal factors.

This will set the agenda for the remainder of the chapter. In Sections 4.6 and 4.7, we will consider whether "response-dependent" representationalism accommodates the role of internal factors. In Sections 4.8–4.11, we will turn to "internalist" representationalism.

4.3 Armchair arguments against response-independent representationalism?

Armchair arguments against response-independent representationalism have been very prominent.

One famous armchair argument concerns the *inverted earth* case (Block 1990). Here on Earth, Sally looks at the blue sky. On the response-independent view, she has a bluish experience because her neural state – call it B_{17} – has the biological function of detecting the blue reflectance of the sky. Now imagine another planet, "inverted earth". On inverted earth, the color of the sky is "inverted": it has the yellow reflectance rather than the blue reflectance. By an amazing coincidence, some creatures evolved on this planet that are very much like humans here on earth. But there is one difference. They evolved with "inverting lenses" in their eyes. Now imagine that one of them – Twin Sally – looks at the sky. Even though the sky is yellow, the inverting lenses mean that she is put into the same neural state – B_{17} – that Sally is in when he looks at the blue sky here on earth. In Sally's species here on earth, this neural state has the biological function of detecting the blue reflectance. In Twin Sally's species on inverted earth, this same neural state B_{17} has the biological function of detecting the yellow reflectance. The same neural state, in the different populations, detects quite different external colors. So, on response-independent representationalism, Twin Sally has a yellowish experience, because B_{17} enables her to experientially represent (experience) the yellow reflectance, which constitutes the quality *yellow*. Therefore, this view implies that Sally and Twin Sally have different experiences, even if their internal neural state B_{17} is exactly the same. Such examples show that response-independent representationalism violates the thesis of the *intrinsicness of experience*: the thesis that "intrinsic" (roughly, internal) duplicates must have the same experiences (see Hawthorne 2004 for a more precise formulation).

Many consider this to be a *reductio ad absurdum* of response-independent representationalism. For how could individuals differ concerning whether they see blue (or have a headache, or whatever) unless they differ in some internal, intrinsic respect? Many philosophers seem to think that we can know *a priori* that this is impossible. That is, we can know "prior to" or "independent of" empirical investigation that experience is an intrinsic or internal affair, just as we can know in this way that 2+2=4. For example, Ned Block (1994: 516, 518) and Tyler Burge (2003: 412, 444) assume the intrinsicness of experience without offering empirical evidence.

Hawthorne (2004: 352) and Horgan and Tienson (2002: 531n.23) explicitly say that this is just something we can know *a priori*.

What should response-independent representationalists say in response? Some well-known proponents, such as Dretske (1995: 151) and Tye (2000: 120), concede that the intrinsicness of experience enjoys *a priori* support. Still, they maintain that the case for their theory is so strong that we must give it up, even if that is a cost.

However, an alternative, more hardline response is available. According to this response, the intrinsicness of experience is just not something we have any *a priori* reason to believe, in the way we have *a priori* reason to believe that 2+2=4. So giving it up has no intuitive cost at all. We can see this by noting that pre-modern thinkers such as Plato, Euclid, and Ptolemy accepted a theory of vision, the *extromission theory*, which runs counter to the intrinsicness of experience (Winer *et al.* 2002). To see this, suppose that Jules and his identical twin, Jim, are looking at different objects, one blue and the other green. The extromission theory holds that there are rays going out from their eyes and toward objects, and they simply experience what the rays hit. So, on this theory, even though they have totally different color experiences, Jules and Jim's internal processes, which generate the ray, might be exactly the same. Jules and Jim are like two identical flashlights directed at differently colored objects.

Of course, our modern theory of vision is the *intromission theory*. We all know that light proceeds from objects to the eye. But my point here is only that the externalism about experience proposed by Plato, Euclid, and Ptolemy could not be ruled out *a priori*. If it could be ruled out just by pure thought (like 2+2=5), then geniuses like Plato, Euclid, and Ptolemy would never have accepted it. If this is right, then we also cannot rule out response-independent representationalism *a priori* just because it violates the alleged intrinsicness of experience (but see the Discussion Box for how a twist on the inverted earth thought-experiment leads to a quite different puzzle for this view).

Here is another armchair argument against response-independent representationalism (Block and Fodor 1972: 172; Shoemaker 1994: 24; Levine 1997: 109; Chalmers 2010: 400, n. 7). Imagine you look at a ball that looks dark blue. The response-independent representationalist identifies having a dark bluish experience with undergoing an internal state that has the function of detecting the "dark blue" reflectance-type. But why should detecting this reflectance-type constitute *that* color experience and not some other? The connection seems totally arbitrary. There is an "explanatory gap".

Discussion Box: The Middle Earth case and the puzzle of experiential indeterminacy

Here is a fanciful twist on the inverted earth thought-experiment, which raises a new puzzle for response-independent representationalists. Suppose that after a while Harry and Sally's earth-like planets, Earth and Inverted Earth, undergo extreme global warming. So they decide to flee to a new planet, Middle Earth, that is midway between their planets. This is when Harry met inverted Sally. Even though Sally's species evolved on a different planet, she happens to be very human-like. As a result, Harry and Sally can interbred and have a child. They name her "Mary". Suppose that she is born blind – in fact she doesn't even have eyes – but she does have a visual cortex. However, even though her visual cortex receives no external stimulation, one day it undergoes spontaneous neural activity. (Compare the spontaneous neural activity of those with Charles Bonnet syndrome, which results in vivid hallucinations. See Chapter 1.) In this way, her visual cortex is put into neural state B_{17}. This situation raises a big puzzle for response-independent representationalists. On this view, Mary will hallucinate a color, but *what* color? Mary's neural state B_{17} has the function of detecting the blue reflectance in her mother's population and it has the function of detecting the yellow reflectance in her father's population. Given the symmetry, they cannot say that she experientially represents (experiences) the one but not the other – that would be bizarre and arbitrary. So maybe they should say that it is "metaphysically indeterminate" whether she experientially represents blue or yellow – it is determinate that she experientially represents one of them but it is indeterminate which one it is. (It is not just that we cannot know which.) But, given representationalism, this would mean that it is indeterminate whether Mary enjoys bluish phenomenology or yellowish phenomenology. And such radical experiential indeterminacy is inconceivable. Lycan (2019a) responds to this kind of problem, but doesn't consider this specific example.

For example, the following "altered spectrum" scenario is conceivable: an individual from a different species could undergo a neural state that has the function of detecting this same reflectance property and yet have a different color experience ("altered spectrum"). For instance, they could have a light blue experience, or even a greenish experience ("color inversion"). Since this scenario is so easy to conceive, we have reason to think it is possible.

But if this is really possible, response-independent representationalism fails. For, on this view, this altered spectrum scenario shouldn't be possible: if they detect the same reflectance, then they must have exactly the same dark bluish experience that you have.

The argument from the intrinsicness of experience depended on the idea that intrinsic duplicates must have the *same* experiences. The argument from the conceivability of altered spectrum depends on the claim that an individual who detects the same reflectance-type as you could have a different experience.

What should we think of the argument from the conceivability of altered spectrum? One problem with the argument is that it works equally well against alternative views. So it may come back to bite those who deploy it against response-independent representationalism. For instance, Block and Fodor (1972) and Shoemaker (1994) use this argument against response-independent representationalism, and go on to defend an alternative "internalist" view that holds that the character of a dark bluish experience is constitutively linked to the internal neural state rather than to the external reflectance-type detected. But the same argument can be re-deployed against this view. For the link between having a dark blue color experience and having a certain neural state appears just as contingent as the link between having a dark blue experience and detecting a certain reflectance. It is easy to conceive that two individuals should have the same total neural state, but different color experiences. In this sense, the "explanatory gap" is just as wide in both cases. Armchair intuitions do not discriminate between the view that the character of experience is fixed by the external reflectance-type detected and the view that it is fixed by the nature of the neural state.

Because the altered spectrum conceivability argument threatens any view on which experience is determined by something physical (whether internal or external), most philosophers think that there must be something wrong with it. The standard response is that "conceivability doesn't entail possibility". Most think our experiences are necessarily pinned down by something physical, even though this is not evident to us in having experiences (just as it is not evident that water is H_2O). So we find it conceivable that experience should vary independently of physical conditions, even though this is not really possible.

4.4 The problem of internal dependence about sensible properties

We have just seen that the armchair arguments of Block, Chalmers, and Shoemaker are questionable. To evaluate response-independent representationalism, we must get out of our armchairs and look at the science of sensory experience. When we do, we find that it fits poorly with empirical findings.

We saw at the end of Section 4.2 that response-independent representationalism can accommodate internal dependence in illusion and hallucination. But in the present section we will see that decades of research in psychophysics and neuroscience support the idea that, even in *normal experience*, the explanation of why you experience one sensible property rather than another resides in the nature of your internal neural state, not the external physical property detected. Response-independent representationalism does not accommodate this kind of internal dependence. In fact, it is directly opposed to it. Their slogan is "the explanation of phenomenal character is to be found in the objective world, not the brain", but the science shows that in many cases the opposite is true. We will illustrate the problem by looking at pain, smell, and color.[3]

To begin with, consider the sensory intensity of pain. For example, suppose that you put your hand in some water that is increasing in temperature within the painful range. The sensory intensity of your pain increases in a fine-grained way. Minute temperature increases cause discriminable increases in sensory intensity. According to response-independent representationalists, this consists in your pain system experientially representing (that is, detecting) increasing values of some fine-grained physical magnitude in your hand. But what physical magnitude? In general, what constitutes the sensory intensity of pain?

One option available to response-independent representationalists is to say that pain intensity is constituted by your experientially representing levels of nociceptive activity. In one version, the relevant activity is peripheral activity in your skin (Armstrong 1968: 315, 319). In another version, it is nociceptive activity in your spinal cord, even if the pain feels to be in your skin (Hill 2017: 65ff).

But, in either version, the nociceptive option doesn't fit with what response-independent representationalists say about other cases. For instance, they do not say that the visual system has the function of detecting (and enabling us to experience) receptor activity in the eyes or in the visual pathway, but rather reflectances of the external object. To be consistent, they should say that the pain system does not have the function of detecting nociceptor activity in the hand or the spinal cord, but a biologically significant property of the stimulus, such as a dangerous temperature level or tissue damage.

This suggests that response-independent representationalists must hold that the intensity of thermal pain is constituted by the representation of skin temperature (or degree of difference from neutral skin temperature).

Maybe the intensity of other pains is constituted by the representation of the size and extent of tissue damage (burn, cut, etc.).

Let us leave the details to one side. Are *any* of these forms of response-independent representationalism about sensory intensity empirically plausible? Psychophysics and neuroscience seem to go against it.

To begin with, psychophysics has shown that there is *bad external correlation*. Even in biologically normal conditions, sensory intensity is very poorly correlated with the external stimulus. For example, for thermal pain and electric shock, there is a power function relationship with an exponent greater than one. So, a small change in the stimulus could lead to a gigantic change in sensory intensity. Sensory intensity is also a function of stimulus size and duration, in a way that cannot be systematized. For pains involving tissue damage (wounds and burns), there is not a good correlation between pain intensity and the size of the tissue damage. Pain intensity is not even well correlated with peripheral nociceptive firing rates.

At the same time, neuroscience has revealed *good internal correlation* (Price and Barrell 2012: 203). There is a simple, uniform, indeed linear relationship between pain intensity and firing rates of cortical neurons in the pain-matrix. Coghill and coworkers (1999) presented subjects with noxious temperatures and then measured the resulting neural activity with fMRI. As they put it: "Many cortical areas exhibit significant, graded changes in activation linearly related to pain intensity" (1999: 1936). Many studies show the same thing.

It's obvious that the explanation of sensory pain intensity resides in the brain, and not in the stimuli. But this conflicts with response-independent representationalism. To make this precise, consider the example depicted in Figure 4.3.

Suppose that, in the actual world, you put your hand in some water that is increasing in temperature within the noxious range between 43°C and 50°C. The bottom line in Figure 4.3 represents the actual relationship between increasing temperatures in the noxious range and the firing rates of neurons in the pain matrix. To some extent, the exact steepness of this curve is a fluke of evolution. So, consider a hypothetical situation where everything is the same, but for one thing: because of fluke differences in humans' evolutionary history, in this hypothetical situation, the psychophysical response curve relating increasing noxious temperature to increasing firing rates of pain neurons is quite steeper than it is in the actual world (Figure 4.3, top curve). In this situation, the increasing temperatures are not more harmful, but the cortical firing rates increase much more rapidly.

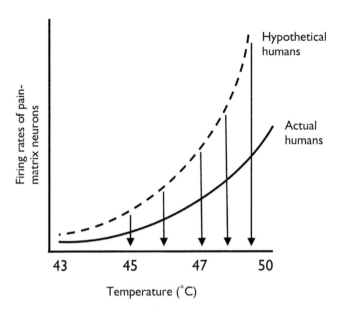

Figure 4.3 The relationship between painful temperatures and neural response in actual humans and in hypothetical humans.

In particular, there is an amped-up neural response in both the "primary somatosensory cortex" (which codes for the sensory intensity of pain) and the anterior cingulate cortex (which codes for the "affective dimension" of pain). So, in the hypothetical situation, people are even more likely to withdraw their hands from the water as it increases in temperature.

Imagine that in this hypothetical situation your counterpart puts her hand in the water going from 43°C and 50°C. Would the sensory intensity of her thermal pain increase more rapidly than your own? The description so far leaves this open. But, of course, given that cortical firing rates are the best and simplest predictor of sensory pain intensity, the most reasonable answer is yes.

But response-independent representationalism delivers the opposite verdict. This is because, even though your counterpart's firing rates increase more rapidly than your own, they have the function of detecting the same external physical properties (whether those be temperature differences, peripheral nociceptor activities, or whatever). This is indicated in Figure 4.3 by the arrows. Compare: two fire alarms might differ in loudness but represent the same thing, namely fire. So, on this view, even though your counterpart's neural response is amped up and she has a stronger tendency to withdraw, she should experientially represent (experience) exactly the same properties throughout the process that you do. So, on this view, there should be no difference in how quickly the sensory intensity of her pain increases in this situation.[4] This picture seems to be undermined by the empirically-demonstrated dependence of pain intensity on internal factors.

A second illustration of response-independent representationalism's inconsistency with internal dependence concerns the experience of smell. As in the case of pain, psychophysics has revealed bad external correlation (Mainland 2018: 15). Cowart and Rawson (2001: 568) write:

> Available evidence indicates that numerous chemical and molecular features (e.g., molecular weight, molecular mass and shape, polarity, resonance structure, types of bonds and sidegroups) can all influence the odorous characteristics of a chemical. However, no systematic description of how these characteristics relate to particular odor qualities has been developed. In other words, chemicals that bear little resemblance structurally can smell the same, and chemicals that are nearly identical structurally can elicit very different experiential qualities.

Here is an actual illustration. Suppose that you consecutively smell the odorants shown in Figure 4.4: citral, R-limonene, and R-carvone. As a matter of fact, you will experience citral and R-limonene as having similar but distinct citrus-like smell qualities and you will experience R-carvone as having a minty smell quality. So, in respect of their qualitative characters, your experience of R-limonene (the middle chemical-type) resembles your experience of citral more than your experience of R-carvone. On response-independent representationalism, this fact about the resemblance-order among your experiences should consist in the resemblance-order of the response-independent *chemical-types* which your olfactory system detects and thereby represents, because these constitute the smell qualities that you experience (Byrne 2003: 645). But, by any natural measure, it is not the case that R-limonene resembles citral more than R-carvone – in fact, if anything, the opposite is true. There is bad external correlation; there is a huge mismatch between the resemblance-order of your smell experiences and the resemblance-order of the chemical-types that the olfactory system has the function of detecting. How then could the sensory resemblance-order of your smell experiences consist in the resemblance-order of the chemical-types your olfactory system detects and thereby represents?

Recent neuroscience suggests that the best explanation is instead to be found in the brain. While there is bad external correlation, there is good internal correlation. For instance, Howard and coworkers (2009) used fMRI to look at distributed spatial-temporal neural patterns produced by

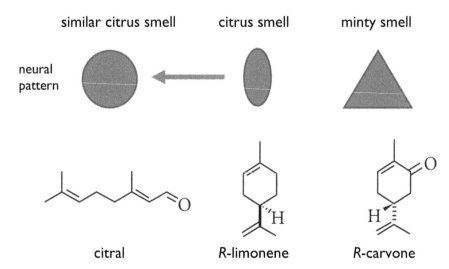

Figure 4.4 The degree of similarity between smell experiences much better matches that between internal PPC neural patterns (represented here by shapes) than that between the external chemical-types detected by those experiences.

different odorants in "posterior piriform cortex", or PPC for short. They analyzed the similarities among these neural patterns and found that neural similarity nicely predicted qualitative similarity, even when chemical similarity did not. Neural similarity, then, is the *only* predictor of smell similarity.

In fact, Howard and coworkers looked at the above example. Even though it is not the case that R-limonene resembles citral more than R-carvone, your PPC *neural representation* (distributed neural pattern) of R-limonene *does* resemble your PPC-neural representation of citral more than your PPC neural representation of R-carvone, in perfect agreement with the resemblance-order of your smell experiences (see also Youngentob *et al.* 2006). This is illustrated in Figure 4.4. Here the shapes represent PPC neural patterns (Prinz 2012: 126–133), and the arrow indicates similarity.

To illustrate the conflict between these scientific findings and response-independent representationalism, consider a hypothetical situation. In this situation, humans' PPC neural representations of citral and R-carvone are the same as in the actual world. But, because of differences in their postreceptoral wiring, their PPC neural representation of R-*limonene* is different than in the actual world; in particular, in the hypothetical situation, it is more similar to their PPC neural representation of *minty-smelling R-carvone* than it is similar to their PPC neural representation of the citrus-smelling citral – the exact opposite of how things stand in the actual world. (So, looking at Figure 4.4, imagine that the "circular" neural state is replaced by a triangular one, similar to but distinct from the one produced by minty smelling R-carvone.) As a result, whereas in the actual world you would put the R-limonene in the same category as the citrus-smelling citral, in the hypothetical situation your counterpart puts it in the same category as the minty-smelling R-carvone. Since neural similarity is the only good predictor of smell similarity, we should say that in this different scenario he experiences R-limonene as minty rather than as citrus-like – similar to but distinct from the way R-carvone smells.

But response-independent representationalism mistakenly delivers the opposite verdict. For we can stipulate that, even though your counterpart's neural representation of R-limonene differs from your actual neural representation, it has the function of detecting the same chemical-type. (An analogy: even though the Spanish word "rojo" differs from the English term "red", it means the same thing.) Then, on this view, the different neural state should enable your counterpart to represent, and thereby experience, the very same citrus smell quality that you experience in the actual world.

Let us turn to a final example involving color experience. Pretheoretically, we are strongly inclined to accept externalism here: color qualities are response-independent qualities out there in the world, and the character of our experience is determined by which of them we experience. That is why we started with examples about pain and smell as warm-up exercises. If empirical findings convinced you that an internalist model is right for pain and smell, then parallel findings about color experience should lead you to accept an internalist model here as well, even if it is contrary to your pretheoretic inclination.

To illustrate, suppose that, at different times, you experience a purple-looking grape, a blue-looking sphere, and a green-looking leaf (see Figure 4.5). Your color experience of the sphere resembles your color experience of the grape more than your color experience of the leaf. On response-independent representationalism, the color qualities you experience are the reflectance properties of these objects that your visual system consecutively detects and thereby represents. So the resemblance-order among your experience consists in the resemblance-order of those reflectance properties (Byrne 2003: 645). The trouble is that the reflectance of the sphere is not more like the reflectance of the grape than the reflectance of the leaf. If anything, the opposite is true (MacAdam 1985).

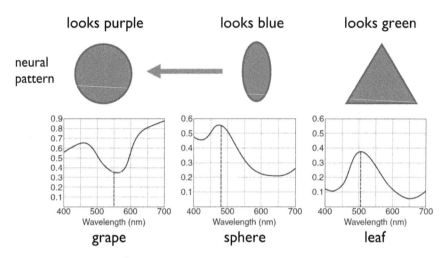

Figure 4.5 The degree of similarity between color experiences much better matches that between V4 neural patterns (represented here by shapes) than that between the reflectance properties of objects.

As in the cases of pain and smell, neuroscience suggests that the best explanation is instead to be found in the brain. While there is "bad external correlation", there is "good internal correlation". For instance, Bohon and coworkers (2016) analyzed the responses of "glob cells" in the posterior inferior temporal cortex (part of the V4 complex). Here is what they found:

> For the glob population, the arrangement of the [neural responses] clearly reflects color space: points of the same hue irrespective of luminance level are plotted next to each other, and the progression of the points forms a circle that proceeds according to the color wheel. Behavioral judgments of the similarity between colors closely match the similarities between the neural responses to these colors by the glob population.
>
> (Bohon *et al.* 2016: 18)

Given this, we can conjecture that, even though the reflectance of the sphere does not resemble the reflectance of the grape more than the reflectance of the leaf, your *V4 neural representation* of the sphere resembles your V4 neural representation of the grape more than your V4 neural representation of the leaf (see Figure 4.5). This is what explains why your color experience of the sphere resembles your color experience of the grape more than your color experience of the leaf.

To illustrate the conflict with response-independent representationalism, we can use a hypothetical situation that parallels the one about smell. In this hypothetical situation, everything is the same except for one thing: because of naturally evolved differences in humans' postreceptoral wiring, their V4 neural representation of the sphere resembles their V4 neural representation of the *green-looking leaf* more than their V4 neural representation of the purple-looking grape – the opposite of how things stand in the actual world. (So, looking at Figure 4.5, imagine that the "circular" V4 neural representation of the sphere is replaced by a triangular one, similar to but distinct from the V4 neural representation of the green-looking leaf.) We can also suppose that, whereas in the actual world people tend to sort the sphere with the purple-looking grape, people in the hypothetical situation sort the sphere with the green-looking leaf.

Now suppose that your counterpart in this hypothetical scenario consecutively looks at these objects. Since the only difference is that their V4 neural representation of the sphere resembles their V4 neural representation of the green-looking leaf more than their V4 neural representation of the purple-looking grape, and since this is the best predictor of color experience, there is reason to think that they would have a greenish experience of the sphere, rather than the bluish experience you have in the actual world.

But response-independent representationalism delivers the mistaken verdict that you and your counterpart have the same color experiences despite the vast neural and behavioral differences. For we can stipulate that your counterpart's V4 neural representation of the sphere, although different from your own, has the function of detecting the same reflectance property of the sphere. In general, your counterparts' neural states have the function of detecting the same reflectance properties. Since your counterpart's color experience of the sphere represents the "blue" reflectance, this view wrongly predicts that your counterpart should have the same bluish experience that you have, despite the radical difference in his V4 color processing and categorization behavior.

In short, on viewing the sphere, you and your counterpart experience distinct color qualities because of the internal neural difference, just as in the previous cases you and your counterpart experience different pain intensities and smell qualities. But you stand in the function-to-detect relation to the same reflectance-type. Therefore, we must reject the claim of response-independent representationalism that experiencing is detecting and color qualities are reflectance-types.

What is unique about these hypothetical examples is that there is massive variation between you and your counterpart in internal neural processing and behaviors but a complete coincidence in what external response-independent properties your sensory systems have the function of detecting. We can call them *coincidental variation cases*. And we can equate *internal dependence* about the sensible properties with the claim that, in some such cases, you and your counterpart have different experiences, despite the complete coincidence in what external response-independent properties your sensory systems have the function of detecting. Response-independent representationalists cannot handle this by employing either the "illusion gambit" or the "selection gambit" discussed in Section 4.2. Since we stipulate that the internal neural states of you and your counterpart's sensory systems, although different, have the function of detecting the same properties under biologically normal conditions, they must hold that you and your counterpart accurately represent the same properties. So they are stuck with the mistaken verdict that you and your counterpart have exactly the same experiences, despite the neural and behavioral differences. They fail to accommodate internal dependence about the experience of sensible properties.

Notice that the empirical evidence for the role of internal processing is strongest for our experiences of "sensible properties". It may be weaker when it comes to our experiences of spatial properties (shape, size, distance, number, motion). For instance, if the apparent length of a line doubles, then the length that your neural state has the function of indicating doubles. This is true even if the experience of the line is a total hallucination. So here, unlike in the cases of pain, smell, and color, there is a "good external correlation" between the character of experience and the character of the physical properties in the world that our neural states have the function of detecting. The problem of internal dependence for response-independent representationalism chiefly concerns the experience of *sensible properties*, such as pain qualities, smell qualities, and color qualities.

In response to this problem, response-independent representationalists might emphasize the virtues of their view. They have a nice explanation of the externally directed character of experience. They also have a nice explanation of illusion and hallucination. True, they must reject internal dependence about our experience of sensible properties in the sense just explained. But maybe that is a price worth paying.

However, the findings of bad external correlation and good internal correlation provide strong evidence for internal dependence about our experience of sensible properties. In fact, if those findings don't convince you, what empirical findings would convince you? And the problems for response-independent representationalism do not end there.

4.5 Other problems about sensible properties

There are two additional problems for response-independent representationalism that we must consider. They concern its identification of sensible properties with response-independent physical properties.

First, there is the *problem of meaning*. This problem arises out of the same empirical findings we reviewed in the previous section. But it is a distinct problem.

Let me introduce the problem with an analogy. If heat is mean molecular kinetic energy, true statements about heat must express (or "mean") truths about molecular kinetic energy. For instance, "object *a* is hotter than object *b*" expresses the truth that *a* has a higher mean molecular kinetic energy than *b*. The problem is there are many true statements about sensible properties that cannot be mapped on to purely response-independent truths about external physical properties.

For instance, suppose that you consecutively smell the chemical-types shown in Figure 4.4 and you are asked to judge their resemble-order. You will then assert:

[1] The second citrus smell resembles the first citrus smell more than the third minty smell.

On response-independent representationalism, these smell qualities are just identical with the corresponding response-independent chemical-types shown in Figure 4.4. So, on this view, your statement [1] is true just in case your use of the predicate "x resembles y more than z" means an entirely response-independent ("objective") relation, *Resembles*, such that the second chemical-type *Resembles* the first chemical-type (on the left) more than the third chemical-type (on the right). But the second chemical-type does *not* in any obvious way objectively resemble the first chemical-type more than the third – if anything, it resembles the third more than the first. This is a case of "bad external correlation". So what in the world could this response-independent *Resembles* relation be? As Cowart and Rawson write in the passage quoted in the previous section, there is simply no kind of chemical resemblance that lines up with smell resemblance. Therefore, response-independent representationalists have no plausible way of accommodating [1]. This is a reason to reject the claim that smell qualities are response-independent chemical-types.

The problem arises for color too. Suppose you look at the grape, the blue-looking ball, and the leaf (Figure 4.5). You will assert:

[2] Blue resembles purple more than green.

Response-independent representationalism implies that [2], if it is true, is a truth about the objective resemblance-order of the reflectance-types shown in Figure 4.5. But there is no evident sense in which the blue reflectance-type is more like the purple reflectance-type than the green reflectance-type. In fact, by a natural measure, the blue reflectance-type is more like the *green* reflectance-type than the purple reflectance-type. So if the colors *just are* the reflectance-types, it's hard to avoid the absurd result that "blue is intrinsically more like *green* than purple"! This is a reason to reject a purely response-independent account of the colors in terms of reflectances.

How might response-independent representationalists respond? We saw in the previous section that resemblances among experienced sensible properties *do* line up nicely with resemblances among distributed neural responses in the brain. So it would be extremely natural to hold that our statements about such resemblances are somehow made true by resemblances among these *neural responses*. But this would be to give up response-*independent* representationalism and move to response-*dependent* representationalism – the kind of representationalism we will consider next. What response-independent representationalists need, if they wish to retain their view, is a purely response-independent account of [1] and [2].

Byrne and Hilbert (2020, 2003) have attempted a purely response-independent account of [1]. First, they assert that there are four basic *hue-magnitudes*, namely, *being reddish, being greenish, being yellowish,* and *being bluish*. They identify each of these four hue-magnitudes with different *disjunctions* of reflectances (Byrne and Hilbert 2003: 55). Thus, for instance, in their view, something is bluish just in case it has the purple reflectance, *or* the blue reflectance, *or* ..., and so on. Call this disjunction D. From the point of view of physics, the disjunction is utterly miscellaneous – the disjuncts have nothing interesting in common. Byrne and Hilbert claim that, when you said "blue resembles purple more than green", somehow you meant something equivalent to the following complex condition (although of course you didn't know that this is what you meant): the blue reflectance and the purple reflectance, but *not* the green reflectance, belong to the miscellaneous disjunction D (that is, they are disjuncts of this disjunction).

However, this may not be an adequate, general answer to the problem of meaning. For one thing, how did your sentence "blue resembles purple more than green" come to mean something about this highly idiosyncratic and unnatural objective relation among reflectances (rather than, say, something to do with our subjective neural responses)? For another thing, nothing like the hue-magnitude account applies in other cases. For example, no such account could be applied to your statement about smell-resemblance [1].[5] For, while smell qualities resemble more or less closely, they do not uniquely fall into special "smell categories" in the way that colors fall into special "hue categories" (Mainland 2018: 15–16). In general, there is no hope of explaining [1] in response-independent terms. There is just no kind of chemical similarity that lines up with smell similarity. The physical correlate of smell similarity is only to be found in our neural responses. And once we give up on a purely response-independent theory of smell, we have little reason to insist on a purely response-independent theory of color.

In fact, the problem of meaning arises equally for brightness, taste qualities, pain qualities, audible qualities, and so on. Structural relations among these qualities (e.g., increases in brightness, equal pitch intervals, ratio relations among loudness-levels) simply do not map onto structural relations among the corresponding response-independent physical properties in the world, since the relationship between those physical properties and perceived quality is often non-linear and messy (Stevens *et al.* 1937, Hardin 1988). There is little hope of providing a response-independent account of all these truths about qualitative structure in response-independent terms.

We shall see in later sections that other forms of representationalism easily solve the problem of meaning. Together, these points provide a strong reason to reject response-independent representationalism and move to one of these alternatives.

So much for the problem of meaning. Next we turn to another problem for the idea that all perceptible properties are response-independent physical properties of things: *the percipi problem*. (This is related to the percipi problem for the act-object theory discussed in Section 1.7.) To appreciate the problem, let's first start with a contrasting example involving color that is *not* a problem for response-independent representationalists.

Suppose that you are looking at a blue sphere. You focus on the bluish quality that seems to pervade the round region. Now consider:

[3] That bluish quality could occur even if no one experiences it.

Response-independent representationalists are committed to [3]. They hold the blue quality that you are referring to is in fact a response-independent reflectance represented by your visual system. And that reflectance could of course occur even though no one is having an experience. This implication of response-independent representationalism is not obviously wrong. So far, so good.

But now suppose you cut your finger. You focus on the pain quality that seems to pervade the finger. Now consider:

[4] *That* very same quality could occur even if no one experiences it.

Now, response-independent representationalism implies [4] just as it implies [3]. For, on this view, although you don't know it, the quality you are focusing on is in fact a response-independent physical property of your finger represented by your pain system, such as *being cut* or *undergoing some peripheral nociceptive activity*. And this physical property could occur even if no one feels pain. Imagine, for instance, a totally disembodied hand being cut and having its nociceptors stimulated. But while we find [3] acceptable, we find [4] absurd. For pain qualities, *esse est percipi*. That is, necessarily, if a pain quality occurs, then someone must have an experience of it. So response-independent representationalism fails in the case of pain (see Cutter 2017b; Bradley 2021).

4.6 Response-dependent representationalism

We have seen that there are reasons to reject response-independent representationalism. The chief problem is that it doesn't fully accommodate internal dependence: the dependence of our experiences of things on our neural responses to those things. This brings us to response-dependent representationalism.[6]

To introduce response-dependent representationalism, we can use the same thermometer analogy we used to introduce response-independent representationalism. Suppose that a mercury thermometer and thermoelectric thermometer (which works by producing a temperature-dependent voltage) are in a room that is 70 degrees. Do they have the same "experience" of the temperature, or do they have different "experiences" due to their different internal states? We saw that, on response-independent representationalism, they have the same experience because they detect and hence represent the same response-independent temperature *70 degrees*, even though they do so via different internal states. Response-dependent representationalism disagrees. On this view, the thermometers represent different things. The mercury thermometer represents the air as *causing the response of mercury level L in itself* (where L is the level caused by 70 degrees). The thermoelectric thermometer represents the air as *causing the response of voltage level V in itself*. So they "experience" the air as having different properties.

Response-dependent representationalists provide a similar account of our experiences. It may solve the problem of internal dependence (Section 4.4) as well as problems about sensible properties (Section 4.5).

Let us begin with the problem of internal dependence. To illustrate, consider our last example in Section 4.4. You and your counterpart view the same sphere. Because of the internal color processing difference between you and your counterpart, you and your counterpart experience the distinct color qualities, blue and green, as pervading a round surface "out there", even though your visual systems have the function of detecting the same response-independent reflectance property of that sphere. Given representationalism, this means that you and your counterpart experientially represent distinct sensible colors "out there".

Response-dependent representationalists' account of your and your counterpart's different experiences resembles the above account of the different "experiences" of the two thermometers. The sphere has the following two properties: it is *disposed to produce V4 neural state n in you* and it is *disposed to produce a different V4 neural state n' in your counterpart*. These dispositional properties belong to the external sphere but they are bound up with your neural responses to the sphere. Response-dependent representationalists put forward the following speculative hypothesis: the bluish quality that you experience just is the first dispositional property of the sphere and the greenish quality that your counterpart experiences just is the second dispositional property of the sphere.

Of course, the bluish quality and greenish quality do not seem to you and your counterpart to be such dispositions – they seem to be intrinsic, non-dispositional features of the ball. Still, according to this theory, that is what they are.

On this view, sensible colors are real properties of external things. But they are response-dependent properties of things: they are defined in terms of the responses they are disposed to cause in the brain. So, before we evolved, things had no sensible colors (although they had reflectances), because they had no dispositions to produce V4 neural states. The sensible colors of things *co-evolved* with perceiving organisms.

Response-dependent representationalism can be extended to the experience of smell and pain. There are countless distinguishable smell qualities and pain qualities. On response-dependent representationalism, each one is identical with a disposition of external items (odor clouds, body parts) to cause a specific, distinguishable neural response. What response-dependent properties you experientially represent depend on your neural responses to those external items.

Response-dependent representationalists presumably do not hold that all the perceptible properties that we experientially represent are response-dependent properties involving our sensory systems. After all, we experientially represent various spatial and temporal properties – shapes, positions, distances, motions – and these are certainly not response-dependent properties of the form *being disposed to produce so-and-so neural response.*[7] The idea is only that the *sensible properties* (sensible colors, smell qualities, pain qualities) we experientially represent are response-dependent properties of this kind. This fits with the point, mentioned in Section 4.4, that the evidence for internal dependence is strongest when it comes to our experience of sensible properties.

In sum, response-dependent representationalists need a complex, non-uniform answer to the *perceptible properties question* – the question of the nature of the properties that the "arrow" is directed at in Figure 4.1. As you view the sphere, the blue sensible property you experientially represent is a complex response-dependent property of the sphere, but the round shape is a response-independent property.[8]

Response-dependent representationalism may also be able to answer the problems about sensible properties we covered in Section 4.5. To illustrate, consider statement [1] above. On a response-dependent theory, the smell qualities are not the response-independent chemical-types shown in Figure 4.4. Rather, they are dispositions of external odorants to cause PPC neural patterns (they are dispositions to produce the neural "shapes" in Figure 4.4). The similarity relations among these PPC neural responses match the similarity relations we judge to hold between the smells. So, on the response-dependent theory, [1] comes out unproblematically true. Similar remarks apply to statement [2] about the resemblance among colors. Finally, since it defines the pain qualities felt in bodily regions in terms of producing certain responses in sentient organisms, response-dependent representationalism may be better placed to accommodate the *"percipi* claim" that pain qualities are necessarily experienced.

In short, unlike response-independent physical properties, response-dependent properties nicely correlate with sensible properties in their resemblance relations. So maybe our "best guess" should be that sensible properties are in fact complex properties of external items involving their dispositions to cause neural responses in us, even though this is not at all perceptually evident.

Could response-dependent representationalism be the solution to the puzzle of how experience is internally dependent as well as externally directed? The answer to this question depends on whether it is a workable view. And there are grounds for doubt.

4.7 Two problems with response-dependent representationalism

The first problem concerns response-dependent representationalists' answer to the perceptible properties question. In particular, that answer violates some very plausible claims about the perceptible properties.

To see this, consider the example where you and your counterpart look at the sphere. To you, it seems that a bluish quality fills a round region in a certain place. To your counterpart, it seems that a greenish quality fills a round region in a certain place. Here are some things we somehow just know. Or, at least, they are intrinsically plausible core beliefs we have about color qualities. (i) These qualities are incompatible with one another – a single surface cannot have both of these qualities at the same time. In the same way, a surface cannot be round and square. (ii) Color qualities are actualities, not mere possibilities. When a surface has a color quality, this is a matter of the actual character of the surface. It is not just a matter of what the surface might do. It is not just a matter of potentiality or possibility. (iii) These qualities can only belong to an item that is extended, that is, that has volume and takes up space. Neither quality, therefore, could belong to a subatomic particle that is point-sized in the sense that it lacks volume. Any theory that violates these beliefs is a mistaken theory of sensible colors.

Response-dependent representationalism violates all of these color beliefs. It violates (i) because it holds that the two qualities are dispositions to produce distinct neural states, both of which dispositions the sphere actually possesses (Shoemaker 2019: 478). It violates (ii) because it holds that these qualities are mere dispositions or tendencies of physical surfaces (McGinn 1996).[9] And it violates (iii). To see this, consider a fanciful scenario. There could be an organism with a super fine-tuned "visual system" that can detect the presence of a single sub-atomic particle that is "point-sized" and has no volume. In this scenario, this point-particle might be disposed to cause neural state n. So, on a simple response-dependent theory, the point-particle would have the color quality *blue* despite not taking up space, violating the link between having a color quality and taking up space (Cutter 2016).

Therefore, there are reasons to think that sensible colors, whatever they are, cannot be dispositions to produce neural states. Response-dependent representationalism's answer to the perceptible properties question is problematic.

The second problem with response-dependent representationalism concerns its ability to answer the representation question. Look back at Figure 4.1. Representationalists face the perceptible properties question and the representation question. Response-dependent representationalists like Shoemaker (1994) answer the perceptible properties question, as we have seen. But they neglect the representation question. How might they explain the "arrow" in Figure 4.1? How do such complex and specific response-dependent properties, rather than response-independent properties, become present out our minds, so that they can shape the character of our experience? Shoemaker (1994: 37) briefly mentions the question but concedes "I have no fully satisfactory answer".

In fact, response-dependent representationalism may be unworkable because there is no answer to the representation question compatible with its answer to the perceptible properties question.[10]

To begin with, recall that response-dependent representationalists claim the following:

> [i] When you and your counterpart view the sphere, there is a relation of experiential representation R (the "arrow" in Figure 4.1) that you bear to the property *normally causing neural state n* and that your counterpart bears to the property *normally causing neural state n'*.

But what could representation relation R possibly be? That is the representation question as it arises for response-dependent representationalists.

Response-dependent representationalists cannot identify R with "the detection relation". For your neural state n doesn't have the function of detecting the response-dependent property *normally causing neural state n*. And your counterpart's neural state n' doesn't have the function of detecting the different response-dependent property *normally causing neural state n'*. Rather, these neural states have the function of detecting the same response-independent reflectance-type.

To appreciate the point, return to our thermometer analogy. The internal states of the mercury thermometer and those of the thermoelectric thermometer do not have the function of detecting different response-dependent properties about how the air affects their own internal states. Rather, they

have the function of detecting the same response-independent temperatures, such as 70 degrees.

In short, a "detectivist" theory of experiential representation fits
with response-independent representationalism but it doesn't fit with
response-dependent representationalism. Response-dependent representationalists cannot say that R in their claim [i] is the detection relation.

Could response-dependent representationalists say that R is some other
relation, yet to be specified? The problem is that it is hard to specify *any*
representation relation that you and your counterpart bear to the relevant
different, idiosyncratic response-dependent properties of the form *normally
causing so-and-so neural response.*

In fact, the problem gets worse. For response-independent representationalists also claim:

> [ii] When you and your counterpart view the sphere, you two also bear experien-
> tial representation relation *R* to the same response-independent shape property,
> *being round.*

According to response-dependent representationalists, then, on viewing
the sphere, you and your counterpart experientially represent two radically
different types of properties. You experientially represent a color property of the sphere, which on this view turns out to be identical with a
response-dependent property of the form *normally causing neural state n*. And
you experientially represent the shape property *being round*. According to
response-dependent representationalists' non-uniform answer to the perceptible properties question, this is a totally different kind of property.
It is not a response-dependent property of the form *normally causing neural
state n*. It is a response-independent property. It follows that response-
dependent representationalists require a peculiar kind of "representational
discontinuity".

This makes it even harder for response-dependent representationalists
to answer the representation question. For they must specify a relation R
that satisfies (ii) as well as (i). Such a relation R would have to be one that
you and your counterpart bear to different response-dependent properties
of the sphere (which on this view constitute the color qualities you experience) *and* that you also bear to the same response-independent shape of
the sphere.

If such a relation cannot be specified, then response-dependent representationalists cannot answer the representation question in a way that is
consistent with the claims they want to make.

4.8 Internalist-nonreductive representationalism: the basic idea

Let us take stock. Experience is internally dependent as well as externally directed. When you view the sphere, you experientially represent blue rather than green in external space because of your internal neural response to the sphere. This chapter is about what variety of representationalism best explains how this is possible.

The varieties of representationalism we have considered so far are "reductive". They *identify* experiences with complex physical states. In this way, they resemble the internal physical state view (Chapter 2), but they explain experience in terms of "external" physical states rather than internal ones. For instance, response-independent representationalism identifies the sensible property blue with a physical reflectance-type, and it identifies experiential representation with a complex "detective" relationship between the brain and such external physical properties. Response-dependent representationalism identifies the apparent blue quality of the external sphere with its disposition to produce a neural response.

But we saw that these views face serious problems. Response-independent representationalism fails accommodate internal dependence. Response-dependent representationalism showed initial promise in accommodating internal dependence, but it faces other problems.

Internalist-nonreductive representationalists think that the history of failed attempts to reduce experientially representing blue to something else suggests that, while experientially representing blue *depends on* internal physical processes in the brain, we cannot *reduce it to* anything physical. In the present section, I will explain the basic idea. In the next sections, we will address questions about the basic idea.

The easiest way to get a handle on internalist-nonreductive representationalism is by starting with pain. Imagine having an experience of a pain in your foot. It is both externally directed and internally dependent. You experientially represent a pain quality as "down there" because of neural processing "in here". (If it were a phantom pain, it would be a misrepresentation.) This quality cannot be reduced to a response-independent physical property of your foot, and your experientially representing it cannot be reduced to detecting it (Sections 4.5 and 4.6). Nor can the pain quality be reduced to a disposition to produce a neural response (Section 4.7). The pain quality is irreducible. It "is what it is and not another thing". Our brains "invented" a novel and horrible quality, and enabled us to experientially represent it as located in parts of our bodies, as a sign of damage.

Internalist-nonreductive representationalists take a parallel view of the experience of color. When you view the sphere, you experientially represent the color quality blue "out there" because of neural processing "in here". You only have access to the quality, not the underlying neural processing. This quality cannot be reduced to a response-independent reflectance-type that was out there before we evolved (Sections 4.5 and 4.6). In fact, the quality blue, just like the pain quality, was just not out there before we evolved (Locke 1869, II.viii.16). The physical world consisted in colorless atoms arranged in the void of space. Nor can the quality blue be reduced to a disposition to produce a neural response. The quality blue is irreducible. To adapt a phrase of Gertrude Stein, "a color is a color is a color". The brain is a productive faculty. Our brains invented the quality blue and other colors, and enabled us to experientially represent them as occurring in an antecedently colorless world, in order to help us recognize and remember objects. As Cosmides and Tooby (1995, xi) put it, "color is an invention that specialized circuitry computes and then projects onto physically colorless objects".[11] So the way our brains came to represent colors is nothing like the way thermometers represent temperatures. It is not the case that colors were out there before we evolved, and we came to experientially represent (experience them) by detecting these pre-existing properties. That origin story is incorrect.

To illustrate the internalist character of this view, return to an example mentioned in Section 4.2, that of a life-long "brain in the void" (BIV), cut off the external world. By some cosmic accident, it undergoes all the same neural states as you. On internalist nonreductive representationalism, the BIV experientially represents the same pain qualities and smell qualities as you. It also experientially represents the same color qualities. When it comes to the experience of sensible properties, bad external correlation and good internal correlation (Section 4.4) suggest that the external cause is irrelevant; all that matters are the internal neural states.

Since experientially representing color qualities requires experientially representing them as filling spatial regions in a certain place, the BIV also experientially represents spatial properties. For instance, BIV has a vivid hallucination of a blue and round thing in front of it (see Figure 4.6). Since the BIV has the same experiences as you, BIV mistakenly believes it lives in a world populated by objects and people in space, but it is all a hallucination. So internalist representationalists generalize their account of the

round shape

BIV hallucinates a blue sphere

Figure 4.6 Your BIV duplicate.

experience of sensible properties to the experience of spatial properties (more on this "generalization argument" in Section 4.10).

Therefore, internalist-nonreductive representationalists hold that the kind of empirical findings reviewed in Section 4.4 (together with the "generalization argument" to be discussed in greater detail in Section 4.10) support across-the-board *experiential internalism*: *all* aspects of experience are fully determined by internal neural states (Section 2.2). This differs from *internal dependence* as formulated in Section 4.4, which only said that internal processing plays a role in our experiences of *sensible properties*.

In sum, internalist-nonreductive representationalists' answer to the perceptible properties question is that many of them − namely sensible properties like pain qualities, smell qualities, and color qualities − are irreducible. Their answer to the representation question is that your experientially representing items having perceptible properties is something we cannot reductively explain in other terms (e.g., in terms of undergoing neural states that detect those properties). In other words, the fact that it experientially seems to you that the world is filled with certain perceptible items cannot be identified with any more fundamental fact. This is a basic notion. This does not mean it is totally inexplicable. It is fully explained by your internal neural processing.[12]

Internalist-nonreductive representationalism resembles the sense datum view (Chapter 1). On both views, experiences are fully dependent on internal neural states, but they are something more than those internal neural states (contrary to the internal physical state view discussed in Chapter 2). However, the two theories differ on what that "something more" is.

On the sense datum view, your brain has an innate capacity to generate sense data with various colors and shapes, and to enable you to stand in a special experience relation to those sense data.

By contrast, on internalist-nonreductive representationalism, your brain has an innate capacity to enable you to experientially represent that there are objects with colors and shapes. So the brain does not really generate sensible properties or objects with sensible properties. Rather, it merely generates "seeming-states" in which it seems that there are such objects. Our experiences are those seeming-states. There don't exist sense data; there only seem to exist sense data.

So if you like the way in which the sense datum view solved the "external-internal" puzzle, but you don't like sense data, then you may like internalist-nonreductive representationalism. It is like the sense datum view but without sense data. It is the sense datum view on the cheap.

That, then, is internalist-nonreductive representationalism. Why believe it? The case for it is an inference to the best explanation. It may best explain how experience is externally directed and internally dependent. In fact, external directedness and experiential internalism lead directly to it.

To see this, consider the following little argument involving the brain in the void (also discussed in Section 2.6). The empirical evidence for internal dependence (Section 4.5) suggests that the BIV could have the same blue-sphere experience that you have. Given that representationalism is the best explanation of essential external directedness, in having this experience, the BIV stands in the experiential representation relation to the property of being round (among other properties). True, on this view, the BIV doesn't experience a non-physical sense datum that possesses that property – there only seems to be such an object. But the *property* still exists, and the BIV is mentally related to it. In particular, the BIV experientially represents that something has this property (in more ordinary language, it seems to the BIV that something has the property). In Figure 4.6, this is indicated by the solid arrow. However, the BIV doesn't have any interesting physical relationship to that property, such as the detection relation. It is physically cut off from interaction with all round things. In Figure 4.6, this is indicated by the dotted arrow being crossed out. So the experiential representation relation (solid arrow) is distinct from the detection relation (dotted arrow). Even when you view a blue sphere and experientially represent the property of being round, that is not reducible your undergoing a neural state that detects that shape, because the BIV example shows that these two things are separable. In short, internal dependence and external directedness imply that the experiential representation relation is irreducible to any physical relationship, even if it depends on the internal physical state of the subject's brain (Speaks 2015: 272; Block 2019: 426). That is just what internalist nonreductive representationalism says.

In addition, unlike the other forms we have discussed, internalist-nonreductive representationalism can accommodate our core beliefs about colors. On this view, sensible properties are irreducible properties, distinct from both response-independent physical properties (e.g., reflectance-types, bodily damage) and response-dependent dispositions to cause neural states. So we can credit them with all the structural features they seem to have. For instance, we can say that blue is more like purple than green, even if it is not the case that the blue-reflectance is more like the purple-reflectance than the green-reflectance (Section 4.5). We can say that pain qualities are mind-dependent ("the *percipi* intuition"), even if the types of bodily disturbance that cause them are mind-independent. And we can say that distinct colors are incompatible in that a single surface cannot have two distinct colors at the same, even if a single surface can have multiple dispositions to produce different neural states (Section 4.7).

There is a final advantage of internalist-nonreductive representationalism. Versions of representationalism that try to reductively explain experiential representation in terms of your sensory systems having the function of detecting external conditions imply that in some cases it is radically indeterminate what experiences an individual undergoes because it is indeterminate what their sensory systems have the function of indicating (see the Discussion Box in Section 4.3). Internalist-nonreductive representationalism avoids this problem. What you experientially represent is always fixed by your neural states, which cannot be radically indeterminate.

The basic approach of internalist-nonreductive representationalism ("internalist representationalism" for short) raises many questions. In the following sections, we will look at a few. First, as I formulated the view above, it holds that, before sentient creatures evolved, colors-as-we-see-them did not belong to physical objects. So does this view violate our commonsense color beliefs, such as "tomatoes are red"? Must internalist representationalists *treat color as wholly illusory?* Second, while the internalist model is plausible for pain and color, it is hard to believe when it comes to spatial experience. We tend to think that spatial properties are "out there" and that in experience we simply detect these pre-existing properties. Is internalist representationalism *plausible for spatial experience?* Finally, the view holds that the brain has an intrinsic capacity to experientially represent a variety of perceptible properties that are not in the world or brain. Is internalist representationalism *too mysterious to be believed?*

4.9 Must internalist representationalists treat color as illusory?

Internalist-nonreductive representationalists hold that sensible properties are simple and irreducible properties that the brain "invented". They also hold that they did not belong to physical objects prior to the evolution of sentient creatures.

Strictly speaking, this is compatible with the view that objects somehow acquired these properties when sentient creatures evolved. And, in fact, some internalist representationalists have taken this option. We will call it the *co-evolution view* of sensible properties. For instance, fruits evolved bright colors when we evolved to experience them as having bright colors.

This view is difficult and strange. It may help to introduce it with an analogy. Suppose that electric charge is fundamental and irreducible. Now imagine a fanciful theory. According to this theory, there is a weird law of nature to the effect that, if we all get together and just believe that a thing has a certain electric charge, then it will thereby acquire that electric charge. The electric charge of things is a fundamental physical property, but it is under the control of our minds, by way of a kind of telekinetic law.

The co-evolution view of sensible properties is similar. The sensible colors that we experientially represent things as having are irreducible and simple. But there is a single brute "law" to the following effect:

Color Law. If (and only if) an object comes to normally cause members of some population to experientially represent that object as having a certain irreducible color, then the object thereby acquires that irreducible color.

For example, suppose you perceive a spherical object (say a stone) that is very old. It existed before humans or other sentient creatures evolved. Before we evolved, it was just a colorless collection of atoms, which reflected equally colorless photons. But then we evolved a visual system that enables us to experientially represent the sphere as having the irreducible property *blue*. In this way, by the Color Law, it thereby acquired this irreducible color, in addition to its reflectance-type and other physical properties. In the same way, the sky came to be blue, lemons came to be yellow, tomatoes came to be red, and so on.

Unlike response-dependent representationalism discussed earlier in this chapter, the co-evolution view doesn't *reduce* colors to dispositions of objects to produce neural responses; rather, it holds that colors are irreducible properties that objects acquire when they are normally experienced as having those properties.

The Color Law only guarantees that all objects have the colors that they *normally* appear to have. So if an ice-cube looks pink because it is bathed in *abnormal* pink light, the Color Law doesn't imply that it acquires the irreducible color pink. Likewise, if in abnormal circumstances you should hallucinate a pink elephant, the Color Law doesn't entail that anything is pink.

This kind of co-evolution view can be applied to other sensible properties. For instance, maybe there is another special law to the effect that, if it *actually* seems to you that there is a pain quality in a bodily region, then *voilà* that pain quality really comes to exist in that region (Bradley 2021).

However, the co-evolution version of internalist representationalism faces problems. While we humans normally experientially represent the sphere as blue, imagine that the members of another species normally experientially represent it as green (as in the case discussed in Section 4.4). The Color Law will imply that the surface of the sphere is blue and green all over (just as the fanciful law about charge we started with would imply that the same object has two electric charges, if two groups have different beliefs about its electric charge). Therefore, it after all violates one of our core beliefs about colors: that such colors are incompatible with one another.

Second, the Color Law is framed using the notion of *normal conditions*. But this notion is unclear. For instance, take the granite of I. M. Pei's East Building of the National Gallery of Art. We experientially represent it as grey in diffuse daylight and pink in direct sunlight. Which lighting conditions count as normal? There are many possible answers. So there are many possible versions of the Color Law, appealing to different precise notions of "normal conditions", that give different verdicts about the distribution of irreducible colors among objects. The co-evolution view requires that one of them is a fundamental metaphysical truth. It is hard to believe that the fundamental metaphysical laws are arbitrary in that way.

Third, the Color Law that is part of the co-evolution view would add to the complexity of the world. It would be an extra, special law in nature going beyond the laws of logic and the laws of physics. Occam's razor counts against it.

Not only are there reasons to disbelieve the co-evolution view. There is no strong reason to believe it. The Color Law is not an *a priori* certainty, like 2+2=4. This is shown by the coherence of the illusion view about to be discussed next, which denies the Color Law. In fact, far from being an *a priori* certainty, the Color Law is quite strange. The only reason to believe the Color Law seems to be that it satisfies our commonsense opinion that things normally have the colors they appear to have. But why should nature be so obliging as to come outfitted with a law that guarantees that our commonsense opinion comes out true?

This brings us to another option: the illusionist version of internalist representationalism.[13] It is much more popular than the co-evolution view among internalist representationalists. It agrees with the co-evolution that before we evolved the sphere was intrinsically colorless – just a collection of colorless atoms in the void. And it agrees that we evolved so that it causes us to experientially represent the irreducible color blue. But it rejects Color Law. It rejects the idea that when this happened the collection of colorless atoms suddenly acquired the irreducible color blue. So our present color experiences are all illusory.

This view is like the sense datum theory, but it goes further. The sense datum view holds that, when you view the sphere, the physical sphere does not have the irreducible color blue, but it does hold that there exists a sense datum in your private visual space that has this property. By contrast, the illusion view we are considering holds that there exists *nothing* that has this property. When you view the sphere, it only seems to you that there exists such an object.

The same illusion view can be applied to all sensible properties: pain qualities, smell qualities, audible qualities, and so on. The illusion view has been popular since the 17th-century scientific revolution. As Galileo (1623/1957) said, "tastes, odors, colors, and so on reside in consciousness".

The illusion version of internalist representationalism is simpler than the co-evolution view because it rejects the arbitrary-looking Color Law.

Moreover, even though it is an illusionist view, it can accommodate many of our core beliefs about colors. For instance, it can accommodate "blue is more like purple than green", even if holds that nothing possesses these colors. Compare: there can be truths about resemblances among complex shapes, even if no objects happen to possess those specific complex shapes. Likewise, illusionists can accommodate our belief that blue and green necessarily exclude. Even if no surface is blue, it may be still be true that if a surface were to be blue then it could not also be green. And illusionists can accommodate the *percipi* intuition about pain in the sense that pain qualities cannot occur outside of experience.

In fact, illusionists might say that, even though the irreducible quality blue is not spread out on the surface of the physical sphere (as proponents of the co-evolution view maintain), "the physical sphere is blue" is true *in a sense*: it has a reflectance that normally causes us to experientially represent it as blue (Jackson 1977: 128; Chalmers 2010: chap. 12).

Far from being strange, the illusion view of sensible properties is perhaps what we would expect. The primary function of the sensory systems is to enhance adaptive fitness − not to represent the way the world really is. There is every reason to expect that this should sometimes involve embellishment or error, depending on an individual's unique ecology. For instance, regardless of whether fruits are objectively bright or sweet, we would have evolved to experience them as bright and sweet.

4.10 Is internalist representationalism plausible for spatial experience?

The empirical findings of good internal correlation and bad external correlation make internalist representationalism quite plausible for the experience of pain, smell, and color. These sensible properties were not out there before sentient creatures evolved. They are inventions of the brain.

But, as we noted at the end of Section 4.4, the empirical evidence for this kind of *internalist model* in the case of the experience of spatial properties is less robust. Here there does seem to be good external correlation. If the apparent length of a line doubles, then the length in the world that your neural state has the function of detecting doubles.

In fact, an internalist model of our experiential representation of spatial properties may appear downright implausible. Consider again your experience of the blue-looking sphere. Nearly everyone accepts that the perceived roundness is a real, response-independent property of the physical sphere. The sphere had this property even before humans evolved. In that case, it's very natural to hold that you came to accurately experientially represent this shape because you undergo a state that has the historical function to detect it, in the same way that thermometers came to represent temperatures. If so, the brain doesn't have an intrinsic capacity to experientially represent spatial properties in the way it has an intrinsic capacity to experientially represent pain, smell, and color. This capacity derives from interaction with external things possessing those properties.

In short, in the special case of experientially representing spatial properties, a *detectivist model* seems to be more plausible than the internalist model. In this case, you might think, response-independent representationalists have the right account.

Nevertheless, internalist representationalists wish to apply the same internalist model to the experience of spatial properties (shape, size, distance, orientation, up-down, left-right) that they apply to the experience of sensible properties (pain, smell, color). What arguments might they give for the internalist model of our experience of spatial properties, and against the natural detective model? We will briefly look at two arguments.

The first argument is a *generalization argument*. As we saw in Section 4.4, the empirical case (based on "bad external correlation and "good internal correlation") for an internalist model of the experience of pain, smell, and color is persuasive. But once we accept an internalist model of the experience of colors, we can use the following argument to "bootstrap" our way to an internalist model of the experience of spatial properties:

(1) Given the internalist model of color experience, the BIV experientially represents the same blue color as you, thanks to its internal neural processing (Section 4.8).

(2) Since colors necessarily appear to fill up space (even in hallucinations), the BIV must experientially represent some spatial properties as well, thanks to its internal neural processing.

The conclusion amounts to an internalist rather than a detectivist model of spatial perception. You could experientially represent spatial properties, even if you were a BIV that never detected their occurrence in the external world. The brain has an intrinsic capacity to experientially represent spatial properties, just like it has an intrinsic capacity to experientially represent colors, smells, and pains. The result is an across-the-board internalist model.

When we introduced response-independent representationalism (Section 4.2), we considered a generalization argument for the opposite conclusion: an across-the-board detectivist model. According to that argument, if the externalist-detectivist ("thermometer") model applies to the experience of spatial features, it is reasonable to extend it to the experience of color. The above argument is also a generalization argument, but it runs in the reverse direction. Since there is overwhelming empirical evidence for the contrary view that the experience of color is internally generated, so too must be the experience of space.

This argument for an internalist account of spatial perception has some persuasive force, but it is somewhat dissatisfying because it piggy-backs on the argument for an internalist account of color perception. Is there a more direct argument?

The *argument from physics* provides a more direct reason to accept an internalist model of the perception of space. Since Galileo and Newton, many prominent thinkers have advocated illusionism about colors, such as the apparent blue of the sphere. The case for this view is that colors are very different from their physical correlates (Section 4.5). Some prominent thinkers have suggested that we must generalize illusionism to spatial properties. Here, for instance, is Bertrand Russell:

> It is not only colours and sounds and so on that are absent from the scientific world of matter, but also *space* as we get it through sight or touch.
>
> (Russell 1912a: 45)

> The "real" shape is a shape in physical space, which has no more resemblance to visual shape than light-waves have to colour. Shape as [experienced] is in just the same position as colour. I suggest that the apparent shape "corresponds" as a rule to a real shape, due to relations having similar logical properties. But it is a case of correspondence, not identity, just as in the case of colours and their physical correlates.
>
> (Russell 1913: 79)

One argument for illusionism about spatial properties derives from Einstein's theory of relativity (Chalmers 2010, 2012). When you view the sphere, you experientially represent it as simply *round*, where that is not relative to anything else. (Likewise, when you experience two flashes as simultaneous, you experientially represent them as standing in a relationship that just depends on how the flashes are related.) But relativity theory tells us that the physical correlate is frame-relative. So what you experience is not out there.

Another argument for illusionism about spatial properties derives from the interpretation of quantum mechanics. In quantum mechanics, the fundamental elements are not things like particles and their positions in a familiar three-dimensional space of our experience, but a "wavefunction" in a high-dimensional "configuration-space" that evolves according to Schrödinger's equation. This suggests illusionism about the spatial properties we experience. As David Albert (1996: 277) puts it:

> The space we live in, the space in which any realistic understanding of quantum mechanics is necessarily going to depict the history of the world as playing itself out (if space is the right name for it - of which more later) is *configuration-space*. And whatever impression we have to the contrary (whatever impression we have,

say, of living in a three-dimensional space, or in a four-dimensional space-time) is *flatly illusory*.

This situation is depicted in Figure 4.7.

If illusionism about spatial properties is correct, then we have a direct argument for an internalist model over a detectivist model of our perception of space:

(1) Just as the quality *blue* does not occur in the world, so the shape *round* as we experience it doesn't occur in the world.

(2) Therefore, it cannot be that we experientially represent *round* by detecting its prior occurrence in the world; rather, the brain generates the experience of the shape *round* on its own, just as it generates the experience of the color blue on its own.

The result is a form of internalist-nonreductive representationalism that is uniform in two respects. First, it upholds a uniform internalism about experience: the experience of both colors and shapes is internally generated by the brain without help from the world. Second, it upholds a uniform illusionism: neither colors-as-we-experience-them nor shapes-as-we-experience-them are really in the world.

These doctrines fit together. If the brain "made up" the experiential representation of all perceptible properties (internalism), as internalist

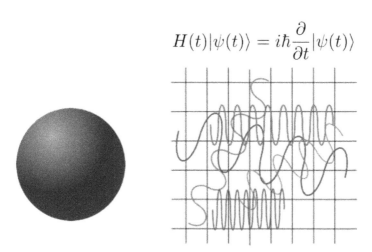

$$H(t)|\psi(t)\rangle = i\hbar \frac{\partial}{\partial t}|\psi(t)\rangle$$

Figure 4.7 Left: The world as you experience it. *Right:* The world as it really is, according to generalized illusionism. Neither blue-as-you-experience it or round-as-you-experience-it is really out there.

representationalism maintains, then it would be an inexplicable coincidence if those properties independently belonged to the objective world before sentient creatures evolved (response-independent realism). The puzzling coincidence is avoided if we deny that those properties independently belong to the objective world (irrealism).

This generalized illusionism is a "virtual reality" model of perception (Chapter 1). The real world is alien, and we are not acquainted with it. You may recoil from this view. But generalized illusionism cannot be easily dismissed. Even though experience provides a highly embellished representation of reality, it might help us navigate the world. The reason – as Russell notes in the above quote – is that there is a kind of structural match between the world as represented in experience and the world as it really is.

Further, we saw above that illusionists can say that "the physical sphere is blue" is true in a sense: it has a reflectance that normally causes us to experientially represent it as blue (Jackson 1977: 128; Chalmers 2010: chap. 6). In the same way, they can say that "the physical sphere is round" is true in a sense: it has an arcane quantum-mechanical property that normally causes us to experientially represent it as round.[14]

4.11 Is internalist representationalism mysterious?

We saw above that, in any form, internalist-nonreductive representationalists solve the puzzle of how experience is both externally directed and internally dependent by asserting the following:

> [#] Your brain has an intrinsic capacity to generate richly externally directed experiences in which you stand in an irreducible experience relation to perceptible properties (the color blue, the shape round), even if those properties don't occur *in* the brain or indeed anywhere at all.

To illustrate, when you view the sphere, the physical sphere in the external world causes you to go into a certain neural state, which in turn results in your experience. However, the world is inessential. Your neural state *on its own* is enough to generate the experience. If you were a brain in the void and you had the same neural state, it would generate a vivid experience in which you stand in an experiential relationship ("experiential representation") to the color quality *blue* and the shape *round*, even if the properties don't occur *in* the brain or indeed anywhere at all. Since in this scenario you wouldn't stand in any interesting physical relationship to these external properties, such as the detection relation, this experiential relationship must be a non-physical, mental relationship.

While [#] solves the external-internal puzzle, it faces some problems. How can you stand in an irreducible experiential relation to properties like *blue* and the shape *round* that are not "in the head", simply by virtue of undergoing neural states "in the head"? How did this capacity evolve? How did the brain manage to "invent" experiences of novel properties which are not instantiated in the brain?

Since the 1950s and 1960s, the philosophy of perception has been closely bound up with the broader project of "physicalism" which seeks to explain the mind in physical terms. We saw in Chapter 1 that most philosophers rejected the sense datum view because it seems to violate physicalism. It seems to require a mysterious and complicated "dualist" theory, with psychophysical laws connecting two things, namely our neural states and our non-physical experiences of sense data. Internalist-nonreductive representationalism gets rid of non-physical sense data, but in asserting [#], it still requires an irreducible relation of "experiential representation". So you may think it also leads to a form of "dualism" that requires a raft of special "psychophysical laws". For instance, one law might state that, if you are in a certain internal neural state, then you experientially represent the color *blue* and the shape *round* in external space. But such laws add to the complexity of our theory of experience. They also look arbitrary.

Other theories of experience reject [#], and therefore avoid these problems. For instance, on the internal physical state view (Chapter 2), your neural state doesn't "generate" an externally directed experience in which you stand in an irreducible experience relation to the external perceptible properties *blue* and *round*. Your experience simply is your neural state. And it doesn't essentially involve standing in any relation – much less an irreducible one – to the perceptible properties *blue* and *round*. Since experiences are identical with neural states, there is no need for psychophysical laws that connect them. On response-independent representationalism (Section 4.2), your neural state does realize an externally directed experience in which you experientially represent the properties *blue* and *round*. But, on this view, this is no more mysterious than the way in which a thermometer represents a temperature, as we saw.

How might nonreductive representationalists respond to these problems with [#]? They might offer a two-pronged defense. They might say that [#] is unavoidable, and that it is also not so bad after all. So the price is worth paying.

They might say that [#] is unavoidable because it is an inevitable consequence of two very well-supported claims about experience: internal dependence and external directedness. Take the blue-sphere experience. The empirical evidence for internal dependence suggests that your neural state is sufficient for this experience, so that even a brain in a void with the same neural state would have the same experience. Further, it is hard to deny that it is essentially externally directed: unlike a headache, it essentially involves the seeming presence of a round object, where that is certainly not a neural property. From these two claims, [#] inevitably follows: your brain has an intrinsic capacity to generate an experience in which you are related to the shape round, a feature that need not be instantiated in the brain. And, by the argument above, this relation cannot be identified with a physical relation. That comports with [#].

Internalist-nonreductive representationalists might add that [#] is not so bad after all. For one thing, it does not require giving up "physicalism" and moving to an antiquated "dualism" (see Section 1.9 to review these views). This is a big issue, but in brief the situation is this. Internalist-nonreductive representationalism rules out an austere "reductive" form of physicalism. But many philosophers already think we must reject reductive physicalism for other elements of the commonsense world, for instance, right and wrong, beauty, and numbers. Instead, they favor "grounding physicalism" (see the Discussion Box in Section 1.9). On this view, it is not possible to *reductively define* all elements of the commonsense world in terms of basic physics. But everything is still ultimately *grounded in* basic physics. If this general anti-reductive picture of the world is correct, then internalist-nonreductive representationalism no longer looks so strange. Our capacity to experientially represent perceptible properties is just another thing that is grounded in the physical (in particular, the brain) without being reducible.

In addition, maybe there are relatively simple, systematic connections between our intrinsic neural patterns and what perceptible properties (shapes, sensible colors, and the like) we experientially represent, even if we have not yet discovered them. And maybe, if we only knew them ("cracked the neural code"), we could look into a human brain, or a BIV, and systematically decode what shapes and other perceptible properties the subject experiential represents (Haynes 2009). Then internalist nonreductive representationalism would begin to look somewhat less complicated and mysterious.

Summary

We have looked at three varieties of representationalism with the aim of seeing whether it can adequately solve the puzzle of how experience is both externally directed and internally dependent.

Response-independent representationalism (the "thermometer model") makes experiential representation unmysterious. But it may not completely accommodate the dependence of experience on internal factors.

Response-dependent representationalism showed initial promise in accommodating internal dependence, but it faces other problems.

Nonreductive-internalist representationalism explains how experience is both externally directed and internally dependent. But it is somewhat mysterious and complicated.

Further Reading

In this chapter, we looked at an in-house dispute between "externalist" or "response-independent" representationalists and internalist-nonreductive representationalists. This is dispute is related to a larger debate in the philosophy of mind between proponents of the *reductive externalist program* (Fodor 1992; Millikan 1995; Neander 2017) and proponents of the *phenomenal intentionality program* (Kriegel 2011; Mendelovici 2018; Bourget and Mendelovici 2019).

We discussed an empirical argument for "internal dependence" based on bad external correlation and good internal correlation. In addition to the references in the text, for relevant discussion, see Adams (1987), Crouzet *et al.* (2015), Gescheider (1997), Haynes (2009), Schmidt *et al.* (2014), and Lee (2020).

As discussed in Section 4.10, a big issue for internalist representationalists is what to say about the experience of space. Kant (1781) defended something like "illusionism" on *a priori* grounds and Russell (1912, 1913, 1927) defended this kind of view on the basis of Einstein's theory of relativity. Chalmers (2010, 2012) similarly defends a kind of generalized illusionism on the basis of relativity theory and quantum mechanics. For relevant discussion, see Cutter (2017a, 2020), Epstein (2018), and Saad (2019). Ney and Albert (2013) is an excellent collection on the interpretation of quantum mechanics.

Notes

1   For defenses of response-independent representationalism, see Armstrong (1968, 1981), Tye (1995, 2000), Dretske (1995), and Byrne and Hilbert (2003, 2020). Lycan (2019a) and Hill (2009) accept something like response-independent representationalism, but they hold that some phenomenal differences among sensory experiences are grounded in functional or "syntactic" differences rather than representational differences. I should mention that there is another, *nonreductive* response-independent theory of perceptible properties called "primitivism". However, it is more popular among contemporary naïve realists than it is among response-independent representationalists. So I will save our discussion of it until Chapter 5 on contemporary naïve realism.

2   For the "function-to-detect" theory of experiential representation, see Dretske (1995), Williams (2020), and Neander (2017). Dretske (1995: 21) and Neander (2017: 201) both appeal to the idea that experiential representation is realized in the brain in an "analog" format in order to explain "novel contents" (e.g., the "missing shade of blue"). This will not play a role in what follows and may be ignored. There are many theories of representation that response-independent representationalists can choose from and they all face problems (Byrne and Hilbert 2003: 8). But all the points we will make about response-independent representationalism are neutral on the details.

3   For the empirical internal dependence argument, see Pautz (2003, 2010b). For discussion, see Allen (2016: 68–73), Berger (2018), Chalmers (2005), Cohen (2009: 82–88), Fish (2013: 58–59), Hill (2017: 65ff), Kalderon (2020: 335–336), and Price and Barrell (2012: 203). For a different argument based on introspection, see Mendelovici (2018: chap. 3).

4   Cutter and Tye (2011) concede that Tye's response-independent representationalism about sensory pain intensity implies that between you and your counterpart there is no difference in *sensory* pain intensity. They maintain that the only difference is that your counterpart's thermal pain bothers him more (an *affective* difference), because it indicates "higher probabilities of harm". But since your counterpart's "primary somatosensory cortex" undergoes an amped up response, and this is the best predictor *sensory* pain intensity, there is reason to think, as against this view, that the sensory intensity of his pain increases more rapidly. Also, in my present example, the increasing temperature is *not* more apt to harm your counterpart. For more discussion, see Cutter (2017b: 34).

5   There are also examples involving colors that Byrne and Hilbert's proposal has difficulty with. For instance, pink is a "singular" color. Even though it is just a light red, *pink is more different from red than (say) light blue is different from blue.* Brown is another singular color. Even though it is just a desaturated orange, *brown is more different from orange than light blue is different from blue.* If response-independent representationalism is true, these are response-independent truths about reflectance properties. But what truths? For instance, in what sense is the pink *reflectance-type* "more different" from the red *reflectance-type* than the light blue *reflectance-type* is different from the blue *reflectance-type*?

6   Response-dependent representationalism has been defended by Shoemaker (1994), Harman (1996), Kriegel (2009), Prinz (2012), and Mehta (2012). In what follows, for the sake of simplicity, I will focus on the version defended by Harman and Kriegel on which sensible properties are dispositions to produce *neural* responses.

7   Tye (2000: 79) holds that, when you view a tilted coin, you represent it as *being-elliptical-from-here.* Is this a counterexample to the claim in the text that the shape

properties we represent are not properties of the form *being disposed to produce so-and-so neural response?* No – Tye thinks that *being-elliptical-from-here* is certainly not such a property, but rather a response-independent but *viewer-relative* property. For a sophisticated view of this kind, see Hill (2009). For an overview, see Green and Schellenberg (2018).

8 Sydney Shoemaker, the originator of response-dependent representationalism, advocates such a non-uniform version of the view (personal communication).

9 Notice that the claim of response-independent representationalism that color qualities are *reflectance-types* also violates (i), since reflectance-types are mere *dispositions* to reflect light.

10 For the representational problem for response-dependent representationalism, see Pautz (2010b), Byrne and Hilbert (2017), and Cohen (2020).

11 The case for internalist-nonreductive representationalism is also very strong in the case of the experience of *phoneme-type*s (see Section 5.6) and *tickles* (Galileo 1623/1957).

12 Internalist-nonreductive representationalism is defended by Chalmers (2010), Crane (2003), Horgan (2014), and Pautz (2006, 2010b). Mendelovici (2018) and Levine (2019) defend related views. For recent discussion, see Block (2019) and Speaks (2015). A clarification: proponents of this view of course allow that what *physical objects* you count as perceiving (which might be considered part of "representational content") is determined by external factors: namely, which physical objects cause your internal processing. Their view is just that what *perceptible properties* you experientially represent are internally determined.

13 The illusionist version of internalist representationalism is defended by Chalmers (2010) and Horgan (2014) (on mostly *a priori* grounds) and Pautz (2006, 2010b) (on empirical grounds). Illusionism goes back to Galileo (1623/1957) and Locke (1869).

14 Besides the generalization argument and the argument from physics, there are several other considerations that favor the internalist model of how we experientially represent spatial and temporal properties over the detectivist model. They concern: (i) *normal misperception* (McLaughlin 2016b, Masrour 2017); (ii) the properties *left/right* and *up/down* that we experientially represent, which are not easily identified with physical properties detected by our visual systems (Cutter 2020); (iii) the experience of *subjective duration* (Lee 2017); and (iv) the possibility of *radical experiential indeterminacy*, which is implied by the detectivist model but avoided by the internalist model (see the Discussion Box in Section 4.3).

5

THE RETURN TO NAÏVE REALISM:
EXPERIENCE AS OPENNESS TO THE WORLD

In the first exuberance of liberation, I briefly became a naïve realist and rejoiced in the thought that the grass really is green, in spite of the adverse opinion of all philosophers from Locke onwards.

—Bertrand Russell (1959)

The character of your experience, as you look around the room, is constituted by the actual layout of the room itself.

—John Campbell (2002)

In the halcyon days before you were corrupted by philosophy, you probably accepted something like naïve realism. You took it for granted that, when you saw a sunset, the colors were out there. You experienced the actual character of the external world, and this fully constituted the character of your experience. Such acquaintance with the external world had intrinsic value.

But then you came into contact with philosophy and science. You learned about the argument from hallucination, the argument from perceptual variation, and so on. They convinced you that experience is not at all what it seems to be. The sensible qualities – sensible colors, audible qualities, smell qualities, and so on – are not objectively out there, and your experience of them is entirely a product of the brain.

Philosophers of the past generally rejected naïve realism. For instance, despite flirting with naïve realism in his youth, Bertrand Russell (1940: 15) famously later said, "naïve realism leads to science and science, if true, undermines naïve realism". The idea that science undermines naïve realism is very common. While naïve realism nicely explains the externally directed character of experience, it is hard to square with the dependence of experience on internal factors. The cognitive scientist Steven Pinker puts it this way:

> The scientific outlook has taught us that some parts of our subjective experience are products of our biological makeup and have no objective counterpart in the world. The qualitative difference between red and green, the tastiness of fruit and foulness of carrion are design features of our common nervous system.
>
> (Pinker 2008: 58)

Once you gave up naïve realism, you were led down a rabbit hole of bizarre views: the sense datum view, the internal physical state view, internalist representationalism, and so on. In fact, as we saw in Chapter 4, some internalist representationalists think that not just colors and tastes, but also space as we experience it, is an invention of the brain.

Contemporary naïve realists think that the bizarreness of these views is a sign that we have gone down the wrong path. The mistake, in their view, was to leave naïve realism behind in the first place. They have come up with new forms of naïve realism that are superior to the kind we criticized in Chapter 1. Their hope is that experience can be the way it seems to be, in spite of the discoveries of science. Thanks to their innovations, naïve realism, once cast aside, is now one of the dominant theories of perception.

In fact, it is generally supposed that the final contenders in the debate over the nature of perceptual experience are naïve realism and representationalism. So in this chapter we will assume, for the sake of argument, that we have narrowed down the options to these two, and ask which one we should prefer.

The plan is as follows. In Sections 5.1 and 5.2, I will describe a basic form of contemporary naïve realism. In Sections 5.3 and 5.4, we will look at two arguments for naïve realism over representationalism: one based on how experience seems and another based on the explanatory role of experience. Then, in Sections 5.5–5.8, we will look traditional considerations against naïve realism and in favor of representationalism concerning hallucination and scientific evidence for the role of internal factors in normal perception.

5.1 A basic form of contemporary naïve realism

There are many forms of contemporary "naïve realism", making it difficult to provide a general formulation. It will be best to start with a basic form of contemporary naïve realism and move on to more complex forms later on (Sections 5.7 and 5.8).

I define "basic naïve realism" as the following collection of claims:

(1) Primitivism about sensible properties (colors, smells, etc.)

(2) The naïve account of normal experience

(3) A simple "causal" or "selectionist" theory of the role of the brain

(4) A different theory of hallucination

These claims are not universally accepted by naïve realists. But they popular, making them a good starting point. To explain them, I will focus on an experience as of a blue sphere, as illustrated in Figure 5.1.

First, basic naïve realism endorses primitivism about colors and other sensible properties (Brewer 2011; Allen 2016; Campbell 2020). While many

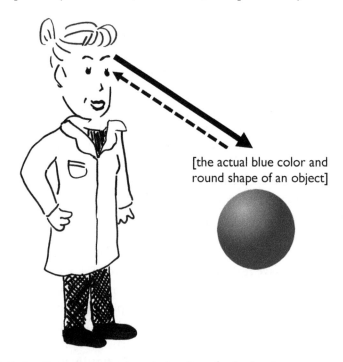

[the actual blue color and round shape of an object]

Figure 5.1   Basic naïve realism. Thanks to Audrey Pautz for the drawing.

philosophers and scientists have said that color is an invention of the brain, naïve realists insist that the quality blue is a primitive property of the physical sphere. The blue color of the sphere is just as objective as its shape and mass. So physical objects had colors before we evolved, even if no one was around to experience them. Furthermore, the color blue is a "primitive" property of the sphere, just as it seems to be. So it is not to be identified with its complex disposition to reflect light. In fact, it is very different from this disposition. The result is a kind of "dualism" at the surfaces of objects. The surface of the sphere has the physical property of reflecting light and *in addition* it has the distinct qualitative property of being bluish.

On primitivism about color, the color blue and the underlying reflectance of the sphere are connected. If you change the reflectance of the sphere (e.g., if you paint it), you might change its color from blue to green. In addition, since you experience the blue quality of the sphere, your visual system must be able to detect it. But your visual system is only able to detect light. So if you are to experiene the blue quality of the sphere, it must be somehow connected to its way of reflecting light, that is, its reflectance (see Figure 4.4 in Chapter 4). This means that there must be a slew of arbitrary-looking "chromatic laws" connecting every color with a corresponding reflectance-type. They have the following form: if an object has so-and-so reflectance, then it has so-and-so distinct primitive color.

In Chapter 4, we discussed how "bad external correlation" makes a problem for realist theories of colors that *identify* colors with reflectance-types of physical surfaces. For instance, blue resembles purple more than green, but it is not the case that R_b likewise resembles R_p more than R_g, where these are the corresponding reflectance-types. So these colors cannot be identical with the reflectance-types. But bad external correlation does not immediately rule out the "primitivist" form of realism proposed by naïve realists. Since this view holds that colors are primitive properties that are *distinct from* but "dependent on" reflectance properties, it can allow that there is a mismatch between the colors and the reflectance properties they depend on (Allen 2016: 128–129; Campbell 2020: 410). This is one of the innovations that have helped put naïve realism back on the table.

Next, the *second* claim of basic naïve realism. We just saw that naïve realists hold that, before we evolved, the physical sphere possessed the quality *blue*. Then brains evolved that enabled something remarkable to happen. For instance, your visual processing enabled you to become *experientially acquainted* with the blue color and round shape of the sphere. The character of your color experience of the sphere is grounded in the blue quality you became acquainted with in this way.

More generally, the second claim of basic naive realism is the *naïve account of normal experience*: Plus or minus a bit, the character your visual experiences, in normal cases, is grounded in your experiential acquaintance with objective, response-independent states of the external world. Differences in veridical experiences are grounded in differences in what states you experience (Campbell 2002: 116; Martin 2004: 64; Fish 2009: 14–15). This is how basic naïve realists answer the *character question* for normal experience – the central question in the philosophy of perception (see the introduction to this book).

A *state* (or "trope") is an actual occurrence of a property. For instance, the state of the blueness of the sphere is something that cannot exist unless the sphere is actually blue. We experience the states of ordinary physical objects as well as states involving pure *visibilia*, like rainbows and the vault of the sky.

Naïve realists say that the character of your visual experiences is fully *grounded in* your experiential acquaintance with states involving objects. This means that external objects aren't just causes of your experiences. Instead, your experiencing the actual states of objects constitutes your experience, somewhat as two people in a certain relationship constitute a dance. In normal experience, differences in the character of experiences just are differences in what external states you experience.

In formulating the naïve account of the character of experience, I said that "plus or minus a bit" differences in veridical experiences are grounded in (constituted by) differences in what states are experienced. The reason is that there may be a couple of exceptions concerning covert attention shifts (as when you are viewing two dots, and shift attention from one to the other without moving your eyes) and visual blur (as when you take off your glasses while viewing the blue sphere). In such cases, it is natural to say "*what* you experience stays the same but *the way* you experience it changes", even if it is a bit obscure what this comes to.

The third element of basic naive realism is what we might call the *simple causal theory* of experiential acquaintance.

For example, when you perceive the sphere, you experience its blue color and its shape, but not its electric charge. Why? According to the basic causal theory, the answer is that your visual system is causally responsive in the right way to its color and shape, but not to its electric charge. You can think of it this way. Experiential acquaintance is a kind of irreducible mental arrow pointed at the states of objects (the solid arrow in Figure 5.1). But, in the actual world, in order for this arrow to be pointed at those external states, there first must be a causal process going in the opposite "direction", from those states to the right processes in the subject's brain (the dashed arrow in Figure 5.1).

In more detail, the simple causal theory of experiential acquaintance holds that, in the actual world, you are experientially acquainted with an external state (say, the state of a physical object having a color or shape) just in case you undergo some or other "suitable" internal subpersonal physical state that is caused by that state in the biologically normal way (Fish 2009: 135–136; Campbell and Cassam 2014: 49).

The simple causal theory can help naïve realists handle variation in normal experience due to differences in the circumstances of perception and the operation of the sensory systems. The idea is that the external world is rich with perceptible properties. On a given occasion, your sensory systems causally detect only some of them. In this way, your sensory systems "select" what perceptible properties you become experientially acquainted with.

For instance, if you go from perceiving the blue sphere in good light to perceiving it in the shade, maybe you experience *blue* and then *blue in the shade*. Or maybe you experience a new, temporary "color-look" of the ball, determined by the light it is currently reflecting. Likewise, if the ball is slowly moved away from you, maybe you experience different viewer-relative but objective size features of it (e.g., *large-from-here*, *small-from-there*). When you perceive the blue sphere in the periphery of your visual field, you merely experience the occurrence of more "determinable" properties like *being over there and moving to the left*, without experiencing a specific color and shape. This is how naïve realists explain perceptual imprecision (Section 1.11).

Naïve realists might also apply the selectionist idea to variation in normal experience due to differences in the operation of the sensory systems. For instance, suppose you and a pigeon with different color vision view the sphere. The pigeon's visual system causally detects an ultraviolet reflectance of the sphere that grounds an alien color that we cannot imagine. So, by the simple causal theory, the pigeon becomes experientially acquainted with that alien color. Likewise, if the blue sphere looks pure blue to you and greenish-blue to your friend, due to slight differences in your color processing, maybe the sphere has both colors (or objective "color-looks"); you pick up one and your friend picks up on the other (Byrne and Hilbert 1997; Fish 2009; Kalderon 2020). The same "selectionist" gambit might also help the naive realist explain certain attentional differences that cause differences in apparent contrast (Block 2010; Brewer 2019a).

Finally, the fourth and last claim of basic naïve realism concerns hallucination and illusion. Imagine you hallucinate a blue sphere. Here the above account doesn't apply. No blue physical object is present for you to be acquainted with. So basic naïve realists need some other account here. Likewise for internally-generated illusions. This means that their account of experience is non-uniform. As we are formulating basic naïve realism, it is neutral about the account of hallucination and illusion. We will set this issue aside for now and return to it in Section 5.5.

So much for the four claims that make up basic naïve realism. Notice that basic naïve realism is radically externalist. John Campbell sums it up this way:

> Looking for the qualitative character of experience in the nature of a brain state is looking for it in the wrong place; we have to be looking rather at the [properties] of the objects experienced [in the external world]
>
> (Campbell 2010: 20).

On the externalist approach of naïve realists, then, the brain plays a mere enabling role, rather than a determinative role. It *selects* what states in the objective world you experience. In this respect, it resembles the "response-independent representationalism" of Tye and Dretske examined in Chapter 4. In fact, Campbell's slogan here is nearly identical to Tye's slogan quoted in Section 4.2.

To illustrate, suppose you and a Martian view the sphere. The neurobiology of your color vision systems might be different. But, given basic naïve realism, your experiences of the sphere might be exactly the same. For, given color primitivism, the blue color quality is an objective feature of the ball. And, given the basic causal theory of experiential acquaintance, even if your and the Martian's neurobiological states are totally different, as long they are appropriately caused by the same color and shape of the ball, you and the Martian will be experientially acquainted with the same color and shape of the ball.

If naïve realism applies to visual experience, it presumably applies to other types of experiences. For instance, Campbell writes:

> The smells and tastes are objective features of the world. What I disagree with is the idea that our brain makes a big contribution to experience. The function [of brain processing] is just to reveal the world to us.
>
> (Campbell 2009)

In the case of the experience of sound, naïve realists might say that audible qualities – loudness, pitch, timbre – are primitive qualities of external audible events (that is, disturbances of the air). They depend in complex ways on physical properties of audible events involving frequency, amplitude, duration, and "critical bands", but they are not identical with those physical properties (just like colors are not identical with reflectance-types). Thus, in pre-sentient nature, when a tree fell in the forest, it made a sound. The brain determines what experiences we have only to the extent that it selects what pre-existing objective properties we become acquainted with.

Likewise, the smell qualities (e.g., minty, caraway, etc.) are primitive qualities of odorants (clusters of molecules). They are grounded in their chemical compositions. Thus, the brain did not generate good and bad smells; good and bad smells were out there well before the evolution of the nervous system. Fortunately, chemicals that turned out to be bad for us (e.g., methane) had bad objective smells, and chemicals that turned out to be good for us had good objective smells. Then our brain selected those objective smells for us to experience.

5.2 How naïve realism differs from representationalism

As I said at the start of this chapter, our focus is on the contest between naïve realism and representationalism. Our first order of business is to understand the difference between them.

To illustrate, start with a normal experience of the blue-looking sphere. The naïve account of this experience described in the previous section is an example of an *act-object account*. The act-object account holds that the character of your experience is constituted by your being experientially acquainted with [the actual blue color and round shape of an object]. Here [the actual blue color and round shape of an object] is a *complex state involving some object*. It is the joint occurrence in the world of these properties in an object. It cannot exist unless the relevant object is actually blue and round.

The sense datum view is another example of a view that endorses the act-object picture. But, while naïve realists hold that the relevant blue and round object is the physical sphere itself (Figure 5.1), sense datum theorists hold that the relevant blue and object is a brain-created "mental object" that is very life-like (somewhat like a hologram).

Representationalists entirely reject the act-object account of the character of your experience. To see this, it will help to start with a hallucination of a blue sphere and then turn back to the normal case.

Suppose, then, that you have a vivid hallucination of a blue sphere. If we were to apply the act-object picture to hallucination, there would have to exist the state [the blueness and roundness of some existing object]. But representationalists say that there doesn't exist a blue and round object in a hallucination case – not even a "mental object" or sense datum. So here representationalists reject the act-object picture altogether.

(Of course, representationalists hold that in your hallucination there *seems* to you to be a blue and round object. But this is not enough for them to count as endorsing the act-object picture, since that picture requires that the character of your experience is constituted by your actually experiencing an existing blue and round object.)

Instead of accepting the act-object picture, representationalists hold that the character of your hallucination is grounded in your experientially representing the *state of affairs* <some object is blue and round>. This state of affairs belongs to a very different ontological category than the actual state [the actual blue color and round shape of some object]. It is the *possibility* that some object is blue and round; it can exist whether or not this possibility is actual (Plantinga 1974). It is a *way things might be*, rather than a *way things are*. This kind of thing can also be called a *proposition*. Put in another way, representationalists hold that for you to have the hallucinatory experience is for it to seem to you that the possible state of affairs <some object is blue and round> obtains. In this case, it doesn't obtain, but it still exists as a possibility.

Now turn back to the case where you experience a blue sphere in a normal case. Representationalists explain the character of your experience in this case in the same way as in the hallucination case (see Figure 5.2).

The representational explanation of the character of your experience in the non-hallucinatory case is very different from the act-object explanation proposed by naïve realists (Figure 5.1). True, in this non-hallucinatory case, some representationalists (of the "realist" variety) might agree with naïve realists there does exist a blue and round physical object. So, in this non-hallucinatory case, they might agree that the objective state [the blueness and roundness of some object] exists out in the world. But they reject the key claim of the act-object theory. The key claim of the act-object theory is that the character of your experience is constituted by your experiencing this actual state – something you could not do unless there actually exists a blue and round object there. By contrast, representationalists hold that the physical object reflects light into your eyes, setting off a cascade of neural processing. This is depicted by the dashed arrow in Figure 5.2. This neural processing enables you to experientially represent the possible state of affairs <some object is blue and round>. This is depicted by the solid arrow. As a result, it seems to you that this state of affairs obtains.

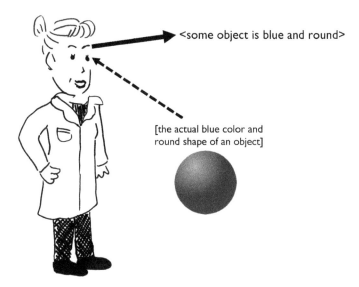

<some object is blue and round>

[the actual blue color and round shape of an object]

Figure 5.2 The representationalist account of your experience.

According to representationalists, it is this which constitutes the character of your experience – not experiencing the actual blue color and round shape of the sphere. The character of your experience is constituted by your being in the same mental state you undergo in a hallucination (or illusion) case in which there doesn't actually exist a blue and round object.

So, on the representational view, the explanation of your experience in the normal case (in which there exists a round object) is the same as in the hallucination case (in which there does not exist such an object). In both cases, having that experience consists in its *seeming* to you that <some object is blue and round> obtains. Even though in the normal case, there may exist a blue and round object, there is a sense in which this is irrelevant to the explanation of the character of our experience, according to representationalists.

To clarify, representationalists allow that, in the normal case, you "perceive" the spherical physical object, in the attenuated sense that the physical object starts off the causal process that results in your experience (Figure 5.1). But the "act-object account" as we are understanding it here is much stronger. It holds that the character of your experience is constituted by your actually experiencing the color and shape of some existing object. And, as we have seen, representationalists deny this.

In sum, naïve realists uphold the act-object account in normal experience, but representationalists reject it across the board. So if you think it's obvious that, in normal cases at least, the act-object account is right (the character of your blue-sphere experience is constituted by your experiencing the round shape and blue color of some actually existing object), then you will not like the representational view (more on this in the next section).

Some forms of representationalism are even more different from naïve realism. Naïve realism holds that the quality blue that you experience is an objective feature of the sphere independent of our nervous systems. By contrast, "illusionist" representationalism agrees with the remarks of Steven Pinker at the start of the chapter. According to illusionist representationalism, the physical sphere, and physical objects more generally, are intrinsically colorless. True, the physical sphere reflects light in a certain way, but this is not necessarily associated with the color quality blue. So, on this form of the representational view, Figure 5.2 needs to be modified: there is no such objective state as [the blue color of the object]. Rather, you experientially represent the sphere as blue only because of your neural response to the sphere. Color qualities are "inventions of the brain". Likewise for pain qualities, smell qualities, audible qualities, and so on.

Having learned the difference between naïve realism and representationalism, we will in the next two sections look at two arguments for naïve realism over representationalism.

5.3 Naïve realism v representationalism: intrinsic plausibility

Suppose again that you are looking at a blue sphere. We just saw there are two incompatible explanations of the character of your experience: the act-object account (Figure 5.1) and the representational account (Figure 5.2). Naïve realism is an example of the act-object account.

The first argument for naïve realism over representationalism that we will consider simply claims that the act-object account is much more "intrinsically plausible" than the representational account.

In fact, as we saw in Chapter 1, for Russell (1912a), Moore (1957), and Broad (1923), the act-object assumption was a starting point in the philosophy of perception. The present argument rehabilitates this thought and uses it to argue for naïve realism (Hellie 2007; Fish 2009; Langsam 2017).

The act-object account is indeed more intrinsically plausible than the representational account when you reflect on your experience. When you look at the sphere, it just seems obvious that there is a blue and round object then and there, and that the character of your experience is fully grounded in your experiencing the concrete color and shape of this object, namely the state [the blueness and roundness of the object]. Any alternative account that denies this will fall short.

In particular, if you think about it, the alternative representational account seems wrong precisely because it rejects the act-object account. Instead, this view holds that the character of your experience is grounded in your experientially representing the state of affairs <something is blue and round>. The state of affairs <something is blue and round> is very different from the concrete state [the blueness and roundness of the object]. It is a mere possibility. It doesn't exist in space. It could exist even if there is no blue and round thing before you, or indeed if there is no blue and round thing in all of reality. The idea that the character of your experience is grounded in your being mentally related to such a weird abstract item – an item that could exist in the absence of a blue and round object – is very implausible (Section 3.7).

So, when you reflect on your experience, the act-object explanation of the character of your experience is more intrinsically plausible than the representational explanation.

But, even if this is right, it does not yet establish naïve realism. The reason is that the basic act-object account is neutral on the nature of the blue and round object that you are experiencing. There are two options here. Naïve realists hold that the relevant blue and round object is the physical sphere itself. But, as we saw in Chapter 1, there is another option. Russell, Moore, and Broad argued that the blue and round object you are experiencing is actually a brain-created "mental image" or "sense datum" that is so life-like that you mistake it for a physical object.

You cannot decide between these options just by reflecting on your experience. Here is an analogy due to J. L. Austin (1962: 50). When you view a lemon, the character of your experience alone does not support the claim that the object is a lemon rather than a decoy piece of soap that has the same visible properties as a lemon. So, to reach naïve realism, we need additional considerations.

At this point, naïve realists can invoke the arguments against the sense datum theory discussed in Chapter 1. For instance, if the blue and round object you are experiencing is a non-physical object created by your brain, where does this peculiar non-physical object reside? A much better candidate to be this blue and round object is simply the physical sphere. So if we retain the act-object account on which the character of your experience is grounded in your experiencing an existing blue and round object, and we deny that this blue object is a non-physical "sense datum", we are led to the naïve realist view that it is the physical sphere. The physical sphere really is blue, in spite of the adverse opinion of all philosophers from Locke (1869, II.viii.16) onwards.

So the argument from intrinsic plausibility for naïve realism has two steps. First, the act-object account is intrinsically plausible. Second, additional considerations show that the relevant object is a physical object. How might representationalists respond to this argument?

One obvious problem concerns hallucination. For imagine a hallucination of a blue sphere. Here there exists no blue and round physical object. And, as just noted, there arguably exists no blue and round mental object ("sense datum"). So here the act-object account does not apply. For this reason, after Chapter 1, we entirely left the act-object assumption behind, and in the rest of the book looked at views that reject it.

But naïve realists have a reply to this particular problem. The right moral is not to reject the act-object account but to restrict it. The act-object account is right for normal experiences but a different account is needed for hallucinations and illusions (as we will discuss in Section 5.5).

However, hallucination creates another problem for the argument from intrinsic plausibility. Even if hallucination doesn't decisively rule out the act-object account because it can simply be restricted to normal experience, it does weaken the argument from intrinsic plausibility argument for the act-object account.

To see what I mean, imagine that you have Charles Bonnet syndrome (to be discussed in Section 5.5) and you have a vivid hallucination of a blue sphere. You will find an act-object account of this hallucinatory experience to be just as plausible as an act-object account of your veridical experience of the sphere. You will find it intrinsically plausible that there exists a blue and round object for you to scan and explore, and that the character of your experience is grounded in your experiencing its color and shape. But contemporary naïve realists will agree with representationalists that in this case your act-object conviction is false. There does not exist a blue and round object – not even a "sense datum". In fact, the rejection of sense data is the second step in the above argument for naïve realism.

Likewise, in Edward Adelson's famous *checker-shadow illusion* (available online), a tile is in fact a quite dark grey but it looks very light grey to you. If you are not tipped off, you will find it intrinsically plausible that the character of your experience is grounded in your experiencing the state of the tile being light grey. But naïve realists agree with representationalists that here your act-object conviction is in error for the simple reason that the tile is not light grey.[1] For naïve realists restrict the act-object account of experiential character to normal cases.

Now turn back to the normal case in which you experience a sphere that really is blue and round. Here you will find the act-object claim "intrinsically plausible". And, according to naïve realists, that is why we must accept it in this case. But representationalists, who deny your act-object conviction here as well as in hallucination and illusion, can point out that your act-object convictions were in error in cases of hallucination and illusion. This shows that your act-object conviction here is not *certain*. If in other cases the character of experience is not grounded in the character of the object (for the simple reason that there is no object with that character), maybe in the normal case the character of experience is not grounded in the character of the object (even though there is an object). Further, there is no theory-neutral reason to think that we are likely to be more reliable about act-object claims in normal perception than in hallucination and illusion. For we are not in a better position to make judgments about the character of our experience when we perceive the world than when we undergo hallucinations or illusions. Since there is no theory-neutral reason to think our act-object claims are more reliable in veridical experience than in the relevant cases of hallucination and illusion, and since they are wrong those cases, this somewhat weakens the support provided by "intrinsic plausibility" for act-object claims in the case of "normal" experience (Fish 2013; Millar 2014; Langsam 2017; Niikawa 2020).

Here is another way to put the point. Representationalists hold that act-object convictions about the grounds of phenomenology are *always* in error, even in veridical cases where an object is present. But, since we all reject the sense datum view of hallucinations and illusions, all of us – including naïve realists – must concede that these very same convictions are *often* in error. And, once we accept they are often in error, it is no longer so bad to say that they are always in error.

In addition, representationalists can explain why we find the act-object claims so compelling, even if they are always false. It is part of their view that for you to have the blue-sphere experience is just for it to vividly seem to you (for you to "experientially represent") that a blue and round object is there. So it is natural that you should surmise that the character of your experience is simply grounded in your experiencing the color and shape of this object, even if arguments about non-veridical experience and the science of color (to be discussed in Sections 5.5 and 5.6) ultimately show that this is not the case.

5.4 Naïve realism *v* representationalism: explanatory role

We next turn to a quite different argument for naïve realism over representationalism due to John Campbell (Campbell and Cassam 2014) and Bill Brewer (2019b). The argument has two steps. First, visual experience plays an explanatory role in providing us with knowledge about colors and shapes. Second, visual experience can play this role only if naïve realism is the correct account of it; visual experience cannot play this role if representationalism is correct. Let's look at these steps in turn.

First, visual experience plays an explanatory role in providing us with knowledge. To illustrate, suppose that someone – call her "Mary" – has never experienced any colors before. Everything in her environment is either black or white (Jackson 2004). And suppose that, for some reason, she has never experienced round things. Maybe everything in her environment is rectangular!

One day she experiences a blue and round sphere for the first time. Campbell and Brewer both say that her experience explains her acquisition of a quite distinctive type of knowledge. Campbell (2014: 13–14, 42) says that she thereby has new "non-propositional knowledge" of *which property blue is* and *which property round is*. Brewer (2019b: 279) says that she thereby has knowledge of "what being blue is" and "what being round is", knowledge that she might express by saying "being blue is being like *that*" and "being round is being like *this*". Campbell (119) holds that visual experience is *necessary* for this special kind of knowledge. A *robot* incapable of experience, however sophisticated, just could never have this special knowledge about colors and shapes. Brewer goes further than Campbell. He implies (286–287) that visual experience is also *sufficient* for this special kind of knowledge. For instance, he says that, necessarily, if Mary has an experience of blue and round thing, and attends in the right way, she automatically has this knowledge (personal correspondence).

In sum, Campbell and Brewer advocate the following:

> **Explanatory link.** There is an essential explanatory link between having an experience as of a color or shape and having knowledge of "what properties colors and shapes are".

Visual experience seems to play an explanatory role in providing us with other, less controversial epistemic and cognitive capacities. For instance, necessarily, if you have an experience as of an object that is F (blue, round), then you thereby have a (defeasible) reason to believe that an F object is present. Necessarily, if you have an experience as of an object that is F (blue, round), and if you have the general capacity for belief, then you thereby have the capacity to believe that something is F. Finally, if you have experiences as of a number of colors or shapes, you are in a position to know their resemblance relations. And this is true even if your experiences are hallucinatory (more on this in Section 5.5). However, in this section, I will focus on Campbell and Brewer's explanatory link, which concerns a somewhat more obscure type of knowledge. Let us just grant this explanatory link for the sake of discussion.

The aim of the second step of the argument is to show that the naïve realist account of the explanatory role of experience in providing knowledge of what colors and shapes are like is superior to the representationalist account. Since they disagree about what experience is (acquaintance or representation), they disagree about what it is that explains such knowledge:

> **Naïve realist account.** There is an essential explanatory link between *experiential acquaintance* with actual *states* of the world involving colors and shapes (or undergoing an indiscriminable illusion or hallucination) and *knowing what those colors and shapes are like.*[2]
>
> **Representationalist account.** There is an essential explanatory link between *experientially representing possible states of affairs* involving colors and shapes and *knowing what those colors and shapes are like.*

Both Campbell and Brewer argue against the representational account of the explanatory role of experience in providing knowledge of what colors and shapes are like. They also argue that only the naïve realist account will suffice. In what follows, we will look at their arguments against the representational account.

First, we must understand the representational account of the explanatory role of experience in providing knowledge of what colors and shapes are like. To illustrate, I will focus on the account of "nonreductive internalist" representationalism. Internalist representationalism may provide the best solution to the puzzle of how experience is both externally directed and internally dependent (see Chapter 4 and also Section 5.3 of the present chapter).

Imagine again that Mary has just been released from her black and white environment and experiences the blue sphere for the first time. On any form of representationalism, the character of her experience is constituted by her experientially representing <some object is blue and round>. This is depicted in Figure 5.2. What her experience is like is due to what blue and round are like. Nonreductive internalist representationalists hold that *experiential representation* (the arrow in Figure 5.2) is an irreducible mental relationship. In Chapter 3, we saw that many representationalists try to reduce experiential representation to a kind of detection. They hold that we experientially represent perceptible properties in much the same way that a thermometer represents temperatures. For short, experiential representation is *d-representation*. Nonreductive internalist representationalists reject all such externalist reductive theories of experiential representation. On their view, experiential representation is fully internally determined. For instance, on internalist representationalism, even a lifelong "brain in a void" could experientially represent <some object is blue and round>, just like Mary, even though its neural state does not have a history of physically detecting the occurrence of blue and round. Indeed, the brain in the void bears no interesting physical relationship to these properties. So the experiential representation relation is a non-physical relationship fundamentally different from mere d-representation. In fact, experiential representation and d-representation are so different it is somewhat misleading to call them by the same name, "representation".

Nonreductive representationalists do not give an elaborate account of the explanatory role of experience in providing knowledge of what colors and shapes are like. They just say that it is the nature of experiential representation that, if Mary (or the BIV) experientially represents <some object is blue and round>, then Mary in a position to know what blue and round are like. There is nothing more to say. Here is an analogy: it is arguably just in the nature of pain that it gives us knowledge of what pain is like and a reason to avoid it.

Now that we understand one representational account of the explanatory role of experience, we can turn to Campbell and Brewer's arguments against it. Their arguments concern representation without conscious experience.

For example, imagine Robo, a hypothetical robot. Robo is an insentient automaton that has no *experiences* of colors and shapes. That is, on the representational view, Robo doesn't *experientially represent* <some object is round> or <some object is blue>. Intuitively, unlike Mary, Robo cannot know *what colors and shapes are like* since Robo doesn't *experience* them. However,

Robo does *d-represent* <some object is round> and <some object has the blue-reflectance>. That is, Robo undergoes internal physical states with a history of detecting the occurrence of these states of affairs, just as a thermometer has states with a history of detecting temperatures. And these states are in turn indirectly connected to Robo's verbal reports. For instance, if Robo is in a neural state that normally detects or indicates <some object is round>, Robo says (in a robotic voice of course) "there is a round thing there".[3]

On the basis of such examples of representation without experience, Campbell raises the following challenge for the representational account of the explanatory role of experience:

> If you think of sensory experience as a matter of representing how things are, then it is not obvious how [experience] can have a fundamental epistemic role to play, since you can have representations without [experience]; *why would not representations without [experience] provide just as good epistemic access to objects and properties?*
>
> (Campbell and Cassam 2014: 47–48; my italics)

For instance, Campbell's challenge to representationalists is to answer the question: if Mary's experientially representing <some object is round> enables Mary to know what being round is like, why doesn't Robo's *d-representing* <some object is round>, without any experience, equally enable Robo to know what being round is like?

However, representationalists seem to have a simple answer to Campbell's question. As noted above, they can just say that it is in the nature of experientially representing <some object is round> that it enables one to know what being round is like. As for mere d-representing (the sense in which thermometers and robots represent), nonreductive internalist representationalists hold that it is *fundamentally different from experientially representing*. It is not in the nature of mere d-representation that a system's merely d-representing <some object is round> enables the system to know what being round is like. Robo can detect shapes without knowing what they are like, just as a thermometer can detect temperatures without knowing what they are like.

In fact, naïve realists like Campbell face a parallel question, and they will presumably provide a parallel answer. By contrast to representationalists, naïve realists hold that Mary's first experience of a blue sphere is constituted by her *experientially perceiving* (or "being acquainted with") the actual states [the round shape of the object] and [the blue color of the object]. (This is the arrow in Figure 5.1.) This enables her to know what being blue and being round are like. But, when Robo views the sphere, there is a sense in which Robo also "perceives" the state [the round shape of the object]. After all, Robo is in an internal physical state that actually registers or detects this external state, allowing Robo to respond to it. Let's say that Robo *d-perceives* [the round shape of the object], even though Robo doesn't experience it. So naïve realists like Campbell face the question: if Mary's *experientially perceiving* [the round shape of the object] enables Mary to know what being round is like, why doesn't Robo's *d-perceiving* [the round shape of the object], without any experience, equally enable Robo to know what being round is like? They will presumably answer that it is just in the nature of experientially perceiving ("conscious acquaintance"), but not the very different relation of *d*-perceiving, that if a subject bears this relation to [the round shape of the object], then they are in a position to know what being round is like. If naïve realists can give this kind of answer, why cannot representationalists give a parallel answer?

Now let us briefly turn to Brewer's argument that representationalists cannot adequately accommodate the explanatory role of experience in providing knowledge of what shapes and colors are like. Recall that Brewer goes further than Campbell. While Campbell holds that having experiences of colors and shapes is necessary for knowing what they are like, Brewer adds that having such experiences is sufficient for this kind of knowledge. Brewer argues that representationalists cannot accept this. For representationalists, it would imply that *experientially representing* states of affairs involving colors and shapes is sufficient for knowing what they are like. But Brewer says that representing properties "is in general manifestly insufficient for" knowledge of what those properties are like (Brewer 2019b: 286–287). For instance, he points out that individuals (like Robo) can *d-represent* properties without knowing what those properties are like. He concludes that "the representational account misidentifies the source" of our knowledge of what colors and shapes are like.

In reply, representationalists can clarify that their view only implies that *experientially representing* states of affairs involving colors and shapes is sufficient for knowing what they are like. It is no objection to this to point out that *d-representing* a state of affairs involving colors and shapes is "manifestly insufficient" for such knowledge. As the "brain in the void" example illustrates, nonreductive internalist representationalists hold that experiential representation is an irreducible mental relation that is fundamentally different from mere *d*-representation.

One last point. Representationalists claim that "experientially representing" states of affairs involving colors and shapes is essentially linked with

knowing what colors and shapes are like. This is not supposed to be immediately obvious. Instead, they arrive at this claim from two premises. First,
Campbell and Brewer are right: it is pretheoretically plausible that experiences of colors and shapes ground such knowledge. Second, as we saw in
Chapter 3, the best hypothesis concerning what experiences are is that they
consist in experientially representing states of affairs involving color and
shapes. So experiential representation must have the power to ground such
knowledge.

5.5 Representationalism *v* naïve realism: hallucination and illusion

So far, we have considered arguments for naïve realism over representationalism. In the next two sections, we turn to arguments on
the other side. We will look at arguments against naïve realism and for
representationalism.

We begin with hallucination and illusion. As we have discussed in previous chapters, people with "Charles Bonnet syndrome" have impaired
eyesight but, due spontaneous to internal neural activity, often have vivid
hallucinations:

> Their hallucinations are seen in perfect detail. They may be so compelling that
> patients are often left uncertain of whether a given object is real or not. Many
> test the reality of such experiences, for example, by reaching out to touch them or
> assessing their plausibility.
>
> (ffytche 2013: 50)

In Chapter 3, we considered Buddy Burmester, an actual person with
Charles Bonnet syndrome. He had vivid hallucinations of purple flowers
with very intricate shapes. Let's work with this example again.

In such a hallucination case, the naïve account of experiential character
does not apply: it is not the case that the character of Buddy's hallucination
of the flower is grounded in his experiencing the state of some physical
object. Consequently, naïve realists need to say something different here.

Recently, John Campbell (Campbell and Cassam 2014: 10–12) has flirted
with accepting a *sense datum view* restricted to the case of hallucinations. In
the case of Buddy's hallucination, there exists a purple and flower-shaped
mental image or sense datum that goes proxy for a physical object. Campbell doesn't endorse this account but he does call it "powerful". If naïve
realists take this view, then they can say that the act-object account of the

character of experience is correct for both veridical experience and hallucination. It's just that the nature of the presented object is quite different in the two cases. In Chapter 1, we called this "normal-abnormal naïve realism".

Campbell also says (Campbell and Cassam 2014: 90) that "hallucination and perception are quite different problems" and that "hallucinations seem at best tangentially related to the study of perception". Campbell seems to be saying that your theory of hallucination needn't impact your theory of veridical experience.

But there is a problem with this idea. For instance, if naïve realists were to accept a sense datum theory of Buddy's hallucination of a flower, they would be under pressure to accept a sense datum theory of a case in which Buddy has a similar normal experience of a real flower, giving up their naïve realist account. After all, in these cases, Buddy's neural state N is relevantly the same (Penfield and Perot 1963; ffytche 2013). The simplest and least arbitrary view is that if N generates a flower-like sense datum for Buddy to experience in the hallucination case, then N also generates a flower-like sense datum for Buddy to experience in the normal case (see Chapter 1). That is to say, in the normal case as well as in the hallucinatory case, Buddy's visual field is a private mental screen containing a very detailed flower-like image, which he mistakes for the physical flower. But then naïve realism is mistaken in the normal case. The sense datum filling his visual field "blocks" or "screens off" the physical flower from directly constituting the character of his experience – the physical flower is only a distant cause of his experience (as when you watch a football match live on the television). The sense datum theory cannot be confined to the hallucination case; if it is correct for the hallucinatory case, it spreads to the veridical case.

The problem here is more general. For instance, suppose we hold that Buddy's hallucination consists in his experientially representing that a flower-like object is present, even if there is not such an object (not even a sense datum). But then, since Buddy undergoes the same relevant neural state N when he actually sees a flower, we must say that even when he actually sees a flower he experientially represents that a flower-like object is present. And now the "screening off" problem rears its head again. We must now say that what grounds the character of Buddy's experience (and explains his related behavior) even in this case is his experientially representing that a flower-like object is present (Figure 5.2). And this apparently prevents us from saying that the character of his experience is grounded in his experiencing the actual state of the flower. The naïve account of the character of veridical experience is pushed out of the picture. Once the representationalist has her foot in the door in the hallucination case, we must buy her view across the board.[4]

Traditionally, this is how things go in the philosophy of perception. Once we give a strange theory of hallucination and illusion, such as the sense datum theory or the representational theory, then we are obliged to spread the strange theory to normal cases, "screening off" the naïve realist account.[5]

How might naïve realists answer this "screening off" problem? The naïve realist M. G. F. Martin (2004) has provided an influential response. He has put forward the following proposal:

> **Indiscriminability theory.** To have an experience with the flower-like character (whether it be hallucinatory, illusory, or veridical) is to be such that it is *as if* you are successfully experiencing a flower; that is, it is to be in a situation *reflectively indiscriminable from (not knowably different from)* experiencing a flower. In general, different visual experiences consist in being in situations indiscriminable from successfully experiencing different states of the world.

Like the sense datum theory and the representational theory discussed in previous chapters, the indiscriminability theory addresses the question "what in general is to have an experience with a certain character?" But it provides a radically different answer. For one thing, it takes the case of successful experience as basic in the analysis of experience; it analyzes experience in general in terms in terms of indiscriminability from the successful case. For another thing, it explains indiscriminability in terms of an inability to know. The result is a "cognitive" or "epistemic" view of experience.

The payoff of the indiscriminability theory is that it is exactly what naïve realists need: it is a general theory of the character of experience that covers hallucination and that also does not screen off the naïve account of the character of veridical experience. In fact, it entails the naïve account as a special case. It is one of the innovations that have helped put naïve realism back on the table as a serious contender. Let us take these points in turn.

Return to Buddy's hallucination. Suppose that, at first, he experiences a blank wall. Then suddenly he hallucinates a flower on the wall, because, due to aberrant activity, he undergoes the same kind of neural state N he undergoes when a flower is present. On the indiscriminability theory of experience, here is what is going on: at first, it *is* knowable by reflection on the situation that it differs from experiencing a flower (that is, it is *not* as if he is experiencing a flower on the wall). But then suddenly it is *not* knowable just by reflection on the situation that the situation differs from experiencing a flower (that is, it *is* for Buddy as if he is experiencing a flower on the wall). (Of course, if Buddy is told by someone else that there is no flower there, then he knows that he is not really experiencing a flower; but it is not possible to know this merely by reflecting on his situation.) On the indiscriminability theory of experience, the change in the character of Buddy's experience *just is* this change in what is knowable.

Now you might wonder: *why* is Buddy's situation suddenly indiscriminable from experiencing a flower? As we saw above, the "screening off" problem prevents naive realists from answering that he suddenly experiences a flower-like sense datum or experientially represents the presence of a flower-like object. Therefore, Martin suggests something surprising: in this hallucination case, there is no such underlying experiential state that explains *why* it is unknowable just by reflection that Buddy's situation differs from experiencing a flower. Buddy's experiential state in this case just *consists* in this inability to know. As Martin puts it, "there is nothing more to the character of the. . . hallucination than that it can't be told apart through reflection from the veridical perception" (Martin 2006: 370).

Of course, Martin recognizes that Buddy's suddenly coming to hallucinate a flower (which on his view consists in an inability to know something) has a *cause*. It is caused by his being put into neural state N, the same kind of neural state he is in when he really sees a flower (Martin 2013: 46). But, as regards the *nature* of the experience, he holds that there is nothing more to its character than an inability to know.

Next, suppose later in the day Buddy is once again put to neural state N, but this time it is because of the real presence of a flower on the wall. Far from screening off the naïve account, the indiscriminability theory entails the naïve account as a special case. For, as a result of undergoing neural state N, Buddy will once again be in a situation indiscriminable from (not knowably different from) successfully experiencing a flower. True, in this case as in the hallucination case, this epistemic fact is grounded in Buddy's neural state N. But, in this case unlike in the hallucination case, it is also grounded in something else: in this case, Buddy's situation is *indiscriminable from* (not knowably different from) successfully experiencing a flower, by virtue of the fact that his situation *is* one of successfully experiencing a flower! Furthermore, since, on this view, having an experience with the relevant character *just is* being in a situation indiscriminable from successfully experiencing a flower, it follows that in the veridical case Buddy has an experience with the relevant character by virtue of the fact that he is successfully experiencing a flower. And this is just what the naïve realist account of the character of experience holds.[6]

In sum, on the indiscriminability theory, Buddy has the same experience-type (an experience with the same "character") when he has a veridical experience of a flower and when he has a hallucination of one. But it has different grounds in the two cases.

Naïve realists can naturally treat internally-caused illusions in the same way they treat hallucinations. For instance, in Adelson's checker-shadow illusion, a dark grey tile looks light grey to you. The tile does not reflect "light grey light" and does not have a light grey "objective look" (Brewer 2011). It looks light grey only because of the internal computational processes of your visual system. So in such illusions as in hallucinations, the character of your experience is not grounded in the objective character of the presented object. So naïve realists might apply to such illusions the same indiscriminability theory they apply to hallucinations (Brewer 2011: 115–117). In Adelson's checkerboard illusion, you are in a situation indiscriminable from seeing a light grey tile, even though you are not seeing light grey tile.

So the indiscriminability theory allows naïve realists to explain hallucination and illusion in a way that avoids the screening off problem. But it faces many other problems. Here we will focus on two.

First, what does it mean to be in a situation *indiscriminable from* (not knowably different from) successfully experiencing the shape and color of an object?

To begin with, suppose we interpret the account as follows:

> **Crude indiscriminability theory.** *S* has a flower-like experience just in case *S* cannot know by reflection that *S* is not experiencing a flower-like object.

However, consider a dog lazing on the porch watching people pass by on the street. The dog can know things about the world but the dog cannot know things about her own experiences because she lacks the concept of an experience. Due to her conceptual unsophistication, she cannot know by reflection *that she is not experiencing flower-like thing* (just like she cannot know *that she is not on the planet Venus*). Therefore, the crude indiscriminability theory wrongly entails that she has a hallucinatory experience as of a flower. By the same reasoning, it implies that the dog has countless experiences: an experience of a tomato, a lemon, a pumpkin, and so on. In fact, it implies that even an insentient stone on the ground has every possible experience because, for every kind of thing F (e.g., a flower), the stone trivially cannot know by reflection that it is not experiencing an F![7]

In view of such problems, Martin (2006: fn.44) rejects the crude theory and accepts an alternative theory that appeals to a special notion of "impersonal knowability":

> **Impersonal indiscriminability theory.** *S* has a flower-experience just in case it is not *impersonally knowable* by reflection that *S* is not experiencing a flower-like object.

This account is also taken up by Bill Brewer (2011: 110–112). The idea is that, even though the dog herself does not know by reflection that she is not experiencing a flower, it is "impersonally" knowable by reflection that the dog is not experiencing a flower. Likewise, even though the stone does not know by reflection that it is not experiencing a flower, it is supposed to be "impersonally" knowable by reflection that the stone is not experiencing a flower. Therefore, unlike the crude version, the impersonal version avoids the mistaken implication that the dog and the stone have every possible experience.

But what exactly does Martin mean "impersonally knowable"? In ordinary English, "knowing" requires a knower. So, in ordinary English, to say something is knowable is say it is possible that some *individual or other* should know it.

However, Martin (2006: fn.44) insists that, when he says that it is impersonally knowable by reflection that the dog (or the stone) isn't experiencing a flower-like object, he does not mean it in this way; he does not mean that it's possible that some individual or other should know this by reflection, if they were in the "same" situation as the dog (or the stone) and had the capacity to reflect on that situation. This is why he calls it "impersonal". So he is not using "knowable" with its ordinary English meaning. But then what *does* he mean?

Here is an analogy. If someone claimed that concrete (e.g., the concrete in a sidewalk) is "impersonally drinkable", but then they said that they do not mean that it is possible that someone should drink it, we would not know what they meant.

Maybe Martin and Brewer are using "impersonally knowable" as a new technical term whose meaning is detached from the meaning of "knowable" in ordinary English. In fact, Brewer (2011: 211) calls it an "unanalyzable notion". But even if it is a technical term expressing a novel unanalyzable notion, it must be explained. Until this is done, no clear view has been put on the table.

Martin (2006: 385ff) emphasizes that it is his view that reflection on experiential character is not to be understood as reflection on a realm that is independent of that reflection. But this does not shed any light on what he means by "impersonally unknowable".

Here is a second problem that confronts any version of the indiscrimibility theory of experience. In the previous section, we saw that one argument for naïve realism concerns the explanatory role of experience. Ironically, the explanatory role of experience is also the source of an argument *against* the naïve realists' indiscriminately theory of experience. The argument concerns the potential explanatory role of certain illusions and hallucinations.

For instance, when Buddy (an actual person) has his vivid hallucination, it appears to him that something has a very idiosyncratic and complex shape. Call it f_{17}. His hallucination is so vivid that he is able to study his hallucination and depict the unusual shape in a drawing. Once he has the hallucination, he can now wonder whether anything is f_{17}. He didn't have this specific cognitive capacity before his hallucination. True, using language, he could wonder whether"something this room is flower-shaped", for instance. But, unaided by experience and imagery, he couldn't wonder whether something is *precisely* f_{17}. He had no way of singling out this precise shape. So, Buddy's hallucination wasn't just a "prod" for a cognitive capacity Buddy already had (in the way that a dream might prod you to exercise a pre-existing capacity to think of your grandmother). Rather, it *explains* his having the capacity to have a *novel* thought.

Here is another fascinating example. The color scientists Billock and Tsou (2010) caused participants in a scientific experiment to have an illusory experience of a new color they had never experienced or even been told about before. They described it as a bit yellowish and a bit bluish (somewhat as purple can be described as a bit reddish and a bit bluish). Call it *newhue*. Let's suppose Mary was one participant. Mary's non-veridical color experience explained her novel capacity to wonder whether anything is newhue. In fact, it explained her acquisition of novel *knowledge*. She now knows "what newhue is like", a kind of knowledge discussed in the previous section. In addition, she knows that newhue is more like yellow than it is like red. Similarly, a hallucination of novel shapes could give Mary knowledge of their resemblances. Hallucination does not give Mary knowledge of particular individuals but it does give her knowledge of universal properties. Strange as this may seem, hallucination, as well as veridical experience, can be a source of new knowledge about the non-mental world.

Naïve realists' indiscriminability theory does not fit with the explanatory role of Buddy and Mary's non-veridical experiences in these cases. On this theory, Buddy's hallucination and Mary's color illusion consist in nothing but in an *inability to know something* (in particular, that one is not successfully experiencing something f_{17}-shaped, or that one is not successfully experiencing the newhue color of some real object). And it is just intrinsically implausible that an *inability to know something* might explain Buddy and Mary's novel cognitive capacities in the examples above. In the case of Mary, it is especially implausible that an *inability to know something* might be a *source of new knowledge*, for instance that newhue is more like yellow than it is like red. Buddy and Mary's non-veridical experiences must be more than a mere inability to know something, if they are to plausibly explain their new cognitive capacities.[8]

To sum up: naïve realists cannot accept a substantive theory of hallucination and illusion, such as the representational theory, because such a substantive theory leads to the screening off problem. In response, Martin (2004) proposed the indiscriminability theory of experience, which is tailor-made to avoid the screening off problem. But it faces serious difficulties.

Representationalists may be able to provide a better account of hallucination and illusion than naïve realists. Their account of hallucination and illusion avoids the two problems we just raised for the indiscriminability theory.

First, the representational view avoids attributing a hallucination of a flower to the lazy dog and the insentient stone without invoking the unexplained technical term "impersonally unknowable". For it denies that they experientially represent a flower. True, representationalists need to explain their own technical term, "experientially represents", but as we saw in Section 3.1 they can explain it using the Ramsey-Lewis method.

Second, the representational view fits better than indiscriminability theory with the potential role of illusory and hallucinatory experiences in explaining novel thoughts. For it holds that experiences and thoughts have a congruent nature: both involve representing that things are a certain way (albeit in fundamentally different modes). So it is plausible that experientially representing that something is newhue or shaped f_{17} should be able to *explain* the capacity to represent in thought that something is newhue or shaped f_{17}, even in illusory and hallucinatory cases where no such object is present. (See also the "best explanation" argument for the representational view in Chapter 3.) This is much more plausible than the idea that a mere inability to know something might play that explanatory role.

As we saw, once we accept the representational view for hallucinatory and illusory cases, we are obliged to accept it across the board, screening off the naïve account of the character of veridical experience.

5.6 Representationalism *v* naïve realism: two arguments from science

If you crack open a textbook of sensation and perception, you are likely to find claims to the effect that science undermines naïve realism. For example:

> There is no color in the wavelengths; it is the nervous system that creates the experience of color. This also holds for other senses. Bitterness and sweetness are not in the molecular structures. They are created by the action of the nervous system. Pressure waves do not have pitch. Pitch is created by how the auditory system responds to the pressure waves.
>
> (Goldstein and Brockmole 2016: 221)

Basic naïve realism requires that sensible properties are primitive, pre-existing features of external items independent of our nervous systems. So if the scientists are right, naïve realism is wrong.

By contrast, representationalism is more flexible. If science supports eliminating sensible properties from the physical world, representationalists can agree. There are "internalist" varieties of representationalism on which experiences of sensible properties are entirely a creation of the brain. What sensible properties we seem to experience ("experientially represent") out in the world are entirely due to our internal neural responses to that world. Experience is externally directed but internally determined. Indeed, representationalists can say that this is only to be expected. After all, the primary function of the sensory systems is to enhance adaptive fitness, not to represent the objective character of the world.

So if the scientists are right, then we have reason to accept internalist representationalism over naïve realism. This is a variation on an old theme in the philosophy of perception. In Chapter 1, we saw that once upon a time many philosophers used science to support the sense datum view which locates sensible properties "in the mind" over naïve realism which locates them in the world. Internalist representationalism is the contemporary descendent of the sense datum view (Section 4.8).

In the present section, we will be replaying this old debate, but we will use some new evidence. We will begin by reviewing some recent scientific evidence for "good internal correlation" and "bad external correlation". Even in biologically normal circumstances, variations in the audible qualities, smells, and colors we experience (similarities and differences, increases in intensity, and so on) are better correlated with variations in our internal neural states than with variations in the external physical properties (pressure waves, reflectance properties, molecular structures) detected by our sensory systems. Then we will consider two arguments based on these findings against basic naïve realism and for internalist representationalism.

To be clear, the target of the arguments of this section is only *basic* naïve realism. In subsequent sections, we will consider whether other forms of "naïve realism" might be able to better accommodate evidence for the role of internal factors in shaping experience.

We start with a fascinating example of "bad external correlation" and "good internal correlation". When you produce a consonant such as /da/ or /ta/, the *voice onset time* (VOT) is defined as the time between the initial release of air and the onset of vocal cord vibration. The VOT has an effect on the acoustic waveform. As Figure 5.3 shows, if you repeatedly hear a speech sound that is increasing in VOT, then for a time you will experience

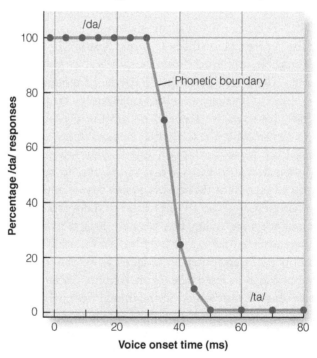

Figure 5.3 A continuous change in physical stimulus with a discontinuous change in auditory quality. From Eimas and Corbit (1973), with permission.

the same consonant (/da/, /da/, /da/), but when it gets to, say, 30 ms, all of a sudden you will experience a quite different consonant (/ta/, /ta/, /ta/). The categorical change in the perceived audible quality corresponds to no categorical change in the stimulus: the stimulus changes gradually (Goldstein and Brockmole 2016; O'Callaghan 2020b). By contrast, Chang *et al.* (2010) found that it corresponds to a categorical change in your neural response. In particular, in response to such a gradual change in the acoustic signal, there occurs a categorical change in neural activations in your posterior temporal gyrus (part of Wernicke's area), perfectly corresponding to the categorical change in your experience of sound.

In addition, even under normal conditions, variations in experienced loudness and pitch are related in an enormously complex, non-linear fashion to variations in several objective physical magnitudes. They are much more closely related to variations in internal neural parameters (Langers 2016).

In Chapter 4, we looked in some detail at examples of bad external correlation and good internal correlation involving smells and colors. Resemblances among smells are poorly correlated with resemblances among chemical-types, but they are well-correlated with resemblances among neural representations in the brain (see Figure 4.4 in Chapter 4). Additionally, sometimes a continuous change in the concentration of a chemical results in a categorical change in quality; in such cases, the only underlying categorical change occurs in the brain (Mainland 2018). Likewise, if you experience the blue-looking sphere along with a purple-looking grape and a green-looking leaf, then the resemblance-order of the color qualities you experience lines up with the resemblance-order of your *internal neural patterns* in visual area V4 of your brain much better than they line up with the resemblance-order of the reflectance properties of these objects (see Figure 4.5 in Chapter 4).

We will now construct two arguments based on these findings for preferring internalist representationalism to basic naïve realism.

The first argument is a *simplicity argument*:

(1) Basic naïve realists' primitivist theory of sensible properties requires "external laws"; given *bad external correlation*, they would be unsystematic and numerous.

(2) Internalist representationalism eliminates "external laws" and only requires "internal laws"; given *good internal correlation*, they will be systematic and simple.

(3) *Conclusion*: simplicity considerations strongly support internalist representationalism over basic naïve realism.

This two-premise argument specifically targets the first tenet of basic naïve realism: the "primitivist" theory of sensible properties, on which they are primitive properties that "emerge from" objective physical properties.

To illustrate, suppose that, somehow, before any sentient creatures evolved, by a cosmic accident, a series of sounds like the speech sounds shown in Figure 5.3 occurred, even though no one was around to produce or to hear them. Suppose that their VOTs gradually increased from 0 to 80 ms. The naïve realist must apparently hold that the gradual change in the physical stimulus grounded, at 30 ms, a discontinuous jump in the objective audible quality, from /da/ to /ta/, even though no one was yet around to hear it. This is an example of the "external laws" mentioned in premise 1.

Likewise, imagine that the grape with reflectance R_p, the sphere with reflectance R_b, and the leaf with reflectance R_g were around before any sentient creatures evolved. Naïve realists hold that these reflectances grounded the distinct primitive colors purple, blue, and green, even though there is a mismatch between the resemblances among these reflectance properties and the resemblances among the colors. And they hold that, even before we evolved, objective smell qualities emerged from clouds of molecules, even though there is no systematic relationship at all between molecular properties and smell qualities.

In short, in the face of "bad external correlation", basic naïve realists might retain their "primitivist" view of sensible properties, at the cost of holding that the "external laws" turned out to be totally unsystematic. This is exactly what John Campbell suggests. In fact, he says (2020: 410) that "it is difficult to see why [bad external correlation] should be thought of as a threat to primitivism" (see also Allen 2016: 128–129).

The reason why bad external correlation is a threat to basic naïve realism is that it means its primitivist theory of sensible properties is extremely complicated, as premise 1 states. It requires a huge list of external laws and, given bad external correlation, they cannot be systematized:

A When VOT reaches exactly 30 ms., this grounds a discontinuous qualitative change from /da/ to /ta/.

B If an object (e.g., the grape) has reflectance R_p (reflects "blue" light), then it has the distinct primitive quality *purple*.

C If an object (e.g., the sphere) has reflectance R_b (reflects "blue" light), then it has the distinct primitive quality *blue*.

D If an object (e.g., the leaf) has reflectance R_g (reflects "green" light), then it has the distinct primitive quality *green*.

E Necessarily, if there is an odor cloud made up of R-carvone, then it has the distinct primitive smell quality *minty*.

F Necessarily, if there is an odor cloud made up of R-limonene, then it has the distinct primitive smell quality *citrus*.

And so on for every sensible property

Bad external correlation means that each and every one of these external laws will have to be taken as basic. For instance, there is no general, systematic *functional dependence* of color qualities on reflectance properties, from which we could predict the specific associations B, C, D. The same applies to the "external laws" governing the emergence of primitive smell qualities from molecular structures (E, F, and so on). So basic naïve realism requires *millions* of brute "external laws" – one for each and every distinct sensible property.[9]

We should avoid this complex and messy account if we can. And internalist representationalism allows us to avoid it. On internalist representationalism, all that was out there before we evolved were sound-frequencies, molecular properties, reflectance properties, and so on. The audible qualities, smell qualities, and color qualities that we experience were not out there. They are eliminated from the objective physical world. So if we accept this view, then we eliminate the millions of unsystematic *external laws* listed above. Sensible properties only appeared when sentient creatures evolved. Therefore, we only need *internal laws* linking our internal neural states with our experiences of (representations of) such properties as occurring "out there". Given good internal correlation, there are systematic functional dependencies between them. So we can hope for a small handful of general, systematic internal laws. For instance:

I. If a person undergoes V4 neural state N, then they experience ("experientially represent") color quality $f(N)$.

II. If a person undergoes PPC (posterior piriform cortex) neural state N, then they experience smell quality $g(N)$.

Here f and g are systematic functions associating neural states organized in neural "similarity spaces" (abstract spaces in which neural states are organized by similarity) with sensible properties in congruent "quality spaces".

In short, instead of naïve realists' mere list of specific associations (like A–F above), the internalist approach promises something more systematic.

Compare how Newton's law of gravity specifies a systematic functional dependence between the masses and distances of bodies and the gravitational forces between them. Since we should prefer interpretations of the evidence that are simpler and more systematic, we have a reason to prefer internalist representationalism to basic naïve realism.

There is a second argument from good internal correlation and bad external correlation to the conclusion that internalist representationalism is to be preferred to basic naïve realism. We might call it the *fluke argument*:

(1) Basic naïve realism doesn't predict good internal correlation even where there is bad external correlation – in fact, it implies that this is a *fluke*.

(2) By contrast, internalist representationalism does predict good internal correlation even when there is bad external correlation.

(3) *Conclusion:* this is a reason to prefer internalist representationalism to basic naïve realism.

Before explaining the argument, let's start with an analogy. You put your hand in very hot water that is increasing in temperature. Imagine a naïve realist about pain. They say – echoing Campbell's slogan (2010: 20) cited earlier – that "looking for the explanation of the increasing sensory intensity in the nature of your neural state is looking in the wrong place" and "we have to look rather at the increasing temperature of the water". On this view, your internal neural firing rates, in response to the increasing temperature of the water, could be whatever you please. They could be related in a non-linear way to the increasing sensory intensity. Your internal neural firing rates could even be *decreasing* as the temperature increases. On the naïve realist view, as long as they detect, and enable you to experience, the *increasing* external temperature, the sensory intensity of your pain increases. For *that* external magnitude is what constitutes the increasing sensory intensity of your pain, according to the naïve realist model of pain.

Now if we discover that your sensory pain intensity is related in a non-linear and messy way to increasing temperature, but it is always linearly related to increasing firing rates of cortical neurons throughout the pain-matrix (equal increases in sensory pain intensities go with equal increases in firing rates), this would strongly count against the naïve realist theory of pain experience. It would suggest, contrary to naïve realism, that pain is not an objective feature of your hand. And your experience of (representation of) pain "out there" is fully determined by your neural response "in here". This internalist view about pain is to be preferred over naïve realism about pain precisely because it *predicts* good internal correlation even where there is bad external correlation. The naïve realist view does not. It must dismiss this finding as a fluke.

No one is a naïve realist about the experience of pain (but see Sections 4.4 and 4.5). However, Campbell and others do defend naïve realism for the experience of smell and color. If we agree that good internal correlation with bad external correlation supports an internalist theory of pain experience over naïve realism, we should agree that parallel findings for the experience of smell and color support an internalist account over naïve realism in these cases as well.

Take the experience of color. As noted above, many studies have indicated that the resemblances among the color qualities you experience generally line up very well with resemblances among your V4 neural patterns, even when they do not line up well with resemblances among the reflectance properties of the objects you experience.

Premise 1 of the fluke argument states that naïve realism does *not* predict that there should always be good internal correlation, even when there is bad external correlation. Instead, it implies that there could have easily been *bad* internal correlation. This is because, on basic naïve realism, the similarity-order of your V4 neural states is *incidental* to the similarity-order of your color experiences. Rather, the similarity-order of your color experiences is fixed by the similarity-order of the primitive colors of external objects that your V4 neural states enable you to experience.

To illustrate this, we can revisit a hypothetical case discussed in Chapter 4. In this hypothetical case, the color vision system evolved a bit differently. In particular, when your counterpart in this scenario consecutively views the grape, the sphere, and the leaf, everything is the same, but for one thing: his V4 neural representation (distributed neural pattern) of the sphere is different from yours, and occupies a different location in neural similarity space. It is more like his V4 neural representation of the *green-looking* leaf than his V4 representation of the *purple-looking* grape. (So, if you look back at Figure 4.5 in Chapter 4, imagine that the "circular" V4 neural representation of the sphere is replaced by a triangular one, similar to but distinct from the V4 neural representation of the green-looking leaf.) Basic naïve realism implies that, in this case, even though your counterpart's V4 neural representation of the sphere is different, it enables him to be experientially acquainted with the same "primitive" *blue* color of the sphere. Compare how, in the human-Martian case mentioned in Section 5.1, different neural states can be "used" to experience the same external color. So basic naïve realism implies that in this case, even though his V4 neural representation of the sphere is more like his V4 neural representation of the *green-looking* leaf than his V4 representation of the *purple-looking* grape, he still has a bluish color experience of the sphere that is more like his purplish color experience of the grape than his greenish color experience of the leaf. That is, it implies that in this case there is *bad* internal correlation.

This case vividly illustrates that basic naïve realism fails to predict good internal correlation even when there is bad external correlation. It implies that there easily could have been bad internal correlation, as there is in our counterparts in this hypothetical situation. So if we accept basic naïve realism, we must dismiss as an inexplicable fluke the finding that in fact there is always good internal correlation even when there is bad external correlation. And basic naïve realists cannot reply that even on their view good internal correlation is to be expected since it is just an artifact of good external correlation, because there is good internal correlation even when there is bad external correlation (Margot 2009: 814).

Premise 2 of the fluke argument states that internalist representationalism about color experience, by contrast, *does* immediately predict good internal correlation even when there is bad external correlation. For, on this view, what sensible colors you experientially represent as "out there" are systematically determined by your V4 internal neural states, just as what pain qualities you experientially represent in parts of your body are systematically determined by your internal neural states. So internalist representationalism about color experience is to be preferred to basic naïve realism.

In sum, the slogan of basic naïve realists is that "the explanation of the character of experience is always to be found in the world and never in the brain". But the finding of good internal correlation even where there is bad external correlation suggests that in many cases basic naïve realists have the matter backward. For many qualitative parameters, the only thing they are well-correlated with are neural parameters in the brain. The only possible explanation of this correlation is that those qualitative parameters are determined by those neural parameters.[10]

5.7 Can internalist-selectionist naïve realism answer the arguments from science?

We have seen that one problem for naïve realism concerns illusion and hallucination (Section 5.5). The representational view may have a better account of these cases. Another problem concerns scientific evidence for the role of internal factors in normal cases (Section 5.6). Again, the representational view may have an advantage here. There are "internalist" forms of representationalism on which how we experientially represent the world is due to our neural response to the world.

In the final two sections of this chapter, we will dwell on the second of these problems about the role of internal factors in shaping our experience of the world. In particular, we will look at two naïve realist responses. They involve rejecting basic naïve realism and moving to different forms. We start with *internalist-selectionist naïve realism*.

In the previous section, we saw that there is evidence for "internal dependence". In many cases what sensible properties we experience systematically depend on our neural processing. Basic naïve realism cannot accommodate internal dependence. Internalist-selectionist naïve realism is designed to accommodate it. Let us take these points in turn.

To begin with, for our purposes, internal dependence can be equated with the possibility of cases like the following (discussed in more detail in Chapter 4):

Smell example. You and an individual from a different species smell a cloud of *R*-limonene molecules. Your smell systems detect exactly the same chemical property of the cloud. But, due to differences in postreceptoral wiring, you and your counterpart's neural representations (distributed neural patterns) of the cloud occupy different locations in the "neural similarity space" for smells. So while you ostensibly experience a citrus-like quality out there, your counterpart ostensibly experiences a minty quality out there. You have different olfactory experiences.

Color example. You and an individual from a different species view the sphere. Your visual systems detect exactly the same reflectance-type *R* of the sphere. But, due to differences in postreceptoral wiring, you and your counterpart's V4 neural representations of the sphere occupy different locations in the "neural similarity space" for color. So while you ostensibly experience blue quality out there, your counterpart experiences greenish quality out there.

Basic naïve realism cannot accommodate internal dependence, that is, cannot accommodate these cases. For instance, consider the color case. As we briefly discussed in the previous section, basic naïve realism implies that you and your counterpart experience the same color quality, despite your different V4 color processing. One reason for this is its *simple causal (selectionist) theory* of the basis of experiential acquaintance. On basic naïve realism, the fact that the sphere has reflectance R grounds the fact that it has the primitive color *blue*. Moreover, since you and your counterpart's different cortical

V4 states causally detect this same property in the biologically normal way, the simple causal (selectionist) theory implies that they enable you and your counterpart to be experientially acquainted with the *same* primitive blue color. So basic naïve realism violates internal dependence. It violates the claim that, even if two individuals' sensory systems detect ("select") the same objective states, they can have different experiences due to differences in internal processing.

Since good internal correlation even when there is a bad external correlation supports internal dependence, we have reason to reject basic naïve realism. One option is to totally reject naïve realism altogether and move to "internalist representationalism", as discussed in the previous section. But maybe naïve realists should say "not so fast". Maybe there are alternative forms of naïve realism that can accommodate internal dependence.

Internalist-selectionist naïve realism is one such alternative (Allen 2016: 72). It modifies primitivism about sensible properties by holding that the reflectance R of the sphere grounds both primitive blue and primitive green. In fact, it grounds *every possible* color quality. All these colors of the sphere are "objective" and independent of our nervous systems. (I realize that this radical but bear with me.)

Next internalist-selectionist naïve realism claims that your visual processing selects the blue primitive color for you to experience, while your counterpart's different visual processing selects the green primitive color for him to experience.

This is at odds with the simple causal theory of experiential acquaintance that is part of basic naïve realism. As noted above, even though your V4 neural patterns are different, they are alike in what they causally detect in the world. So even if the sphere has multiple primitive colors grounded in its reflectance property R, the simple causal theory is insufficient to explain why you and your counterpart are acquainted with different ones.

So, in place of the simple causal theory of experiential acquaintance, internalist-selectionist naïve realists need a more complex internalist theory. The details here have not been worked out. But one rough idea is that being acquainted with the occurrence of a property P in the external world is grounded in (i) undergoing internal processing that is suitably caused by that occurrence of P and (ii) undergoing internal processing that "matches" the occurrence P, where "matching" might be defined in terms of a "second-order isomorphism" (see Shepard and Chipman 1970). Maybe your V4 neural state is in the blue region of neural similarity space, and so "matches" the blue primitive color of the ball. By contrast, your counterpart's V4 neural state is in the "green" region of neural similarity space, and so "matches" the green primitive color of the ball.

Here is how Keith Allen puts the view:

> The same physical properties can realize a number of distinct properties with different qualitative natures that different perceivers [like you and your counterpart] select in virtue of differences in their visual systems considered as a whole – where this includes their post-retinal processing mechanisms.
>
> (Allen 2016: 72)[11]

As we saw in Section 5.1, if naïve realism is true for the experience of color, it is probably true for the experience of other sensible properties, like audible qualities (/da/ and /ta/) and smell qualities (Campbell 2009). Internalist-selectionist naïve realism could be extended to these other cases. Thus, in the smell example above, the cloud of R-limonene molecules objectively instantiates a primitive citrus smell and a primitive minty smell – and indeed every primitive smell. They are just waiting there to be experienced by some creature. Your internal smell processing enables you to experience its objective citrus smell and your counterpart's different internal processing enables him to experience its objective minty smell. If the view is generalized in a consistent way, it implies that every external physical property grounds every possible sensible property.

In sum, here is how internalist-selectionist naïve realism modifies the tenets of basic naïve realism:

- Primitivism about sensible properties. *Complicates*
- The simple causal theory. *Replaces*

Does internalist-selectionist naïve realism avoid the scientific arguments against basic naïve realism?

Internalist-selectionist naïve realism does avoid the fluke argument because it holds that the natures and identities of our neural states play a major role in selecting which of the multitude of pre-existing sensible properties we experience. So it is to be expected that there should always be an isomorphism between our neural states and the qualities that we experience "out there".

But internalist-selectionist naïve realism obviously does not doge the simplicity argument. This is because that argument specifically targets primitivism about sensible properties, and internalist-selectionist naïve realism retains this view. In fact, it radically "complicates" this view. Since it holds that every external physical property grounds a multitude of primitive sensible properties, it not only needs an endless raft of "external laws" A–F (listed in the previous section) to explain the emergence in the external world of the primitive sensible properties that we experience, but even more external laws to explain the emergence of all the primitive sensible properties that we don't experience.

In general, simplicity considerations evidently strongly favor internalist representationalism over this extremely crowded theory of the external world. As we saw, this view needs no "external laws" at all because it entirely eliminates primitive sensible properties from pre-sentient reality. Sensible properties only appeared when sentient creatures evolved. Therefore, this view only needs a handful of systematic *internal laws* linking our internal neural states with our experiences of (representations of) such properties as occurring "out there".

5.8 Can ways-based naïve realism answer the arguments from science?

We just saw that internalist-selectionist naïve realism is still vulnerable to the "simplicity argument" that targets primitivism about sensible properties. The reason is that it retains (indeed complicates) primitivism about sensible properties.

In this final section, we will look at a second, even more radical departure from basic naïve realism. Just like internalist representationalism, *ways-based naïve realism* discards primitivism about the sensible properties on the basis of the simplicity argument. In fact, it holds that sensible properties are not objectively out there at all.

So, for instance, if there was a cloud of R-limonene molecules before we evolved, it did not objectively possess any smell quality, such as citrus-like or minty, just waiting to be experienced. Likewise, if the sphere shown in Figure 5.1 existed before we evolved, it did not objectively possess any particular color quality, such as *blue* or *green*, just waiting to be experienced. Audible qualities, such as /da/ and /ta/, were not out there either. If a tree fell in a forest, it did not make a sound with an objective loudness, pitch, and timbre. So this view avoids all the external laws (such as A–F) required by basic naïve realism and by internalist-selectionist naïve realism.

However, since ways-based naïve realism holds that the sensible properties are not objectively out there, it must also discard the naïve account of experience that is central to basic naïve realism (a version of the "act-object" model of experiential character). For instance, we cannot say that the physical sphere was first blue, and then the character of our color experience is constituted by our becoming experientially acquainted with this pre-existing quality of the sphere.

In place of the naïve account, ways-based naïve realists propose the following view. In normal experience, the character of our experiences of color, smell, and sound is grounded in the "ways" we experience physical objects, and this is internally dependent. So, for instance, a species might experience a cloud of R-limonene in a citrus-way or a minty-way, depending on their internal neural response to it. Or a species might experience the reflectance of the sphere in a "blue way" or a "green way", depending on their internal V4 neural response. So this view also avoids the fluke problem. Good correlation is to be expected, even when there is bad external correlation.

This "ways-based" account can be extended to variation in spatial experience. For instance, you might experience the sphere in any "oval way". This would be an illusion. As for hallucination, here we don't experience external physical objects in certain ways – in hallucination we don't experience external physical objects at all. So ways-based naïve realists need a different account here, such as the indiscriminability theory. However, we will set to the side this problem for naïve realism, because we already covered it in Section 5.5.[12]

What should we think about ways-based naïve realism? It is designed to avoid the arguments from science. But is it otherwise satisfactory? Is it just as good as an internalist variety of representationalism?

So far, ways-based naïve realism is underspecified. To illustrate, let us focus on a particular case. Suppose that Mary views a white sphere. However, because of some aberrant neural activity, the white sphere looks $oval_{17}$ and $blue_{23}$ to Mary, where $oval_{17}$ is a specific oval shape and $blue_{23}$ is a specific shade of blue (see Figure 5.4).

The ways-based naïve realist will say that the character of Mary's experience is grounded in her experiencing the white sphere in an "$oval_{17}$-and-$blue_{23}$ way". But what does this mean? Until this question is answered, no clear view has been put on the table. Different answers to this question result in quite different views.

We will develop a dilemma for ways-based naïve realism. In one elaboration, it is just a terminological variant of internalist representationalism, and so not a genuine rival to representationalism. In another elaboration, it

Figure 5.4 A white and round sphere looks blue and oval to Mary.

is a genuine rival to representationalism, but in that version it is unsatisfactory. Let us consider these options in turn.

The first option I have in mind uses a theory defended by William Alston (1999). Alston holds that the character of normal experience is grounded in a special perceptual relationship between three things: the *subject*, an *object*, and the *apparent properties*: "subject x experiences physical object y as having property F". In an illusion, physical object y doesn't actually have property F.[13] Now ways-based naïve realists might say that for a subject x to experience an object y in an "F-way" is just for subject x to experience object y as F, where this can be determined by internal factors. In that case, their account of Mary's experience comes to this:

> [1] The character of Mary's experience is constituted by her *experiencing* the white sphere as *oval$_{17}$* and *blue$_{23}$*, even though the sphere does not possess these properties.

But notice that Alston's account of Mary's experience is just a verbal variant of internalist representationalism: for we could choose to express the same view by saying that the character of Mary's experience is constituted by her "experientially representing" the sphere as oval$_{17}$ and blue$_{23}$ (so that it seems to her that it has these properties), even though the sphere does not possess these properties.[14]

In general, if proponents of ways-based naïve realism accept Alston's view, their view effectively becomes a form of internalist representationalism, rather than a rival to it. On the resulting view, before we evolved, external items did not have audible qualities, smells, or colors. (Recall that

I assumed at the outset that ways-based naïve realists agree with internalist representationalists on this point.) Then, due to our internal processing, we came to experience objects out there (we could also say we came to "experientially represent" objects out there) as having certain audible qualities, smell qualities, and colors.[15] We also came to experience them as having various spatial properties. That is the sense in which we experienced them in various "ways".

In addition, if we accept what is effectively a representational account of normal experience, we might as well accept a representational account of hallucination (rather than the problematic indiscriminability theory criticized in Section 5.5). That is, if we hold with Alston that physical objects can experientially appear other than they are (as in Mary's illusion), why not explain hallucination by saying that it can appear to you (you can "experientially represent") that there is an object even if there is not one?

So let us turn to a second option for elaborating "ways-based" naïve realism. On *neurocomputational naïve realism*, ways of experiencing are just types of neural states.[16] So the right account of Mary's illusory experience is as follows:

[2] The character of Mary's experience consists in her experiencing the round and white sphere by way of internal neural state N_o and internal neural state N_b.

Here N_o and N_b are the internal neural correlates of the experience of $oval_{17}$ and the experience of $blue_{23}$. Normally, their occurrence in the brain is caused by the presence of an oval and blue thing, but in this abnormal case their occurrence in Mary's brain is caused by the presence of a round and white sphere.

In general, on neurocomputational naïve realism, before we evolved, external items, such as a cloud of R-limonene or the physical sphere, did not objectively have specific smells or colors. Then we came to experience them in certain ways: for instance, in a citrus-like way or a blue-way. We also came to experience external items in a "round" way, an "over-there" way, and so on. This consists in our experiencing them by way of certain neural states. So our experiences partly depend on those neural states. Neurocomputational "naïve realism", then, is somewhat similar to the "internal physical state view" that was the subject of Chapter 2.

Unlike Alston's view, neurocomputational "naïve realism" is indeed a genuine rival to internalist representationalism, rather than simply a version of it. What should we say about neurocomputational naïve realism?

Unlike basic naïve realism, it does avoid the arguments from science. But is it just as good as an internalist variety of representationalism?

To begin with, it is not obvious why neurocomputational naïve realism should be preferred over internalist representationalism. The case for *basic* naïve realism over representationalism was that it is more "intrinsically plausible" (Section 5.3). The reason is that, unlike representationalism, basic naïve realism endorses the intuitive act-object account of the character of experience: plus or minus a bit, differences in the character of experience are constituted by our experiencing actual differences in the objects of experience (e.g., differences in their colors and shapes). But, somewhat like the internal physical state view, "neurocomputational" naïve realism rejects the act-object account. Differences in the character of experience are constituted by differences in the "ways" we experience objects, which are just differences in neural responses.

On the other hand, there is also a problem with neurocomputational naïve realism that internalist representationalism avoids. Neurocomputational naïve realism violates the following pretheoretically plausible claim:

> [#] The shape property oval$_{17}$ and the color quality blue$_{23}$ *somehow* figure in the account of what constitutes the character of Mary's illusory experience of the white sphere, even if they are not possessed by the sphere. For part of what it is to have the experience is to ostensibly experience these properties together.

This is not a specific theory of experience. It is rather a pretheoretically plausible constraint on an adequate theory.

Let me explain why neurocomputational naïve realism violates claim [#], why this is problematic, and why internalist representationalism accommodates [#].

Neurocomputational naïve realism clearly violates [#]. The neural states N_o and N_b figure in its account [2] of what constitutes the character of Mary's experience. But the shape property oval$_{17}$ and the color quality blue$_{23}$ nowhere figure in that account. Similarly, the internal physical state view violates [#], as we saw in Section 2.5.

This is a problem because [#] is pretheoretically plausible. To appreciate this, just look at Figure 5.4. Clearly, the shape oval$_{17}$ somehow figures in the account of what it is to have this experience, in accordance with [#]. To paraphrase Peacocke (2008: 10), "if we do not mention the shape oval$_{17}$ in characterizing what constitutes the visual experience, we omit a subjective feature of the experience". Because it violates this, neurocomputational naïve realism is immediately implausible. In violation of [#], it wrongly implies that Mary's experience is akin to a head pain caused by getting hit by a sphere, in that it can be fully characterized without mentioning the shape $oval_{17}$.

There is another reason to accept [#], besides its pretheoretical plausibility. By having an experience with the relevant character, Mary can immediately think that the object is $oval_{17}$, by taking her experience at "face-value" and thinking *the object is "that way"*, where this demonstrates the specific way the sphere seems to her. (Since her experience is illusory and the sphere is not $oval_{17}$, this thought would be false.) Likewise, she can immediately think that the object is $blue_{23}$. This is part of the explanatory role of experience that naïve realists themselves emphasize (Sections 5.4 and 5.5). If, by having an experience with the relevant character, Mary can immediately think that the object is $oval_{17}$, then the shape $oval_{17}$ must somehow figure in the account of what constitutes the character of the experience, even though the sphere does not possess this shape. Because it violates [#], neurocomputational naïve realism is at odds with the fact that, simply by having her experience, Mary can think about the shape $oval_{17}$.

By contrast, internalist representationalism accommodates [#]. So does Alston's equivalent view. On this view, the character of Mary's experience is constituted by her experiencing (or "experientially representing") the white sphere as $oval_{17}$ and $blue_{23}$, as a *result* of her neural states N_o and N_b. In this way, the properties figure in the account of what constitutes her experience, even if they are not possessed by the sphere. (Likewise, traditional sense datum theory of Russell 1912a and Peacocke 2008 accommodate [#], because it holds that Mary experiences an $oval_{17}$ and $blue_{23}$ sense datum in a private visual field.) This is pretheoretically plausible. And it fits with the potential explanatory role of her experience. For example, since her experience consists in her experientially representing the round sphere as $oval_{17}$, her experience immediately enables her to represent precisely *this* shape in thought.

In sum, either ways-based naïve realism can be developed so that it accommodates [#], or else not. A version that does accommodate [#], such as the Alston-inspired version we discussed, is effectively a form of representationalism, rather than a rival to it. A version that does not accommodate [#], like neurocomputational naïve realism, is problematic, because there are strong reasons to accept [#].

Summary

In this chapter, we looked at the contest between contemporary naïve realism and representationalism. We started with "basic" naïve realism and later moved on to more complex forms.

Basic naïve realism is more "intrinsically plausible" than representationalism. But it faces two problems.

First, any form of naïve realism has trouble with hallucination and illusion. Representationalism may have some advantages here.

Second, basic naïve realism doesn't fit well with scientific evidence for the role of the brain in shaping experience (good internal correlation and bad external correlation). On the other hand, there are internalist varieties of representationalism that nicely accommodate this evidence.

This led us to consider other forms of naïve realism that may fit better with this evidence: internalist-selectionist naïve realism and ways-based naïve realism. But they are not clearly superior to representationalism.

In sum, naïve realism nicely accommodates the externally directed character of experience but has difficulty accommodating internal dependence.

Further Reading

There are arguments for naïve realism over representationalism besides the arguments from intrinsic plausibility and explanatory role we have considered in this chapter. For example, Fish (2009: 75–79) and Campbell (2010: 20) argue that naïve realism helps close the "explanatory gap" between the physical and the experiential. For discussion, see Logue (2012a), Fish (2013), and Niikawa (2014). Martin's main argument for naïve realism over representationalism is based on an alleged datum about the relationship between perceptual experience and sensory imagination. For critical discussion, see Burge (2005), Logue (2009), and Dorsch (2010). For a helpful overview see Soteriou (2016).

For recent discussion of the arguments from science against naïve realism discussed in Section 5.6, see Allen (2016), Beck (2018), Campbell (2020), MacGregor (2015), Fish (2013), Kalderon (2020), and Logue (2017).

An old but interesting and serious problem with naïve realism we were unable to consider concerns "time-lag". For instance, when you see a star, the star may not exist anymore, because it takes time for the light from the star to reach your eyes. See Russell (1927) and Moran (2019b).

Notes

1   In the checker-shadow illusion, there does exist an object that you "perceive", namely the tile. But the act-object claim is still false in this case because it requires more than that you perceive an object such as the tile. It requires the character of your experience is grounded in your experiencing the actual state of its being light grey – but no such state exists.

2   The parenthetical qualification "or having an indiscriminable illusion or hallucination" is needed because, as we shall see in Section 5.5, Mary's having a hallucinatory or illusory experience of a color or shape would be enough for her to know what the color or shape is like. This casts doubt on the naïve realists' claim that experiential acquaintance with actual occurrences of colors and shapes in the world is *necessary for* knowledge of what those colors and shapes are like. However, I will set this aside.

3   The pathological condition called "blindsight" is another example of representation without experience (Weiskrantz 1986).

4   One response here is that in the normal case (but not the hallucination case) Buddy's experientially representing a flower-shaped object is grounded in the naïve realist property of his being acquainted with a flower-shaped object (Pautz 2010a: 296; Logue 2012b: 179). So there is no screening off. But this grounding claim is *ad hoc* and doesn't follow from any account of experiential representation.

5   Allen (2015) and Moran (2019a) are naïve realists who give positive theories of hallucination but then attempt in similar ways to avoid generalizing them to normal experience. This idea was briefly discussed in Section 1.4. See Sethi (2019) for a quite different way of resisting the generalization step.

6   Martin thinks that the solution to the screening-off problem crucially depends on an idea about explanatory "inheritance" (for details see Martin 2004: 68–70). But if the problem is only to explain hallucination in a way that retains the key naïve realist claim "in the normal case the fact that Buddy successfully experiences the flower grounds the fact that he has an experience with the flower-like character", then the solution only requires (a) the indiscriminability theory of experience in terms of an inability to know and (b) the general principle that the fact that p grounds the inability to know one is in a situation in which it is *not* the case that p.

7   This kind of objection is due to Williamson (1995: 562) and Siegel (2004: 98).

8   For the general point that non-veridical experience can provide "knowledge of universals", see Russell (1912a: chap. X) and Johnston (2004). For how it can enable novel thoughts (an idea that is neutral on the existence of "universals"), and why this might make a problem for the indiscriminability theory in particular, see Pautz (2010a: 277, 289), Brewer (2011: 112ff), Hellie (2010: fn.5), Alford-Duguid and Arsenaul (2017), and Gupta (2019: 175–177).

9   A clarification: it is only "primitivist" realism about sensible properties that faces the complexity problem. If you are instead a "reductive" realist who holds that sensible properties (sensible colors, smells) are *identical with* complex properties of external items, then you don't need a complex raft of "external laws" to explain their correlation (Byrne and Hilbert 2003: 7). However, as we saw in Section 4.5, bad external correlation creates another type of problem for this view: the "problem of meaning".

10 Basic naïve realism faces another problem. On this view, before sentient creatures evolved, every object had many objective colors belonging to different color spaces (so that every class of objects, however miscellaneous, have one primitive color in common). Further, which of those colors a species can perceive is merely determined by which of them they happen to detect (which objects happen to be

"metameric matches" for that species: see Byrne and Hilbert 2003). If so, why aren't there species that are only capable of perceiving (detecting) some *but not* all colors from one color space, and some *but not all* colors from another color space? Why aren't we such a species?

11   Johnston (2007) also proposes a view in the general vicinity of internalist-selectionist naïve realism. This type of view has a long history: see Price (1932: 41ff) and Broad (1925: 161ff).

12   Views in the general vicinity of "ways-based" naïve realism are defended by Langsam (1997), Alston (1999), Logue (2012a), Beck (2018), and French and Phillips (2020). Block (2007: 89) and Chirimuuta (2015: 142) also appeal to "ways of perceiving" but would not describe themselves as "naïve realists".

13   For earlier discussions of this view, see Moore (1918: 23–25) and (Broad 1923: 237) and Jackson (1977: 90). Russell (1912a) defended a similar theory of judgment. French and Phillips (2020: 13 and personal communication) similarly hold that the fact that Mary's has an illusory experience with the relevant character is constituted by the fact that she experiences the external state of the sphere *in such a way that it "strikes" her as blue and oval*, even if it is not blue and oval.

14   In fact, on our "Ramsey-Lewis" formulation of the representational view in Chapter 3, representationalism becomes the claim that experience involves a "neutral" relation that plays a certain explanatory role. Since Alston's view endorses this idea, it *is* a version of representationalism, on this formulation.

15   Like "illusionist representationalists", Alston could say that, even though we evolved to experience external things as having sensible properties, they do not possess those sensible properties. Alternatively, he could co-opt the "co-evolution" view of other representationalists (like Shoemaker 1994 and McGinn 1996) according to which external items somehow acquired sensible properties as we evolved to experience them as having those sensible properties. See Chapter 4 for these options.

16   Beck (2019; personal communication) defends a form of neurocomputational naïve realism that violates [#]. Logue (2012a: 223) is a naïve realist who explains variation in the character of experience in terms of "features of the subject". So she may also reject [#].

6

CONCLUSION

Here we have one of the distinctions that cause most trouble in philosophy –
the distinction between appearance and reality.

—Bertrand Russell (1912a)

Don't you wonder sometimes about sound and vision?

—David Bowie (1977)

It is time to bring the matter to a close.

Our central question has been the character question. What is it to have
an experience with a certain character – a certain specific "type" of experience? What do differences in the character of experience consist in?

The external-internal puzzle is the reason why this question is so difficult to answer. Experiences are to varying degrees externally directed. They
are essentially "spatial". But they are also internally dependent. There are
internally-generated illusions and hallucinations. And psychophysics and
neuroscience suggest that, even in normal perception, our experience of
sensible properties is especially dependent on our internal neural processing. There is no formal or logical conflict between these ideas. But it is very
hard to come up with a plausible theory of experience that fully accommodates both of them.

	External directedness	Internal dependence
Basic naïve realism Response-independent representationalism	Yes	No
Internal physical state view	No	Yes
Sense datum view Internalist representationalism	Yes	Yes

Figure 6.1 Table of Views.

Figure 6.1 shows how different views respond to this puzzle.

Let us conclude by reviewing these views and their responses to the external-internal puzzle.

6.1 Explaining essential external directedness at the cost of denying internal dependence

Basic naïve realism and response-independent representationalism are different. Basic naïve realism provides an "act-object" explanation of the character of experience, while response-independent representationalism provides a representational explanation. However, in another way, basic naïve realism and this specific form of representationalism are very similar. They both hold that the sensible properties – colors, smell qualities, audible qualities – were "out there" before sentient creatures evolved, just as shapes and sizes were out there. Then brains evolved that detected these pre-existing properties in the right way. Thus we came to experience them. Our brains simply "open the window shade" to enable us to experience the objective world. Plus or minus a bit, the character of experience is constituted by what properties we in this way experience, or seem to experience.

These views provide an attractively *simple* and *unmysterious* explanation of the externally directed character of experience. For instance, on response-independent representationalism, we experientially represent external perceptible properties in the same way a thermometer represents temperatures.

But they do not accommodate internal dependence about our experience of sensible properties, as formulated in Section 4.4. In fact, proponents of basic naïve realism and response-independent representationalism are up front about their rejection of internal dependence in this sense. Consider the very similar quotations from the response-independent representation-alist Michael Tye and the naïve realist John Campbell:

> Peer as long as you like at the detailed functioning of the brain. That is not where phenomenal character is to be found. Neuroscientists are looking in the wrong place.
>
> (Tye 1995: 162–163)

> Looking for the qualitative character of experience in the nature of a brain state is looking for it in the wrong place; we have to be looking rather at the [properties] of the objects experienced [in external world].
>
> (Campbell 2010: 20)

Tye and Campbell, then, hold that the correct solution to the external-internal puzzle is to deny one of the ideas that generate the puzzle. They nicely explain the externally directed character of experience. But they deny internal dependence when it comes to our experience of sensible properties (as formulated in Section 4.4). They hold that the brain merely plays an enabling role, rather than a determinative role.

However, the empirical evidence for internal dependence is quite per-suasive. For many qualitative parameters, *the only thing they are well correlated with are neural parameters in the brain.* So it may be hard to avoid the conclusion that the brain plays a determinative role and not merely an enabling role. This is especially clear in the case of pain. What pains you experience "out there" in regions of your body depends on neural processing "in here". But the evidence is the same for other types of experiences. So consistency demands that we also hold that what smell qualities, audible qualities, and color qualities we experience "out there" in external space depends on neural processing in the brain.

6.2 Explaining internal dependence at the cost of denying essential external directedness

The internal physical state holds that experiences just are internal physical states, for instance neural states. Differences in experiences just are dif-ferences in these neural states. The problem with this view is the oppo-site of the problem with basic naïve realism and response-independent representationalism. While it accommodates a strong form of internal dependence in a simple and unmysterious way, the price is that it is apparently at odds with essential external directedness.

Of course, internal physical state theorists may say that the price is worth paying. For example, David Papineau explicitly rejects essential external directedness. But others will insist that essential external directedness is just an undeniable comment about the character of experience. For instance, contrast a headache with the experience of an orange and round item moving to the right. Here is an obvious comment about the phenomenology of the head pain: it does *not* essentially involve the seeming presence of a round thing moving to the right. It is an equally obvious comment about the phenomenology of the orange-experience that it *does* essentially involve the seeming presence of a *round item moving to the right*. So these spatial terms figure in the account of what it is have the experience. They do not figure in the account of what it is to have a neural state – a neural state can be *completely* described in terms of *types of neurons* and the *times, directions,* and *intensities* at which they fire. So the visual experience must be distinct from the neural state – something more than the neural state – even if it depends on the neural state. If this is right, essential external directedness rules out the internal physical state view. We need a view that accommodates both essential external directedness and internal dependence.

6.3 Accepting both essential external directedness and internal dependence

This brings us to the sense datum view and internalist (nonreductive) representationalism. The sense datum view is a kind of internalist "act-object" theory, while internalist representationalism rejects the act-object model.

But in another way these views are quite similar. In fact, internalist representationalism can be seen as the contemporary descendent of the sense datum view. On both views, the sensible properties were not out there before we evolved. The brain is inventive. We came to experience novel sensible properties "out there" due to neural processing in the head. Experiences are enabled by neural states but they are something more than neural states. On the sense datum view, experiences are relations to sense data in private spaces created by our brain states. By contrast, on internalist representationalism, they are representational states in which sense data *seem* to exist in space. Our neural processing generates our experiences but we only have access to how things seem as a result of the neural processing.

These views accommodate both essential external directedness and a very strong form of internal dependence. But they face serious problems. Since the sense datum view is generally rejected, let us focus on internalist representationalism. To begin with, internalist representationalism is mysterious and complicated. On this view, experiential representation is not reducible to detection or indeed anything else. The way in which we experientially represent perceptible properties is very different from the way in which thermometers represent temperatures. Rather than "opening the window shade" to reveal the world it is, the brain constructs a "virtual reality" for us to experience. This is all very mysterious. How did this capacity evolve? How did the brain manage to "invent" experiences of novel properties that are not instantiated in the brain? This view seems to require a complex raft of brute associations between different brain states and the experiential representation of different sensible properties.

There is another problem with internalist representationalism. Since experientially representing color qualities requires experientially representing them as filling spatial regions, if the experiential representation of color qualities is internally determined, then so must be the experiential representation of spatial properties. But the internalist model is not so plausible for the experiential representation of spatial properties. For we think that the spatial properties we experience *were* out there before we evolved. And if this is right, it is very natural to think that the brain doesn't have an intrinsic capacity to enable us to experientially represent them; rather, we came to experientially represent them only because our brains have a history of detecting their occurrence in the world (in the way a thermometer represents temperatures).

A great deal turns on whether these problems can be solved. The mysteriousness of internalist representationalism might be somewhat allayed by future research in neuroscience showing that what perceptible properties you experientially represent can be systematically "decoded" by looking at internal processing alone (Adams 1987; Haynes 2009; Prinz 2012). The problem about spatial perception might be resolved by future research in physics. If our best physical theories suggest that space-as-we-experience-it is no more objectively out there than color-as-we-experience-it (Albert 1996; Chalmers 2012; Ney and Albert 2013), this would be a boon to across-the-board internalist representationalism. On the other hand, it would also be quite a blow to commonsense: it would mean that the real world is alien and we are totally cut off from it. (This is also an implication of the sense datum view: see Section 1.8.) So, somewhat surprisingly, issues in the philosophy of perception turn out to be closely bound up with issues in physics.

The puzzle of perception – the puzzle of "appearance vs reality" – has been a focal point of philosophy from the start. For instance, Democritus (c. 460–c. 370 BC) said: "the objects of sense are supposed to be real and it is customary to regard them as such, but in truth they are not: only the atoms and the void are real." We have made progress since then. There have been advances in science and innovations in philosophy. But here as elsewhere in philosophy, there is no perfect solution. So the puzzle of perception remains alive and well.

Further Reading

Now that you have some background in the philosophy of perception, you can move on to more advanced texts. Some recent (2000s) monographs in the philosophy of perception include Block (2020), Breckenridge (2018), Burge (2010), Campbell (2002), Campbell and Cassam (2014), Brewer (2011), Fish (2009), Foster (2000), Hill (2009), Fulkerson (2014), Gupta (2019), Matthen (2005), Nanay (2014), O'Callaghan (2007, 2020a), Orlandi (2014), Mendelovici (2018), Montague (2016), Price and Barrell (2012), Schellenberg (2018), Siegel (2010), Smith (2002), Soteriou (2016), Speaks (2015), Tye (2009), and Watzl (2017).

This book has been primarily focused on "the character question": what constitutes the qualitative character of experience? The views we have addressed are in the first instance answers to this basic question. However, there are many other questions in the philosophy of perception that we have only addressed tangentially: What is it to perceive an object? How does perception enable us to think about objects and form a conception of the world? How does it give us knowledge of that world? There are also many questions tackled by scientists that are of interest to philosophers. What is the format of object-file representations? What is the extent of top-down influences on perception? What is the correct account of "amodal" perception? What kinds of cross-modal interactions are there? Does the brain literally perform Bayesian "inherences" to construct perceptual representations? Many of the books listed above contain more discussion of these other questions.

GLOSSARY

Act-object assumption A starting point of early 20th-century philosophy of perception (Russell, Moore, Price). The act-object assumption doesn't just claim that we perceive objects, or that we seem to perceive objects – claims everyone will accept. It claims that the character of experience is *constituted by* or *grounded in* our experiencing the states of actual objects, for instance their shapes and colors. The sense datum view is an example of an across-the-board act-object theory, where the "objects" are non-physical images. Contemporary basic naïve realists hold that the relevant objects are physical objects and restrict the act-object assumption to normal perception.

Character question The central question of this book. The question of the *definition* of what it is to have different experience-types (experiences with different "characters"), such as the tomato-experience or the orange-experience or the blue-sphere experience. On another interpretation, the question of what *grounds* or *constitutes* having different experience-types. Some naïve realists hold that the same experience-type can be constituted by or grounded in different things in veridical and non-veridical cases.

Essential external directedness A pretheoretically plausible constraint on a correct answer to the character question. It states that the correct definition of what it is to have certain visual experience-types will mention spatial features, like *round* and *moving to the right*. Also called the "spatial datum". It doesn't require an act-object theory. One element of the "external-internal puzzle" that is a focus of this book.

Experience-type When you see a red tomato, or see an orange tomato in red light, your experiences might be "exactly the same" or "have the same character", even though the physical stimulus is different. You have the same type of experience, or "experience-type". Most philosophers hold that you could have the same experience-type in a hallucination case as well.

External-internal puzzle The central organizing puzzle of this book. The puzzle is about how to come up with an answer to the character question that respects both essential external directedness and internal dependence. It is easy to sketch an answer that accommodates one of these ideas at the expense of the other; it is very hard to come up with an answer that accommodates both.

Good internal correlation, bad external correlation Even in *normal experience*, variations in the *sensible properties* (similarities and differences) we experience are much better correlated with variations in our neural responses than with variations in the external states those internal responses have the function of detecting.

Illusion, hallucination In a veridical experience of a tomato, you in some sense perceive a physical item (e.g., a tomato), and it seems to you the way it is (red and round). In an illusion, you perceive a physical item, but it seems different from the way it really is. In a hallucination, you have an experience, but you fail to perceive any real physical item at all.

Internal dependence There are two types. (a) Internal dependence in illusion and hallucination. You can have illusory and hallucinatory experiences as a result of internal processes. (b) Internal dependence about our experience of sensible properties. In hypothetical "coincidental variation cases", you and your counterpart can experience different sensible properties due to differences in internal processing, even though your sensory systems have the biological function of detecting ("selecting") the same objective states. It is supported by bad external correlation and good internal correlation.

Internalism Experiential internalism goes beyond internal dependence. It holds that *all* aspects of the character of your experiences are fully and necessarily determined your internal neural states, so that even a life-long "brain in a void" could have the same experiences as you. Examples of views that endorse experiential internalism include the sense datum view, the internal physical state view, and internalist representationalism. The sense datum view endorses a "dualist" form where the determination is mediated by basic "psychophysical laws".

Property, state, state of affairs A *property* is a general way things might be, such as red and round. A *state* the concrete occurrence of a property in an object, for instance, the redness of an object. It cannot exist unless the object really has the property. A *state of affairs* is a very different entity. For instance, imagine there is nothing in the space before you. Still, there exists the *possible* state of affairs *some object there being red*. It is a kind of abstract item. If an actual red thing is brought into this space, the same abstract item now obtains in the sense that it "corresponds to reality".

Seems-gambit A way of rejecting the general act-object assumption that was once dominant in early 20th-century philosophy of mind. If you should hallucinate a tomato, the right thing to say is that it vividly *seems* to you that a red and round object exists then and there but, contrary to the general act-object assumption, there does not actually exist such an object.

Sensible properties, perceptible properties In this book, we use "perceptible properties" as a catch-all term for all the properties that we can "experience" or "perceive", including spatial and temporal properties. We use "sensible properties" (also "sensible qualities") to refer to a special subset of perceptible properties. The term is hard to define, but examples include sensible colors, audible qualities, smell qualities, taste qualities, and pain qualities. Properties in this group are difficult to locate in the quantitative world of physics. The question of what to say about them has been a central concern in the philosophy of perception since the 17th-century scientific revolution.

REFERENCES

Adams, R. 1987. Flavors, Colors, and God. In his *The Virtue of Faith and Other Essays in Philosophical Theology*. Oxford: Oxford University Press.

Albert, D. Z. 1996. Elementary Quantum Metaphysics. In J. Cushing, A. Fine, and S. Goldstein (eds.), *Bohmian Mechanics and Quantum Theory: An Appraisal*. Dordrecht: Kluwer, pp. 277–284.

Alford-Duguid, D. and M. Arsenault. 2017. On the Explanatory Power of Hallucination. *Synthese* 194: 1765–1785.

Allen, K. 2013. Blur. *Philosophical Studies* 162: 257–273.

Allen, K. 2015. Hallucination and Imagination. *Australasian Journal of Philosophy* 93: 287–302.

Allen, K. 2016. *A Naïve Realist Theory of Colour*. Oxford: Oxford University Press.

Alston, W. 1999. Back to the Theory of Appearing. *Philosophical Perspectives* 13: 181–203.

Anscombe, G. E. M. 1965. The Intentionality of Sensation: A Grammatical Feature. In R. Butler (ed.), *Analytic Philosophy, Second Series*. Oxford: Blackwell.

Armstrong, D. 1968. *A Materialist Theory of Mind*. London: Routledge.

Armstrong, D. 1981. The Causal Theory of the Mind. Reprinted in D. Chalmers (ed.), *Philosophy of Mind*. Oxford: Oxford University Press.

Austin, J. 1962. *Sense and Sensibilia*. Oxford: Oxford University Press.

Ayer, A. 1940. *The Foundations of Empirical Knowledge*. London: Macmillan.

Barnes, W. 1944–1945. The Myth of Sense-Data. *Proceedings of the Aristotelian Society* 45: 89–117.

Battaglia, P., J. Hamrick, and J. Tenenbaum. 2013. Simulation as an Engine of Physical Scene Understanding. *Proceedings of the National Academy of Sciences* 110: 18327–18332.

Batty, C. 2010. A Representational Account of Olfactory Experience. *Canadian Journal of Philosophy* 40: 511–538.

Bayne, T. 2010. *The Unity of Consciousness*. Oxford: Oxford University Press.

Bealer, G. 1982. *Quality and Concept*. Oxford: Oxford University Press.

Beck, O. 2018. Rethinking Naïve Realism. *Philosophical Studies* 176: 607–633.

Berger, J. 2018. A Defense of Holistic Representationalism. *Mind and Language* 33: 161–176.

Berkeley, G. 1713. *Three Dialogues between Hylas and Philonous*. https://www.earlymoderntexts.com/assets/pdfs/berkeley1713.pdf

Billock, V. and B. Tsou. 2010. Seeing Forbidden Colors. *Scientific American* 302: 72–77.

Block, N. 2020. *The Border Between Seeing and Thinking*. Manuscript.

Block, N. 1990. Inverted Earth. *Philosophical Perspectives* 4: 53–79.

Block, N. 1994. Qualia. In S. Guttenplan (ed.), *A Companion to the Philosophy of Mind*. Oxford: Blackwell, pp. 514–520.

Block, N. 2007. Wittgenstein and Qualia. *Philosophical Perspectives* 21: 73–115.

Block, N. 2010. Attention and Mental Paint. *Philosophical Issues* 20: 23–63.

Block, N. 2015. The Puzzle of Perceptual Precision. In T. Metzinger and J. M. Windt (eds.), *Open Mind*: 5(T). Frankfurt am Main: Mind Group.

Block, N. 2019. Arguments Pro and Con on Adam Pautz's External Directedness Principle. In A. Pautz and D. Stoljar (eds.), *Blockheads!* Cambridge: MIT Press.

Block, N. and J. A. Fodor. 1972. What Psychological States Are Not. *Philosophical Review* 81: 159–181.

Boghossian, P. and D. Velleman. 1989. Colour as a Secondary Quality. *Mind* 98: 81–103.

Bohon, K. S., K. L. Hermann, T. Hansen, and B. R. Conway. 2016. Representation of Perceptual Color Space in Macaque Posterior Inferior Temporal Cortex (the V4 Complex). eNeuro 3(4): ENEURO-0039.

Bourget, D. 2019. Relational vs Adverbial Conceptions of Phenomenal Intentionality. In A. Sullivan (ed.), *Sensations, Thoughts, Language: Essays in Honor of Brian Loar*. New York: Routledge, pp. 137–166.

Bourget, D. and A. Mendelovici. 2019. Phenomenal Intentionality. https://plato.stanford.edu/entries/phenomenal-intentionality/

Bowie, D. 1977. Sound and Vision. In the album *Low*. RCA Records.

Bradley, A. 2021. The Paradox of Pain. *Philosophical Quarterly*. Advance Article.

Breckenridge, W. 2018. *Visual Experience: A Semantic Approach*. Oxford: Oxford University Press.

Brewer, B. 2011. *Perception and Its Objects*. Oxford: Oxford University Press.

Brewer, B. 2017. The Object View of Perception. *Topoi* 36: 215–227.

Brewer, B. 2019a. Attention and Direct Realism. In. A. Pautz and D. Stoljar (eds.), *Blockheads!* Cambridge: MIT Press.

Brewer, B. 2019b. Visual Experience, Revelation, and the Three Rs. In J. Knowles and T. Raleigh (eds.), *Acquaintance: New Essays*. Oxford: Oxford University Press, pp. 277–292.

Broad, C. D. 1923. *Scientific Thought*. London: Routledge & Kegan Paul.

Broad, C. D. 1925. *The Mind and Its Place in Nature*. London: Routledge & Kegan Paul.

Brown, D. 2012. Losing Grip on the World: From Illusion to Sense-Data. In M. Raftopoulos (ed.), *Perception, Realism and the Problem of Reference*. Cambridge: Cambridge University Press. pp. 68–95.

Burge, T. 2003. Qualia and Intentional Content: Reply to Block. In M. Hahn and B. Ramberg (eds.), *Reflections and Replies: Essays on the Philosophy of Tyler Burge*. Cambridge, MA: MIT Press, pp. 405–415.

Burge, T. 2005. Disjunctivism and Perceptual Psychology. *Philosophical Topics* 33: 1–78.

Burge, T. 2010. *The Origins of Objectivity*. Oxford: Oxford University Press.

Byrne, A. 2001. Intentionalism Defended. *Philosophical Review* 110: 199–240.

Byrne, A. 2003. Color and Similarity. *Philosophy and Phenomenological Research* 66: 641–665.

Byrne, A. 2009. Experience and Content. *Philosophical Quarterly* 59: 429–451.

Byrne, A. 2013. Review Kriegel *Phenomenal Intentionality*. Notre Dame Philosophical Reviews.

Byrne, A. 2018. *Transparency and Self-Knowledge*. Oxford: Oxford University Press.

Byrne, A. and D. Hilbert. 1997. Colors and Reflectances. In A. Byrne and D. Hilbert (eds.), *Readings on Color: Volume 1*. Cambridge, MA: MIT Press.

Byrne, A. and D. Hilbert. 2003. Color Realism and Color Science. *Behavioral and Brain Sciences* 26: 3–21.

Byrne, A. and D. Hilbert. 2017. Color Relationalism and Relativism. *Topics in Cognitive Science* 9: 172–192.

Byrne, A. and D. Hilbert. 2020. Objectivist Reductionism. In D. Brown and F. MacPherson (eds.), *The Routledge Handbook of Philosophy of Colour*. New York: Routledge.

Campbell, J. 2002. *Reference and Consciousness*. Oxford: Oxford University Press.

Campbell, J. 2009. Berkeley's Puzzle. Philosophy Bites podcast. https://philos-ophybites.com/2009/10/john-campbell-on-berkeleys-puzzle.html

Campbell, J. 2010. Demonstrative Reference, the Relational View of Experience, and the Proximity Principle. In R. Jeshion (ed.), *New Essays on Singular Thought*. Oxford: Oxford University Press, pp. 193–212.

Campbell, J. and Q. Cassam. 2014. *Berkeley's Puzzle*. Oxford: Oxford University Press.

Campbell, K. 2016. The Problem of Spatiality for a Relational View of Experience. *Philosophical Topics* 44: 115–120.

Campbell, K. 2020. Does That Which Makes a Sensation of Blue a Mental Fact Escape Us? In D. Brown and F. MacPherson (eds.), *The Routledge Handbook of Philosophy of Colour*. New York: Routledge.

Casati, R. and A. Varzi. 1994. *Holes and Other Superficialities*. Cambridge, MA: MIT Press.

Chalmers, D. 1996. *The Conscious Mind*. Oxford: Oxford University Press.

Chalmers, D. 2005. Representationalism Showdown. https://fragments.consc.net/djc/2005/09/representationa.html

Chalmers, D. 2010. *The Character of Consciousness*. Oxford: Oxford University Press.

Chalmers, D. 2012. *Constructing the World*. Oxford: Oxford University Press.

Chang, E., J. Rieger, K. Johnson, M. Berger, N. Barbaro, and R. Knight. 2010. Categorical Speech Representation in Human Superior Temporal Gyrus. *Nature Neuroscience* 13: 1428–32.

Chang, L. and D. Tsao. 2017. The Code for Facial Identity in the Primate Brain. *Cell* 169: 1013–1028.

Chirimuuta, M. 2015. *Outside Color*. Cambridge, MA: MIT Press.

Chisholm, R. 1950. The Theory of Appearing. In M. Black (ed.), *Philosophical Analysis*. Ithaca, NY: Cornell University Press, pp. 102–118.

Coghill, R., C. Sang, J. Maisog, and M. Iadarola. 1999. Pain Intensity Processing within the Human Brain: A Bilateral, Distributed Mechanism. *Journal of Neurophysiology* 82: 1934–1943.

Cohen, J. 2009. *The Red and the Real*. Oxford: Oxford University Press.

Cohen, J. 2020. Colour Relationism. In D. Brown and F. Macpherson (eds.) *The Routledge Handbook of the Philosophy of Colour*. New York: Routledge.

Cosmides, L. and J. Tooby. 1995. Foreword. In S. Baron-Cohen (ed.) *Mindblindness*. Cambridge, MA: MIT Pres.

Cowart, B. J. and N. E. Rawson. 2001. Olfaction. In E. Goldstein (ed.), *The Blackwell Handbook of Perception*. Oxford: Blackwell Publishers.

Crane, T. 2003. The Intentional Structure of Consciousness. In A. Jokic and Q. Smith (eds.), *Consciousness: New Philosophical Perspectives*. Oxford: Oxford University Press, pp. 1–27.

Crouzet, S. M., N. A. Busch, and K. Ohla. 2015. Taste Quality Decoding Parallels Taste Sensations. *Current Biology* 25: 1–7.

Cutter, B. 2016. Color and Shape: A Plea for Equal Treatment. *Philosophers' Imprint* 16: 1–11.

Cutter, B. 2017a. Spatial Experience and Special Relativity. *Philosophical Studies* 174: 2297–2313.

Cutter, B. 2017b. Pain and Representation. In J. Corn (ed.), *Routledge Handbook of the Philosophy of Pain*. New York: Routledge, pp. 29–39.

Cutter, B. 2020. A Puzzle About the Experience of Left and Right. *Noûs*. Advance Article.

Cutter, B. and M. Tye. 2011. Tracking Representationalism and the Painfulness of Pain. *Philosophical Issues* 21: 90–109.

Dainton, B. 2018. Temporal Consciousness. https://plato.stanford.edu/archives/win2018/entries/consciousness-temporal/

Dehaene, S. 2014. *Consciousness and the Brain: Deciphering How the Brain Codes Our Thoughts*. New York: Viking Press.

Dennett, D. 2012. A Phenomenal Confusion. https://www.youtube.com/watch?v=AaCedh4Dfs4

Dorr, C. 2016. To Be F Is to Be G. *Philosophical Perspectives* 30: 39–134.

Dorsch, F. 2010. Transparency and Imagining Seeing. *Philosophical Explorations* 13: 173–200.

Dretske, D. 1995. *Naturalizing the Mind*. Cambridge: MIT Press.

Dretske, D. 2003. Experience as Representation. *Philosophical Issues* 13: 67–82.

Duncan, M. 2020. The Puzzle of Impossible Experiences. Manuscript.

Eimas, P. D. and J. D. Corbit. 1973. Selective Adaptation of Linguistic Feature Detectors. *Cognitive Psychology* 4: 99–109.

Epstein, P. 2018. Shape Perception in a Relativistic Universe. *Mind* 127: 339–379.

Farkas, K. 2013. Constructing a World for the Senses. In U. Kriegel (ed.), *Phenomenal Intentionality: New Essays*. Oxford: Oxford University Press, pp. 99–115.

ffytche, D. H. 2013. The Hallucinating Brain: Neurobiological Insights into the Nature of Hallucination. In F. Macpherson and D. Platchias (eds.), *Hallucination*. Cambridge, MA: MIT Press.

Fine, K. 2012. Guide to Ground. In F. Correia and B. Schnieder (eds.), *Metaphysical Grounding*. Cambridge: Cambridge University Press, pp. 37–80.

Fish, W. 2009. *Perception, Hallucination, and Illusion*. Oxford: Oxford University Press.

Fish, W. 2013. Perception, Hallucination, and Illusion: Reply to My Critics. *Philosophical Studies* 163: 57–66.

Fodor, J. 1992. *A Theory of Content and Other Essays*. Cambridge, MA: MIT Press.

Foster, J. 2000. *The Nature of Perception*. Oxford: Oxford University Press.

French, C. and I. Phillips. 2020. Austerity and Illusion. *Philosopher's Imprint* 20: 1–19.

Fulkerson, M. 2014. *The First Sense: A Philosophical Study of Human Touch*. Cambridge: MIT Press.

Galileo, G. 1623/1957. *The Assayer*. Translated by Stillman Drake. New York: Doubleday.

Garcia-Carpintero, M. 2001. Sense-Data: The Sensible Approach. *Grazer Philosophische Studien* 62: 17–63.

Geach, P. 1957. *Mental Acts*. London: Routledge & Keegan Paul.

Gescheider, G. 1997. *Psychophysics: The Fundamentals*. New Jersey: Lawrence Erlbaum Associates.

Goldstein, B. and J. Brockmole. 2016. *Sensation and Perception*. Boston: Cengage Learning.

Goodman, N. 1951. *The Structure of Appearance*. Cambridge, MA: Harvard University Press.

Green, E. J. 2016. Representationalism and Perceptual Organization. *Philosophical Topics* 44: 121–148.

Green, E. J. 2017. Psychosemantics and the Rich-Thin Debate. *Philosophical Perspectives* 31: 153–186.

Green, E. J. 2020. The Puzzle of Cross-Modal Shape Experience. Manuscript.

Green, E. J. and S. Schellenberg. 2018. Spatial Perception: The Perspectival Aspect of Perception. *Philosophy Compass* 13: 1–16.

Gross, C. 1999. The Fire That Comes from the Eye. *Neuroscientist* 5: 58–64.

Gupta, A. 2019. *Conscious Experience: A Logical Inquiry*. Cambridge: Harvard University Press.

Hansen, T., L. Pracejus, and K. Gegenfurtner. 2009. Color Perception in the Intermediate Periphery of the Visual Field. *Journal of Vision* 9: 1–12.

Hardin, C. L. 1988. *Color for Philosophers: Unweaving the Rainbow*. Indianapolis: Hackett.

Harman, G. 1990. The Intrinsic Quality of Experience. *Philosophical Perspectives* 4: 31–52.

Haynes, J. 2009. Decoding Visual Consciousness from Human Brain Signals. *Trends in Cognitive Science* 13: 194–202.

Harman, G. 1996. Explaining Objective Color in Terms of Subjective Reactions. *Philosophical Issues* 7: 1–17.

Hawthorne, J. 2004. Why Humeans Are Out of Their Minds. *Noûs* 38: 351–358.

Hawthorne, J. and D. Manley. 2012. *The Reference Book*. Oxford: Oxford University Press.

Hellie, B. 2007. Factive Phenomenal Characters. *Philosophical Perspectives* 21: 259–305.

Hellie, B. 2010. An Externalist's Guide to Inner Experience. In B. Nanay (ed.), *Perceiving the World*. Oxford: Oxford University Press.

Hill, C. 2009. *Consciousness*. Cambridge: Cambridge University Press.

Hill, C. 2017. Fault Lines in Familiar Concepts of Pain. In J. Corn (ed.), *Routledge Handbook of the Philosophy of Pain*. New York: Routledge.

Hintikka, J. 1969. On the Logic of Perception. In N. S. Care and R. H. Grimm (eds.), *Perception and Personal Identity*. Cleveland, OH: Case Western Reserve University Press.

Hoffman, D. 2019. *The Case Against Reality: Why Evolution Hid the Truth from Our Eyes*. New York: W. W. Norton & Company.

Horgan, T. 2014. Phenomenal Intentionality and Secondary Qualities. In B. Brogaard (ed.), *Does Perception Have Content?* Oxford: Oxford University Press.

Horgan, T. and J. Tienson. 2002. The Intentionality of Phenomenology and the Phenomenology of Intentionality. In D. Chalmers (ed.), *Philosophy of Mind: Classical and Contemporary Readings*. Oxford: Oxford University Press.

Howard, J. D., J. Plailly, M. Grueschow, J. D. Haynes, and J. A. Gottfried. 2009. Odor Quality Coding and Categorization in Human Posterior Piriform Cortex. *Nature Neuroscience* 12: 932–939.

Hubel, D. and T. Wiesel. 1959. Receptive Fields of Single Neurones in the Cat's Striate Cortex. *The Journal of Physiology* 148: 574–591.

Huemer, M. 2011. Sense-Data. https://plato.stanford.edu/entries/sense-data/

Jackson, F. 1977. *Perception: A Representative Theory*. Cambridge: Cambridge University Press.

Jackson, F. 2004. Representation and Experience. In H. Clapin (ed.), *Representation in Mind: New Approaches to Mental Representation*. Oxford: Elsevier, pp. 107–124.

Jackson, F. 2012. Michael Tye on Perceptual Content. *Philosophy and Phenomenological Research* 84: 199–205.

Johnston, M. 2004. The Obscure Object of Hallucination. *Philosophical Studies* 120: 113–183.

Johnston, M. 2007. Objective Minds and the Objectivity of Mind. *Philosophy and Phenomenological Research* 75: 233–268.

Kalderon, M. 2020. Color Pluralism. In D. Brown and F. MacPherson (eds.), *The Routledge Handbook of Philosophy of Colour*. New York: Routledge.

Kant, I. 1781. *The Critique of Pure Reason*. https://www.earlymoderntexts.com/authors/kant

Kentridge, R., Heywood, C., and Cowey, A. 2004. Chromatic Edges, Surfaces and Constancies in Cerebral Achromatopsia. *Neuropsychologia* 42: 821–830.

Kim, J. 2005. *Physicalism, or Something Near Enough*. Princeton: Princeton University Press.

Kind, A. 2003. What's So Transparent About Transparency? *Philosophical Studies* 115: 225–244.

Kriegel, U. 2009. *Subjective Consciousness*. Oxford: Oxford University Press.

Kriegel, U. 2011. *Sources of Intentionality*. Oxford: Oxford University Press.

Kuehni, R. 2004. Variability in Unique Hue Selection: A Surprising Phenomenon. *Color Research and Application* 29: 158–162.

Langers, D., P. van Dijk, E. Schoenmaker, and W. Backes. 2007. fMRI Activation in Relation to Sound Intensity and Loudness. *NeuroImage* 35: 709–718.

Langsam, H. 1997. The Theory of Appearing Defended. *Philosophical Studies* 87: 33–59.

Langsam, H. 2017. The Intuitive Case for Naïve Realism. *Philosophical Explorations* 20: 106–122.

Langsam, H. 2018. Why Intentionalism Cannot Explain Phenomenal Character. *Erkenntnis* 85: 375–389.

Lee, G. 2014. Temporal Experience and the Temporal Structure of Experience. *Philosopher's Imprint* 14: 1–21.

Lee, G. 2017. Making Sense of Subjective Time. In I. Phillips (ed.), *The Routledge Handbook of the Philosophy of Time*. New York: Routledge.

Lee, G. 2020. *The Search for the Inner Light: Explanation and Objectivity in the Study of Consciousness*. Manuscript.

Levine, J. 1997. Are Qualia Just Representations? *Mind and Language* 12: 101–113.

Levine, J. 2019. On Phenomenal Access. In A. Pautz and D. Stoljar (eds.), *Blockheads!* Cambridge MA: MIT Press.

Lewis, D. 1970. How to Define Theoretical Terms. *Journal of Philosophy* 67: 427–446.

Lewis, D. 1994. Reduction of Mind. In S. Guttenplan (ed.), *A Companion to the Philosophy of Mind*. Oxford: Blackwell, pp. 412–431.

Locke, J. 1869. *An Essay Concerning Human Understanding*. http://www.earlymoderntexts.com

Logue, H. 2009. *Perceptual Experience: Relations and Representations*. MIT doctoral dissertation.

Logue, H. 2012a. Why Naïve Realism? *Proceedings of the Aristotelian Society* 112: 211–237.

Logue, H. 2012b. What Should the Naïve Realist Say About Total Hallucinations? *Philosophical Perspectives* 26: 173–199.

Logue, H. 2017. Are Experiences Just Representations? In B. Nanay (ed.), *Current Controversies in the Philosophy of Perception*. New York: Routledge, pp. 43–56.

Lycan, W. 2019a. Block on Representational Theory of Qualia. In A. Pautz and D. Stoljar (eds.), *Blockheads!* Cambridge MA: MIT Press.

Lycan, W. 2019b. Representational Theories of Consciousness. https://plato.stanford.edu/entries/consciousness-representational/

MacAdam, D. L. 1985. *Color Measurement*. New York: Springer-Verlag.

MacGregor, A. 2015. *A Natural View of Perceptual Experience*. Glasgow Dissertation.

MacPherson, F. 2006. Ambiguous Figures and the Content of Experience. *Noûs* 40: 82–117.

Mainland, J. 2018. Olfaction. In J. Wixted (ed.), *Stevens' Handbook of Experimental Psychology and Cognitive Neuroscience, Fourth Edition*. New York: John Wiley & Sons.

Margot, C. 2009. A Noseful of Objects. *Nature Neuroscience* 12: 813–814.

Martin, M. 1995. Perception. In A. Grayling (ed.), *Philosophy 1: A Guide to the Subject*. Oxford: Oxford University Press.

Martin, M. 1998. Setting Things Before the Mind. *Royal Institute of Philosophy Supplement* 43: 157–179.

Martin, M. 2004. The Limits of Self-Awareness. *Philosophical Studies* 120: 37–89.

Martin, M. 2006. On Being Alienated. In J. Hawthorne and T. Szabo Gendler (eds.), *Perceptual Experience*. Oxford: Oxford University Press, pp. 354–410.

Martin, M. 2013. Shibboleth: Some Comments on William Fish. *Philosophical Studies* 163: 37–48.

Masrour, F. 2017. Space Perception, Visual Dissonance and the Fate of Standard Representationalism. *Noûs* 51: 565–593.

Matthen, M. 2005. *Seeing, Doing, and Knowing*. Oxford: Oxford University Press.

McClurkin, J., J. Zarbock, and L. Optican. 1996. Primate Striate and Prestriate Cortical Neurons During Discrimination. *Journal of Neurophysiology* 75: 496–507.

McGinn, C. 1996. Another Look at Color. *Journal of Philosophy* 93: 537–553.

McLaughlin, B. 2016a. Hill on Phenomenal Consciousness. *Philosophical Studies* 173: 851–860.

McLaughlin, B. 2016b. The Skewed View from Here: Normal Geometrical Misperception. *Philosophical Topics* 44: 231–299.

Mehta, N. 2012. Exploring Subjective Representationalism. *Pacific Philosophical Quarterly* 93: 570–594.

Mendelovici, A. 2018. *The Phenomenal Basis of Intentionality*. Oxford: Oxford University Press.

Millar, B. 2014. The Phenomenological Problem of Perception. *Philosophy and Phenomenological Research* 88: 625–654.

Millikan, R. 1995. *White Queen Psychology and Other Essays for Alice*. Cambridge, MA: MIT Press.

Mogk, L. and Mogk, M. 2003. *Macular Degeneration*. New York: Ballantine Books.

Montague, M. 2016. *The Given: Experience and Its Content*. Oxford: Oxford University Press.

Moore, G. E. 1903. The Refutation of Idealism. *Mind* 12: 433–453.

Moore, G. E. 1914. The Status of Sense-Data. *Proceedings of the Aristotelian Society* 14: 355581.

Moore, G. E. 1918. Some Judgments of Perception. *Proceedings of the Aristotelian Society* 19: 1–29.

Moore, G. E. 1942. The Subjectivity of Sense Data. In A. Schilpp (ed.), *The Philosophy of G E Moore*. La Salle, IL. Open Court, pp. 653–660.

Moore, G. E. 1953/1910. *Some Main Problems of Philosophy*. London: George, Allen and Unwin.

Moore, G. E. 1957. Visual Sense-Data. In C. Mace (ed.), *British Philosophy in Mid-Century*. London: George Allen & Unwin, pp. 203–211.

Moran, A. 2019a. Naïve Realism, Hallucination, and Causation: A New Response to the Screening Off Problem. *Australasian Journal of Philosophy* 97: 368–382.

Moran, A. 2019b. Naïve Realism, Seeing Stars, and Perceiving the Past. *Pacific Philosophical Quarterly* 100: 202–232.

Morrison, J. 2016. Perceptual Confidence. *Analytic Philosophy* 57:15–48.

Munton, J. 2016. Visual Confidences and Direct Perceptual Justification. *Philosophical Topics* 44: 301–326.

Nanay, B. 2014. *Between Perception and Action*. Oxford: Oxford University Press.

Neander, K. 2017 *A Mark of the Mental*. Cambridge, MA: MIT Press.

Ney, A. and D. Albert. 2013. *The Wave Function: Essays on the Metaphysics of Quantum Mechanics*. Oxford: Oxford University Press.

Niikawa, T. 2014. Naïve Realism and the Explanatory Gap. *An Anthology of Philosophical Studies* 8: 125–136.

Niikawa, T. 2020. Where Is the Fundamental Disagreement Between Naïve Realism and Intentionalism? *Metaphilosophy* 51: 593–610.

Noorlander, C., J. J. Koenderink, R. J. den Ouden, and B. W. Edens. 1983. Sensitivity to Spatiotemporal Colour Contrast in the Peripheral Visual Field. *Vision Research* 23: 1–11.

O'Callaghan, C. 2007. *Sounds*. Oxford: Oxford University Press.

O'Callaghan, C. 2020a. *A Multisensory Philosophy of Perception*. Oxford: Oxford University Press.

O'Callaghan, C. 2020b. Speech Perception: Empirical and Theoretical Considerations. Supplement to Auditory Perception. https://plato.stanford.edu/entries/perception-auditory/supplement.html

Orlandi, N. 2014. *The Innocent Eye: Why Vision is not a Cognitive Process*. Oxford: Oxford University Press.

Palmer, S. 1999. *Vision Science: Photons to Phenomenology*. Cambridge, MA: MIT Press.

Papineau, D. 2014. Sensory Experience and Representational Properties. *Proceedings of the Aristotelian Society* 114: 1–33.

Papineau, D. 2016. Against Representationalism (About Experience). *International Journal of Philosophical Studies* 24: 324–347.

Pautz, A. 2003. Have Byrne and Hilbert Answered Hardin's Challenge? *Behavioral and Brain Sciences* 26: 44–45.

Pautz, A. 2006. Can Color Physicalists Explain Color Structure in Terms of Color Experience? *Australasian Journal of Philosophy* 84: 535–564.

Pautz, A. 2007. Intentionalism and Perceptual Presence. *Philosophical Perspectives* 21: 495–554.

Pautz, A. 2010a. Why Explain Experience in Terms of Content. In B. Nanay (ed.), *Perceiving the World*. Oxford: Oxford University Press.

Pautz, A. 2010b. Do Theories of Consciousness Rest on a Mistake? *Philosophical Issues* 20: 333–367.

Pautz, A. 2016. What Is My Evidence That Here Is a Cup? *Philosophical Studies* 173: 915–927.

Peacocke, C. 1983. *Sense and Content*. Oxford: Oxford University Press.

Peacocke, C. 2008. Sensational Properties: Theses to Accept and Theses to Reject. *Revue Internationale de Philosophie* 62: 7–24.

Penfield, W. and P. Perot. 1963. The Brain's Record of Auditory and Visual Experience: A Final Summary and Discussion. *Brain* 86: 595–696.

Perkins, R. and T. Bayne. 2013. Representationalism and the Problem of Vagueness. *Philosophical Studies* 162: 71–86.

Pinker, S. 2008. The Moral Instinct. *New York Times Magazine*, pp. 32–58.

Place, U. T. 1956. Is Consciousness a Brain Process? *British Journal of Psychology* 47: 44–50.

Plantinga, A. 1974. *The Nature of Necessity*. London: Oxford University Press.

Polger, T. 2004. *Natural Minds*. Cambridge, MA: MIT Press.

Price, D. and J. Barrell. 2012. *Inner Experience and Neuroscience*. Cambridge, MA: MIT Press.

Price, H. 1964. A Mescaline Experience. *Journal of the American Society for Psychical Research* 58: 3–20.

Price, H. H. 1932. *Perception*. London: Methuen.

Price, H. H. 1959. The Nature and Status of Sense-Data in Broad's Epistemology. In P. A. Schilpp (ed.), *The Philosophy of C. D. Broad*. New York: Tudor Publishing Co, pp. 457–485.

Prinz, J. 2012. *The Conscious Brain: How Attention Engenders Experience.* Oxford: Oxford University Press.

Prior, A. N. 1968. Intentionality and Intensionality. *Proceedings of the Aristotelian Society Supplementary Volume* 42: 73–106.

Pryor, J. 2000. The Skeptic and the Dogmatist. *Noûs* 34: 517–549.

Putnam, H. and H. Jacobson. 2014. The Needlessness of Adverbialism, Attributeism and Its Compatibilty With Cognitive Science. *Philosophia* 42: 555–570.

Quine, W. V. 1948. On What There Is. *The Review of Metaphysics* 2: 21–38.

Reid, T. 1785/2002. *Essays on the Intellectual Powers of Man.* In D. Brookes (ed.), University Park: Pennsylvania State University Press.

Robinson, H. 1994. *Perception.* New York: Routledge.

Rock, I. 1997. *Indirect Perception.* Cambridge, MA: MIT.

Rosenholtz R, J. Huang, A. Raj, B. J. Balas, and L. Ilie. 2012. A Summary Statistic Representation in Peripheral Vision Explains Visual Search. *Journal of Vision* 12: 1–17.

Russell, B. 1912a. *The Problems of Philosophy.* London: Williams and Norgate.

Russell, B. 1912b. Review James *Essays in Logical Empiricism.*

Russell, B. 1913. The Nature of Sense-Data: A Reply to Dr. Dawes Hicks. *Mind* 22: 76–81.

Russell, B. 1914. *Our Knowledge of the External World.* New York: Routledge.

Russell, B. 1927. *An Outline of Philosophy.* New York: Routledge Press.

Russell, B. 1940. *An Inquiry into Meaning and Truth.* London: Allen and Unwin.

Russell, B. 1959. *My Philosophical Development.* London: Allen and Unwin.

Saad, B. 2019. Spatial Experience, Spatial Reality, and Two Paths to Primitivism. *Synthese.* Advance Article.

Sacks, O. 2012. *Hallucination.* New York: Vintage.

Schellenberg, S. 2018. *The Unity of Perception: Content, Consciousness.* Oxford: Oxford University Press.

Schiffer, S. 2004. Skepticism and the Vagaries of Justified Belief. *Philosophical Studies* 119: 161–184.

Schiffer, S. 2003. *The Things We Mean.* Oxford: Oxford University Press.

Schmidt, B., M. Neitz, and J. Neitz. 2014. Neurobiological Hypothesis of Color Appearance and Hue Perception. *Journal of the Optical Society of America* 31: 195–207.

Sethi, U. 2019. Sensible Overdetermination. *Philosophical Quarterly* 70: 588–616.

Shepard, R. N. and S. Chipman. 1970. Second-Order Isomorphism of Internal Representations. *Cognitive Psychology* 1: 1–17.

Shoemaker, S. 1994. The Phenomenal Character of Experience. *Noûs* 28: 21–38.

Shoemaker, S. 2019. Phenomenal Character and Physicalism. In A. Pautz and D. Stoljar (eds.), *Blockheads!* Cambridge: MIT Press.

Siegel, S. 2004. Indiscriminability and the Phenomenal. *Philosophical Studies* 120: 91–112.

Siegel, S. 2010. *The Contents of Visual Experience.* Oxford: Oxford University Press.

Siegel, S. and A. Byrne. 2017. Rich or Thin? In B. Nanay (ed.), *Current Controversies in the Philosophy of Perception.* New York: Routledge.

Siewert, C. 1998. *The Significance of Consciousness.* Oxford: Oxford University Press.

Smart, J. C. 1959. Sensations and Brain Processes. *The Philosophical Review* 68: 141–156.

Smith, A. D. 2001. Perception and Belief. *Philosophical and Phenomenological Research* 62: 283–309.

Smith, A. D. 2002. *The Problem of Perception.* Cambridge MA: Harvard University Press.

Smith, A. D. 2008. Translucent Experiences. *Philosophical Studies* 140: 197–212.

Smithies, D. 2019. *The Epistemic Role of Consciousness.* Oxford: Oxford University Press.

Soteriou, M. 2016. *Disjunctivism.* New York: Routledge.

Speaks, J. 2015. *The Phenomenal and the Representational.* Oxford: Oxford University Press.

Speaks, J. 2017. Reply to Critics. *Philosophy and Phenomenological Research* 95: 492–506.

Speaks, J. 2020. Content and the Explanatory Role of Experience. In J. Genone, R. Goodman, and N. Kroll (eds.), *Singular Thought and Mental Files.* Oxford: Oxford University Press, pp. 52–70.

Stevens, S., J. Volkmann, and E. Newman. 1937. A Scale for the Measurement of the Psychological Magnitude Pitch. *Journal of the Acoustical Society of America* 8: 185–190.

Stoljar, D. 2010. *Physicalism.* New York: Routledge.

Strawson, G. 2020. What Does "Physical" Mean? A Prolegomenon to Physicalist Panpsychism. In W. Seager (ed.), *The Routledge Handbook of Panpsychism.* New York: Routledge.

Sundström, P. 2018. On Representationalism, Common-Factorism, and Whether Consciousness Is Here and Now. *Philosophical Studies* 176: 1–12.

Thomasson, A. 1999. *Fiction and Metaphysics*. Cambridge: Cambridge University Press.

Tononi, G. and K. Koch. 2015. Consciousness: Here, There and Everywhere. *Philosophical Transaction of the Royal Society* 370: 1–18.

Travis, C. 2004. The Silence of the Senses. *Mind* 113: 57–94.

Tye, M. 1995. *Ten Problems of Consciousness*. Cambridge: MIT Press.

Tye, M. 2000. *Consciousness, Color and Content*. Cambridge: MIT Press.

Tye, M. 2009. *Consciousness Revisited*. Cambridge: MIT Press.

Tye, M. 2019 What Uninformed Mary Can Teach Us. In S. Coleman (ed.), *The Knowledge Argument*. Cambridge: Cambridge University Press, pp. 269–280.

Tye, M. 2020. Filling In and the Nature of Visual Experience. *Harvard Review of Philosophy* 28: 1–16.

Tyler, C. 2015. Peripheral Color Demo. *i-Perception* 6: 1–5.

Van Cleve, J. 2015. *Problems from Reid*. Oxford: Oxford University Press.

van Inwagen, P. 2004. A Theory of Properties. *Oxford Studies in Metaphysics* 1: 107–138.

Vogel, J. 1990. Cartesian Skepticism and Inference to the Best Explanation. *Journal of Philosophy* 87: 658–666.

von Fieandt, K. 1966. *The World of Perception*. Belmont, CA: Dorsey Press.

Watzl, S. 2017. *Structuring Mind*. Oxford: Oxford University Press.

Weiskrantz, L. 1986. *Blindsight: A Case Study and Implications*. Oxford: Oxford University Press.

Wertheimer, M. 1912/2012. Experimental Studies on Seeing Motion. In L. Spillmnn (ed.), *On Perceived Motion and Figural Organization*. Cambridge: MIT Press.

Williams, R. 2020. *The Metaphysics of Representation*. Oxford: Oxford University Press.

Williamson, T. 1995. Is Knowing a State of Mind? *Mind* 104: 533–565.

Williamson, T. 2000. *Knowledge and Its Limits*. Oxford: Oxford University Press.

Williamson, T. 2005. Replies to Commentators. *Philosophy and Phenomenological Research* 70: 468–491.

Winer, G. A., J. E. Cottrell, V. Gregg, J. S. Fournier, and L. A. Bica. 2002. Fundamentally Misunderstanding Visual Perception: Adults' Beliefs in Visual Emissions. *American Psychologist* 57: 417–424.

Yi, B. 2018. Nominalism and Comparative Similarity. *Erkenntnis* 83: 793–803.

Youngentob, S. L., B. A. Johnson, M. Leon, P. R. Sheehe, and P. F. Kent. 2006. Predicting Odorant Quality Perceptions from Multidimensional Scaling of Olfactory Bulb Glomerular Activity Patterns. *Behavioral Neuroscience* 120: 1337–1345.

Zeki, S. 1983. Colour Coding in the Cerebral Cortex: The Reaction of Cells in Monkey Visual Cortex to Wavelengths and Colours. *Neuroscience* 9: 741–765.

INDEX

act-object assumption 27–29; naïve
realists' restriction of 55–56,
200–201; representationalists'
rejection of 195–198
afterimage 2, 74
alien colors 146, 193
Allen, Keith 112, 224–226
Alston, William 228–229
Anscombe, Elizabeth 56
armchair arguments 147–151

bad external correlation 68, 153, 216;
different from illusion 160
belief: different from experience
96, 127–128, 130–131; reasons-
responsive theory of 124–125
blindsight 127–128, 233n3
blurry vision 2, 70, 76, 111–113, 192
Bowie, David 235

brain in a vat (BIV): as argument
for irreducibility of experiential
representation 173–174; as problem
for internal physical state view
81–84, 92n8; as skeptical challenge
120–122
Brewer, Bill 202–207, 212–213
Burmester, Buddy 94–95, 207–215
Byrne, Alex 117–119, 162–163, 186n5

Campbell, John 116, 126–128,
202–208, 218
character question 4, 16n1
Charles Bonnet syndrome (CBS) 3,
32, 70, 94, 200, 207
checker-shadow illusion 200–201,
212, 233n1
coincidental variation cases 160
conceptualism 137n11

degreed perceptual justification
   123–124
dress 2
dual component theories 26–27, 95,
   108
duck rabbit 3–4

essential external directedness 74; as
   argument against internal physical
   state view 77–81, 92n8; in history
   of philosophy of perception 89,
   92n9; Papineau's rejection of
   84–90
experience first 14, 125
experience-type 3–4
experiential indeterminacy 150, 174
experiential representation relation
   141; identified with detection
   relation 143; irreducibility of 159,
   173–174
explanatory role of experience: as
   argument for naïve realism 202–
   207; as problem for naïve realism
   213–214, 223n8
external-internal puzzle 6, 42–43,
   235–236; about illusion and
   hallucination 6–7, 152; about
   sensible properties 7–10, 152–160
extromission theory of vision 20, 149

fluke argument 220–222

Galileo 21, 177, 180
gestalt 3, 26, 113–116
good internal correlation 68, 153, 216
greeble 117–118; giant image of 118

grounding 16n1, 49
grounding laws 49

hallucination 3, 30–36, 207–215
Hilbert, David 162–163, 186n5
hue-magnitudes 162–163

illusion 2–3; naïve realist accounts
   of 211, 227–231; representationalist
   account of 147
illusionism: about sensible
   properties 21, 36–42, 175–178;
   about spatial properties 180–182
imagery 54, 103
inference to the best explanation: as
   answer to skepticism 121–123; as
   argument for representationalism
   102–110
internal dependence 160; as problem
   for response-independent
   representationalism 151–161;
   different from internalism 172;
   violated by basic naïve realism
   223–224
internalism 65–68, 172–173
intrinsic plausibility: as favoring
   act-object assumption 30–31,
   198–202; as objection to
   representationalism 128–130,
   198–202, 138n13

knowledge 45–48, 121–122
knowledge-first 125

laws of appearance 130–135
Logue, Heather 234n16

Leibniz's law 77, 84; used against internal physical state view 77–81, 92n8

Macpherson, Fiona 114–116
many-property problem 91n1
Martin, M. G. F. 69–71, 209–214
mescaline 32
Middle Earth 150
motion illusions 54

neural code 61–62, 184, 239
Newton, Isaac 21, 37, 180, 220
novel colors 81, 98, 213–214

Papineau, David 15, 84–90, 91n4, 129–130, 138n12, 238
Peacocke, Christopher 57n8, 74, 86, 89, 110–111, 230–231
perceptible properties 141
perceptual imprecision: dilemma for sense datum view 52–56, 58n13; naïve realist explanation of 55–56, 193; representationalist explanation of 103–107
perceptual presence: Campbell's objection from 126–128, 135; Papineau's objection from 138n12
percipi problem: for response-independent representationalism 163–164; for sense datum view 44–45
peripheral vision 19, 52–56, 58n12, 103
physicalism 13, 48–49; grounding 49, 183–184; reductive 67, 83–84, 170, 184

poison dart frog 40–41
Price, H. H. 30–32, 50, 54, 107, 129; drug user 32
properties 25, 81, 97–98; as objects of hallucination 92n5, 98, 138n12
psychophysical laws 33–34, 44, 48–49, 51, 183
pure motion 54–55, 103

Ramsey-Lewis method 100–102, 109–110, 117, 120, 128, 137n2, 214, 234n14
real definition 16n1, 74
representational format 97, 132–133, 186n2
representation question 141; as problem for response-dependent representationalism 168–169, 187n10
robot 14, 62, 117–118, 202–206

Schellenberg, Susanna 119–120, 125, 136
seamless transition 125
seems-gambit 35, 63, 67, 75, 95
selectionism 146, 193–195; undermined by coincidental variation 160, 223–226
sensa 134; different from sense data 134
sensible properties 8; as primitive and irreducible 38, 170–171, 175–177, 186n1, 190–195; as reducible 142–143, 165–166; as response-dependent 165, 175–177; as response-independent 143, 190–195

Siegel, Susanna 116–119
simplicity argument: against
    primitivism about sensible
    properties 217–220; against
    sense data 48–50
singular colors 186n5
singularism vs generalism
    119–120
spatial argument 77
state of affairs 101, 128, 196
Stein, Gertrude 171
Swift, Taylor 2

transparency observation 68–72;
    hallucination as problem for 70,
    92n5
The Truman Show 123

virtual reality model 22, 182
visual crowding 53

waterfall illusion 55; possible content
    of 138n14
Wilde, Oscar 64
window shade model 20, 28, 236